On the Road
to Kathmandu

by

Daphne Dawson

British Library Cataloguing in Publication Data.
A catalogue record for this book is available
from the British Library

ISBN 978 0 86071 873 4

A Commissioned Publication Printed by

MOORLEYS
Print, Design & Publishing
info@moorleys.co.uk · www.moorleys.co.uk

Chapter 1. Beginnings

The morning of Tuesday the second of September 1975 found me swinging precariously by rope over the tailpin of an orange converted fire engine parked by the Old Brompton Road, London. It was one of two trucks (the other painted blue) in which 44 of us were setting out on an 11 week journey overland from London to Kathmandu. The bright colours of the trucks ensured that the local authorities in the countries we were to travel through didn't think the army had arrived, and the simian swing on the rope was to be the first of many learning experiences encountered on the trip of a lifetime.

But how had I come to think of making such a journey? For two years beforehand I had been working as a physiotherapist in Lausanne, in French-speaking Switzerland. Though I loved the country and its outdoor pursuits, my ex-pat friends of several different nationalities, and most of the work too, I could get rather tired of the political antics of the Swiss themselves. They kept holding referendums to vote foreigners out of their country. Unsurprisingly we foreigners revolted and in October 1974 I wrote my parents...

> 'It's been quite an exciting campaign. Even *I* tried sticking up a poster in Physio. It was up for half-an-hour, and then mysteriously vanished! We were rather wishing secretly that they'd turf us all out and see how they managed without us! However ... the vote went very much in our favour. I should think so too! I resent receiving ... forms actually asking *me* to give money and support the anti-foreigner cause!'

It's worth noting here that there was only ever one Swiss physiotherapist in our department of some 15 people during my two years in the hospital. Swiss physios found Private Practice more lucrative, and foreigners had to work for 5 years in the country before being able to practice similarly. Thus I was already considering returning to Britain during the coming year. Only the way in which I might take some time out between jobs was in doubt.

> 'I've been day-dreaming lately about possible trips I might do next autumn. I was looking through brochures on overland journeys to

Kathmandu, via Austria, Yugoslavia, Greece, Turkey, Iran, Afghanistan, Pakistan and India. That would be super, and reasonably priced! I wonder.'

It had been a much-travelled new member of our physio team who had talked to me of such journeys, and I was very ready to listen. Journeying overland across Asia was a popular activity among the young of the sixties and seventies. Plenty things had combined to make Asia attractive to my generation, the baby boomers. First, we went to school just as Everest was climbed for the first time. Then I had come across popular travel writing on the area by Dervla Murphy[1] and on my parents' bookshelves were such writers as Peter Fleming[2] and Heinrich Harrer[3], telling of the rarely travelled silk roads across Asia, and of Tibet, a country forbidden to travellers for many years. The strange philosophies and religions of the East interested some; images of ancient civilisations were seductive to others; and of course there were always the attractions of Thai and Balinese dancing girls!

Cross-continental travel was already favoured by young people travelling to Europe from Australia and New Zealand, but the visit of the Beatles to India in the late sixties made the subcontinent a must-visit destination for many among Europe's and America's youth too, travelling in the opposite direction. Overland to India – how exotic and exciting! And what better way to experience the East? The journey was long and not without its risks, but the adventurous wanted to go; all they needed was an inexpensive option. Thus the overland organisations came into being. Using old buses and trucks, companies were springing up everywhere. The options ranged from the deluxe tours run by such companies as Penn Overland in London, which cost several hundred pounds, down to Magic Bus from Amsterdam which offered a 4 week, 24 hours a day, trip to Delhi for as little as £98.

It was over 8,000 miles one way from London to Kathmandu and usually averaged 76 days travelling through up to 15 countries. I could see no

---

[1] *Full Tilt* (1965) and *The Waiting Land* (1967).
[2] *News From Tartary* (1936).
[3] *Seven Years in Tibet* (1952).

reason to rush the journey. I think I already knew that it wasn't so much the journey's end that was the goal, but the journey itself ... moving slowly round the globe (our top speed was little more than 50 miles an hour), seeing people in their individual environments (these often seeming extremely enticing and different from mine) – not zooming across them in a plane, for once. Nowadays we tend to think of decreasing carbon emissions and helping to save the planet by travelling overland, but that was not our reasoning back in the seventies. We just had an interest in seeing more of the earth and its inhabitants at a slower pace.

The company I decided on, Encounter Overland (usually referred to as Encounter or E.O.), used converted fire trucks with Perkins engines like our orange vehicle, or dual cab ex-military Bedford trucks (of which our blue truck was one), 3-ton four-wheel-drive vehicles powered through eight forward gears by five litre diesel engines. These had seats along the sides in the rear plus a couple with their back to the driver's cab, all facing inwards, and a canvas canopy with clear Perspex 'windows' for warmer cover and to protect passengers from dust on the road. In our truck there was also room for five people up in the cab, apart from the driver. The blue truck's dual cab seating meant they had only 20 passengers where we had 24. It was pretty basic, but a lot was fitted in. There was a four burner gas hob to cook on in the corner behind the driver's cab and plenty space under the seats to store tinned and dried food as basic or emergency rations if fresh food was hard to come by locally. Water was carried in jerry cans, under the body of the truck (to lessen evaporation in hot climates).

At a pre-departure meeting in London a month before setting out, those of our group able to attend met Ian, our leading driver and guide. He had taken an electrical engineering degree, after which he had failed to settle in an office job and soon starting trekking. He had only been a short time with Encounter but had four years' previous experience of our journey, crossing Asia some fourteen times over that period.

He gave us some very useful security information. It made sense not to travel in good clothes and with expensive jewellery. "Keep to the most functional simple gear", he told us, "and pack a rucksack rather than a case." These would be stowed with care in trailers attached behind the trucks. Some items needed extra care: camera film should be carried in plastic bags. Our valuables, passports, cash and travellers' cheques would be safest in a money-belt worn round our waist at all times as we travelled, even in our sleeping bags at night too.

Ian suggested we prepare to bring about £1 a day for basic expenses, with money for any presents in addition. It was best to carry well known travellers' cheques, perhaps fifty-fifty sterling-dollars. This gave me pause for thought as the currency I would be taking was Swiss francs. The franc was good strong currency though: surely there would be no problem. I was to find that Ian's idea was rather better and certainly would have made life easier in one or two instances when I least expected difficulties.

Really useful was the list of Poste Restante addresses at post offices in major towns that Ian now gave us, with the approximate dates of our arrival at each. It would enable my parents, and other relatives and friends, to stay in contact with me as I travelled. One of the biggest changes since I undertook my Asian Odyssey has been the influence of the mobile phone.

He had information about day to day living on the move too. We would share cooking and washing up duties once a week. The trucks had 6ft folding tables on which to set out our meals, and fresh food would be bought daily to supplement our stores. Turkey and Iran had the best markets. Also we would need to clean out the trucks occasionally with disinfectant. The tents too would possibly need a clean if we met with a wind storm in the desert region of Iran.

Ian stressed that he be told straight away if there were any health problems during the trip. There was no need to bring a mosquito net, but a good anti-insect protective cream or spray would be essential. Once we reached eastern Iran we should all take anti-malarial medication twice a week, and this needed to continue for a month after our journey was over. He then told us extremely firmly that no hard drugs were to be taken onto the trucks. He reserved the right to refuse to carry any of us who did so.

Because there were two trucks we could cater for majority decisions on changes of route in one or two places, changing which truck we travelled on as necessary. Also Ian favoured taking the northern route through Afghanistan and was planning to obtain a permit to do so. I'd read Dervla Murphy's *Full Tilt* and knew she'd attempted to go by the northern route too, when she cycled to India in the 1960s. She'd been prevented by the awkward situation vis à vis Russia pertaining in 1963, but had described it as "by far the most beautiful and interesting" way through Afghanistan[4]. So Ian's plan sounded really good. He had also arranged the already mooted extension trip to Assam from Kathmandu. It would be "exciting reconnaissance" he enthused: again this was stimulating talk, but I wouldn't be doing that, for I meant to fly on to Australia from Kathmandu. He finally warned us that an overland journey was not to be attempted lightly; in his experience things could go wrong and often did.

At this point it's worth remembering the life our drivers were leading. Most of them did the round trip of 17,000 miles in about 5-6 months. It was anything but a 'cushy number'; the inevitable bouts of stomach trouble and having to keep a group of travellers amused and safe took its toll. And not all the punters were in it for the right reasons. One driver has commented,

> "Many thought that if they could just get to India the world would suddenly have meaning: how many times did I hear them say "I'm going to India to study religion and music"? That was shorthand for smoking dope. Most of these soon lost their money, or worse, ended up in a local prison."[5]

So experience and safety were top of the priority list as far as the drivers were concerned and our two main drivers, Ian and Ben, were well prepared. Ian had the travelling experience and Ben had run his own car mechanics business. In some ways they displayed very different personalities, Ian being the more gregarious of the two, but both were thoroughly reliable, prepared to drive consistently well for long periods at a time. We were in good hands.

---

[4] Murphy (2010), page 50.
[5] Tyre News (1974).

From the evidence of this preparatory meeting, Encounter, while catering to the price sensitive part of the market, still managed to attract an interesting set of young folk, averaging around 26 years of age. There were nurses, civil servants, a teacher or two and a sprinkling of older couples. When I say 'older' that was around 30 years of age. There was an upper age limit of 40. I was fairly relieved not to see too many thoroughly hippy type travellers. One of her neighbours had not shared my mother's own enthusiasm for the trip and worried her considerably by talking of hippie drug-taking. My response was that I wanted to see the world and how other people lived...

> '– yes, in dirt, squalor, poverty, the lot. I hope it'll make me realise just how lucky I am ... My idea is that if you want to do something with life, you must first go out and look at it as it is, drugs, hippies and all.'

It seems clear that I had developed something of the '*nostalgie de la boue*' as the French call it (literally 'nostalgia for mud'), an idealistic seeking after a simpler life. It pleased me no end, however, that I could tell my mother that Ian insisted that there be no drugs anywhere near the trucks as we travelled. It seemed that most true hippies might make for a cheaper and quicker route: they didn't want to waste time getting to the Indian subcontinent.

At that time you could go by truck with E.O. across South America (a journey of 17 weeks duration), Africa (15 weeks) or Asia (11 weeks), so I was doing the least adventurous trip, if time spent travelling came into the equation. However the Asian brochure advertised the journey as being 'To the Roof of the World', with a smiling lass sitting in the lap of a serene, lotus-positioned Buddha[6] – which struck me as wonderfully romantic and exotic! Africa and South America hadn't quite that same appeal. I also wished to visit a few of my friends in Australia and New Zealand afterwards, and going across Asia to Kathmandu took me half way there.

---

[6] The photograph on the cover of this book.

So I set about finding the books recommended in the *To the Roof of the World* brochure as good preparation and took a few notes from two of them – *Turkey and the Turks* by Bernard Newman and *The Land of the Great Sophy* by Roger Stevens. Both were full of quirky stories and plenty historical background. What fascinating empires had existed across this region! There was much here that was completely new to me, or had only just been touched upon in my school history lessons. It all confirmed my decision to choose to cross Asia.

I had stayed at Earl's Court Youth Hostel to attend the pre-departure meeting and found myself comparing notes with a volunteer on the reception desk there. He too was planning to set off for India soon, but under his own steam. This was something that attracted but also thoroughly scared me. I had in mind Eric Newby's (occasionally terrifying to me) escapades in *A Short Walk in the Hindu Kush* and stories in a similarly amateur-style 'outward bound' vein. I was not yet an experienced solo traveller, ready to face anything fate might throw at me, and wanted my hand held a little at first. Full of admiration I quipped "See you at the Pakistan-India border!" as we parted. I never dreamed that I should.

The 11 weeks were to cost £360. It had only been £330 the year before, but the pound was in trouble and these trips were getting ever more expensive. This didn't worry me too much, for I'd just been earning very good money in Switzerland, and what better way to spend it than in a long journey to take in some of the greatest sights on earth? Penn Overland's equivalent trip cost over £600, but they had steps that let down to allow them to gain access to the rear of their truck in a very sedate manner, while Encounter's swing over the tailpin was almost regarded as a badge of courage by their punters. Penn also used local inns as accommodation, while we were going to camp most of the route. I'd been on a couple of brief camping trips, but never on as long a holiday under canvas as this would be, so I wasn't sure how I would like it. It felt right to travel as simply as possible in poorer countries though, not flaunting our superior wealth in any way. I also somehow had the feeling I should get to know the lands I was to pass through better if I was actually in contact with their soil, as it were, could see their stars at night from the entrance to my tent and hear the sounds of their wildlife around me: it was all part of the adventure.

I was not doing this on my own, though in a way I would have preferred to! Sharing my tent would be an Irish radiographer, Virginia, who had lived in the next room to mine in the staff quarters of the Hôpital Orthopédique when I first arrived to work in Lausanne. She was a friend OK, but I wasn't too sure she would make a suitable travelling companion for a long journey. She had had a tendency to follow wherever someone led, rather than make decisions for herself, and then complain bitterly if things went wrong. I regretted telling her early on what I aimed to do, for her immediate reaction had been to suggest she joined me, and it had been difficult to say "No". Time would tell how she fared, but I did worry that our relationship would be put badly under strain.

Chapter 2. We Get Under Way

The night before I was due to begin my journey I travelled up to London, left my rucksack at Earl's Court Youth Hostel again, where I was to meet Virginia, and made a visit to the Encounter Overland offices. This was to confirm arrangements for onward travel from Kathmandu, and they had my ticket *out* to Australia all ready for me. But I had to go and collect the return ones back to London myself: when phoned, the company that had booked them (Trailfinders – a very new company then) said they had just come through! This continuing travel had been worrying me, for then I should be entirely on my own and long-haul travel was new to me. It was a close thing: the flight offices closed three minutes after I got my ticket, so I was lucky. I just got back to the Youth Hostel in time to meet Virginia at 6pm. We had tea out and went to bed early.

By 7.30 on the Tuesday morning we were already at the meeting spot on the Old Brompton Road. The trucks were drawn up on the wide pavement, and loading of the trailers with our luggage was beginning. Lists of the party were pinned on each vehicle's trailer so that we knew which truck we were to travel in. Virginia and I were not the only people to be alone, but plenty friends and relations had come along to say 'good-bye' to others. They were milling all around us.

However I noted a darkly handsome girl, with an equally dark-haired youth who gave the impression of being only important to each other, even in this crowd, to the point of dressing identically in rust-coloured jumper and jeans. This struck me as so unusual that they featured in the first photograph I took of our expedition with my Kodak Instamatic camera. I would learn that they were Sabrina, at 20 the youngest on the trip, and her boyfriend, Dieter, both from Switzerland. And it's interesting that what I had guessed even at the start was correct: they were the only ones on the trip to keep themselves almost completely to themselves, though, as a mechanic, Dieter turned out to be helpful. I eventually learnt that his goal was to farm in New Zealand, but otherwise never felt I knew him and his girlfriend particularly well.

Ten minutes before departure time the police turned up too! "That little sign over there allows you to park in the road, not on the pavement!" they told Ian. This struck us as very silly, for if the vehicles had been parked in the road, what problems they'd have had with traffic jams!

We set off south soon after 8am, aiming to catch the 11.15 Dover ferry for France, only to get lost near Blackheath trying to cut across to the Dover Road! Of-course someone now cheerily commented that losing our way this early bode extremely well for the trip! The next time we went wrong was at Dover Harbour, where we went round in circles attempting to board the ferry. People were very helpful – and very curious. A customs official at Dover noted my occupation in my passport and commented with a smile that I "might come in quite useful over the course of the journey". I rather hoped not, though I supposed that the luxury of massage might be of value to one or two fellow travellers.

Our ferry docked at Calais in the early afternoon and, now driving on the right hand side of the road (it would be eight weeks before we returned to the left), we slowly made our way on to Dunkerque. An amusing moment occurred then, when a Citroën got wedged between our two trucks in a traffic jam. "Where are you off to?" demanded the French driver. How amazed he was when he was told Kathmandu!

In the back of our truck people were getting to know one another, and those from nearer London had been commenting on the route. Ian was travelling with us while James, the trainee driver, who I remembered from the pre-departure meeting, was nominally in charge of our vehicle and was driving us through Europe. I had been intrigued by the history of this young man who decided to take some time out at the end of his law degree to travel across Asia and ended up choosing this life instead of practising as a barrister on his return home. Slim, with a sparse beard and moustache, he tended to mince along, giving the impression of being both posh and slightly effeminate compared to both Ian and the blue truck's driver Ben: I could imagine them quietly laughing at him. He'd done the obligatory truck mechanics training of a few months in the Encounter Overland workshops, but he was bound to be new to some issues. It was good however that Ian could take over in those circumstances.

Our 'Orange Truck' party consisted of the Swiss couple, eight British folk, one Irish (my friend Virginia), two New Zealand lads, an American girl and six Australians. Couples were one husband and wife, Peg and Mark from Sydney, who had known each other since childhood; an engaged couple, Cockney Sue's accent barely distinguishable from that of her Australian fiancé Jim's; and Sabrina and Dieter, the 'good friends'. Each of these couples shared a tent of-course. The others had come in ones and twos, some friends sharing like Virginia and me (next door neighbours Maddie and Rosie, fellow Kiwis Dave and Rob, and work colleagues Jane and Liz). The others were put slightly randomly together, always by gender though and where possible by nationality. Almost all were going on to Australia, either to return home, or to visit the country and friends there, like myself, or with the intention of travelling still further, New Zealand being the favourite destination then.

I had decided to keep a diary of the trip and soon started writing it during what I deemed to be this more everyday stretch of the journey. My diary entries were never particularly elaborate for I was mostly writing while travelling, noting the stranger things I saw, and this became quite taxing when there was a poor surface on the road! During the first few days of travel along autobahns this was not an issue though and, alongside the general account of our route and activities, I made an effort to write thumbnail sketches of my travelling companions. Apart from anything else, I needed to learn their names and something of their background. We were perforce going to get to know each other pretty intimately on the trip so my aim was to find out all I could about them. But I kept such writing for quiet periods in the tent, and allotted the back pages of my notebook to this, lest my companions might chance on negative comments about themselves!

We were such a mixed bunch that I found it something of a challenge at first to be in close proximity with all these unknown people, from so many different countries. Not only would we be sharing food together and camping very near each other, but we would become less clean together (camp sites with shower facilities would be a rarity in Eastern Turkey, Iran and Afghanistan) and we were going to go to the toilet together – at least with our own sex - and from time to time might suffer the indignity of being ill in each other's company, if only, in the case of the girls, when we had period pain. It did strike me that I had heard that women who worked together gradually began to have their menstrual cycles in unison.

If so, and if it pertained for our journey of just under three months, we might have to put up with a bad dose of PMT all-round as we reached our destination! I admit I found the prospect of communal living quite daunting. I had never had problems being on my own, coming from my background of being an only child with few others of my age nearby. Crowds could become oppressive though.

From the start Ian and the more extrovert members of the party made efforts to amuse their companions. Ian taught those interested to play poker dice, a game I had not met before. Instead of having number pips, the Poker dice had representations of playing cards upon their six sides, an Ace, King, Queen, Jack, ten and nine, and these were used to form a poker hand.

Meanwhile a pleasant girl with a West Country accent got people telling jokes. This was Maddie, who as a school teacher had some experience of breaking the ice in the classroom. She had an excellent sense of humour and a pleasantly uninhibited style. Soon people were far more at ease thanks to her efforts. Some of the jokes arising from this activity led to strange nicknames being allotted too. Almost from day one, Geoff from Stevenage became known as 'Luigi', thanks to his brilliant impersonation of an Italian in one of the jokes he told us. Maddie herself became known as 'Scrumpy' hailing as she did from cider country.

We eventually pitched camp at Le Mont Noir, 'Domaine de la Sabliére' site, near Lille, after one abortive attempt elsewhere. My first diary entry noted that it was cloudy and chill that evening, but not raining, so there were good conditions for trying out the camping arrangements for the first time. The tents were traditional in design and brand new. Virginia and I had relatively little trouble erecting ours, something about which we had worried beforehand. It was especially nice to find we had the luxury of camp beds too.

I also noted in my diary that we had a 'lecture' from Ian that evening. This was to be a routine event whenever we approached new country and it was particularly important as we began the expedition. Ian started by stressing that we would use what daylight there was, which meant getting going early. He was aiming for a start of 6.30 each day. Getting everything packed away by that time was going to take some work. In Switzerland I had been working from 8am rather than the UK's 8.30 or 9am, but I hadn't had to take down and pack away a tent first thing!

Weather-wise what Virginia and I most dreaded was rain: getting a tent up in a downpour and having to stow it away wet, the canvas sticking to you clammily, were ever present nightmares. Tents were stowed in the trailer along with our rucksacks and, to prevent any damage being done to either, the method of packing was important. Thus an important part of Ian's 'lecture' was the organisation of parties of the men on each of the two trucks to unload efficiently and quickly when we stopped each day, and similarly to load the trailer safely every time we set off.

Next we were told of the bell system to call the cab driver from the rear of the truck. One ring or buzz of the bell indicated a photo stop request, two buzzes a loo stop, three buzzes meant something had fallen out of the truck and four buzzes was for some*one* falling out. Ian commented that it was to be hoped that the latter would never be used for this particular reason (this raised an uneasy laugh), but it could be used to alert the driver of other emergencies too.

Then came the organisation of shopping and cooking parties, groups of four people designated to shop en-route each day, sort out lunch and cook the evening meal, lastly preparing breakfast the following morning. The next group washed up after breakfast and then took on the duties for that day. I was with Virginia, Sarah, a nursing sister from Charing Cross Hospital that I'd met and liked at the pre-departure meeting, and Tim, a tall quiet lad from Kent. In a day or two I was to tell my parents...

> 'I rather dread cooking night which comes round every 6 nights (we're divided into parties of four, with at least one man – for bazaar shopping later). Cooking three-course meals for 24 is not too easy on four gas rings, but even worse is knowing how much of everything to buy.'

This first evening Ian got us preparing food we'd brought from London. This was stored under the rear seats, and consisted of a great many tins of such items as three bean salad and corned beef, as well as jars of Piccalilli sauce, plus fruit and plenty fresh vegetables, mainly potatoes. Everyone mucked in and I found myself preparing the potatoes with Heidi and Hannah, Swiss girls from the blue truck. It sounded a comparatively simple task, but it was for 44 people. How many did we allot each person and what pans could we use for such quantities? This aspect of the trip was quite a steep learning curve for me, for I had very little experience of cooking for more than three or four people at a time, and knew my culinary skills to be extremely basic. The Swiss girls seemed to take to it much better and left me feeling a bit inadequate. "Ah well", I thought, "Everyone will have their particular gifts to offer to the whole", and wondered what mine might turn out to be.

*** *** ***

I slept remarkably well that night, considering the unusualness of my environment, and was up at 5.45 next morning, fixing on the money-belt I should have to get used to wearing round my waist from now on and trying out the campsite's facilities. I have a feeling that, by making a bit of a racket, Ian or one of the other drivers made sure that we woke early. It was common, in the future weeks, for one of those preparing breakfast to make enough noise to ensure everyone was awake. Ian had to gradually get us used to an early start, making sure it became a routine before we were in countries where this would matter more. In Asia we drew crowds wherever we stopped, which made progress slow: if we got going early in the day, when people were busy getting up and ready for work, we might make better headway. He also wanted to avoid heavy traffic in cities. It was less hassle all round if we made every use of daylight on the roads, especially as autumn days grew shorter.

That first day, we breakfasted together hunting through the trucks' supplies to find where everything was; then the first cooking group washed up and we struck camp by 7.30, which was a very reasonable start. We drove through Lille and were soon at the Belgian frontier. Driving on through rather uninteresting country, we read, wrote diaries and letters, and chatted until mid-morning when we stopped at St. Ghislain, to the south of Brussels. This introduced us to the routine of mid-morning shopping wherever we happened to be. There was time for a coffee, while I wrote a quick postcard to my parents. The shopping group had little trouble here, even trying out their French. But how would we manage in some strange Asian town? Would we have to learn to barter? In sign language?

Then we made for lunch off the autobahn just over the German border. From there it was but a short distance to Cologne. Passing through Europe was not seen as a major part of this trip, just a preliminary to the real areas of interest, but it was good to catch a glimpse of regions I'd only seen briefly if at all up to then. From 1965 until the train's discontinuation in 1987, one of the first-class-only Trans Europe Express (TEE) trains, the Rheingold, operated between Geneva and Hoek van Holland, near Rotterdam, a distance of 663 miles. I'd treated myself to the journey up the Rhine valley on it going home for Christmas from Switzerland the year before. Much of the journey at that time of year had sadly been in the dark, but Cologne cathedral, flood-lit across the river, remained in my memory. Otherwise I knew very little of southern Germany and Austria, so even this near home I was interested in our surroundings.

But as we travelled south eastward on the autobahn I had to admit that the scenery was rather boring. I was only too glad to hear and join in with the jokes and stories that were circulating in the back of the orange truck. Maddie told us of her experiences teaching 37 seven to eight year-olds, of almost as many different nationalities, in a primary school in one of the poorer districts of London; Jim used colourful language to describe his time as a mining foreman in South Africa; and Geoff (Luigi) spoke of his travels in the Middle East and Kashmir. Really good news was that both the Kiwi lads, Dave and Rob, were prepared to entertain us. They were cheerful souls, Dave's favourite phrase being "She'll be right, mate" and Rob's "Don't worry; soon be Christmas!" And now we found that Rob had brought his guitar with him, and that he and Dave were happy to sing us some songs before long. It would be great to have live music. Ian had brought most of the current pop favourites with him on tape, "something for everyone" as he put it, and we could have this amplified from the cab of an evening, but, as it was one of my hobbies, I was looking forward to singing along occasionally – not always appreciated other than in the live setting!

We finally came to a halt near Limburg, before it got dark. The boys got out the gear from the trailer and up went the tents. Virginia and I collected our luggage and set up home for the night, while the cooking team got their act together. We were getting the hang of our tent and creating a routine of where our things belonged, so as not to get in each other's way.

The next morning there was trouble starting the truck, the first of several recurrent problems with our vehicles, but we were still off by 7.15. This was a slightly scary day for me though, my first as a member of our cooking team. Thus we washed up after breakfast and planned to do our shopping at the first appropriate stop.

To make the day more pleasant, our cooking team took the opportunity to travel in the cab with the driver, James. I took the seat next to him (which soon became known as 'the hot seat'; not only were you in the full sun, should it shine, but being over the engine made for warmer conditions), while Virginia, Sarah and Tim sat behind us, along with Scott, a quieter Australian chap, who, unlike most of the men, was starting the trip clean-shaven. I saw travelling in this position as something special. First it was a chance for more in-depth conversation with my companions. In the back there was a lot of banter, but some less extrovert people just read or enjoyed a nap. Keeping yourself to yourself was much less easy up front, and you really had a chance to get to know these people better. I suppose it also gave the drivers an opportunity to find out about their punters and how they were feeling. During this day's journey for instance we learnt that Scott had learnt to fly before he could drive a car! Wow, life must be different in Australia, I thought, and, with a frisson, realised I should see for myself in three months' time.

Then I expected to get the best views of the countryside from the cab, and I did indeed find it great to have a wide view of the scenery ahead, but that morning it was just a long stretch of wet autobahn, as we gradually moved south eastward, passing Frankfurt, Würzburg, Nuremberg and Ingolstadt. And 'passing' was the operative word. I should have liked to see one or two of these towns, one of them at least having an infamous reputation post-World War II. However we were pushing on, to ensure we reached Salzburg in plenty time, for it was there that we in the orange truck were to pick up our last travelling companion, Lukas. We'd been told he was the oldest of our party at 37. I wondered what tales *he* had to tell.

Once onto the Munich autobahn, we prepared lunch at one of the service areas. The comment in my diary was brief and brutal.

'Our effort was poor; tea very late!'

On we went to Munich, and then on through more and more fields of hops, some being harvested, into increasingly hilly Bavarian countryside, to reach the Austrian border just after 6pm. Austria was lovely after all the monotonous German autobahn. We continued to the Stadtblick campsite on the outskirts of Salzburg, boasting a panoramic view across the city to the mountains beyond. Virginia and I felt thoroughly at home here in the heart of Europe, having spent the last two years in the vicinity of the Savoy Alps. I felt my spirits lift, despite the fact that it was now almost dark and becoming drizzly. We could see the twinkling lights of the city out there, a place with a magical reputation as far as I was concerned.

But as everyone started eating, we remembered that we still had to put up our tent – oh no! We'd concentrated so hard on getting a reasonable evening meal together (we were not wrong in considering food to be an important element of the expedition) that we had forgotten the need to either put the tent up quickly first, or see that one of us, or maybe one of our companions, tackled the tent before joining the others in cooking duties. Another step along the learning curve! We felt tired out, and the nightmare was happening – we were camping in the rain.

***   ***   ***

However the next morning the weather had improved, and we were rested. I noted in my diary that we had a lie-in till 6.45! Breakfast went well. Tim had helped cook in hotels during the summers while doing his electronics degree at Uni, and he showed us an excellent way to pep up scrambled eggs with some grated cheese. He was definitely going to be an asset on our cooking team, we girls felt.

We packed up and stowed away the tents, discussing what we knew of Salzburg, the birthplace of Mozart and home to the famous festival. Virginia also knew it as the setting of *The Sound of Music*. Now to explore the place itself for a morning: I really looked forward to even this brief glimpse. Our arrival was delayed however, for the orange truck had to tow the blue one to start with, so we only got going after 9 o'clock. We were dropped in the city centre, while Ian went to meet Lukas.

We started with some window-shopping and then bought postcards. I chose an octagonal card with a beautiful illuminated night scene of the city with its famed fortress on the cliffs above the domes and spires of the graceful buildings below, to send home, plus another of Mozart's birthplace for my one-time singing teacher in Edinburgh. (I returned to visit Mozart's home eight years later, the only time to date that I've revisited anywhere I'd been on this quick trip across Europe.) We then found a coffee shop, where we could write while enjoying our drink and a huge, delicious cream cake each. Luxury! We then strolled the elegant streets, gazed at a statue of Mozart, a baroque church or two, neatly tailored jackets in a shop window and finally were delighted by the sight of a gentleman in real lederhosen. We were looking out for the tourist jaunts with a difference we'd heard about, and yes, there they were: horses and carriages with smartly dressed grooms, complete with Tyrolean hat, up on each box. We spent the next half hour seeing the sights of town across the backs of the gently clopping chestnut horses, their bridles a-jingling.

All too soon we had to reconvene at the truck, there to compare notes with others on what we'd managed to see in the short time available, and to meet the newcomer to the trip. We were glad to find that his English was excellent and that he showed signs of being very sociable. Heavily bearded, he looked fitter than most to undertake a rough journey. He had a good camera, though with less lenses that James's Pentax, which I had noted earlier had a special case of its own to house them all.

We boarded our truck and were soon driving up the alpine pass in Styria, our goal to journey via Graz to the Austria/Yugoslav border. The scenery in Austria was definitely the best we'd seen so far, lovely neat little houses by green meadows, under steep sided mountains. I could imagine alpenhorns calling the cows in of an evening. Peering through the rear windows of the truck, I fervently wished I had chosen to travel in the cab today rather than yesterday!

But I soon got a better view of my surroundings. We had passed through the spa town of Bad Ischl when we saw looking back that the blue truck had come to a halt behind us. We alerted the driver, using the 4 bell call, as for an emergency, and returned to find that they had broken down. The drivers looked into the problem and decided a spare part was needed, so we all milled around taking photos and getting some exercise while this was sent for. The truck in working order once more, we moved on to Tauplitz, but the light was failing, so we pitched camp near the village of Ketten, at Camping Puttersee, by the lakeshore and surrounded by mountains. The ground was damp thanks to the recent rain, but the view across the lake was highly romantic. On a rise in the land stood a schlössel, with a typical squared steep-pitched roof, half hidden in the trees. One of the lesser known Grimm's Fairytales might have been set there, or, better still, it could be the backdrop for a production of Schiller's *Wilhelm Tell Spiele*, like the one I'd seen in Interlaken a couple of years before.

After dark Ian gave us information regarding our itinerary through Yugoslavia and Macedonia. Then we enjoyed the first of many sing-songs around the trucks till quite late. It was led by New Zealanders, Dave and Rob, from our truck, and from the 'bluies' (as we now called those from the blue truck), by two quite talented guitar playing entertainers. One was a lad from Toronto, Michael, a chiropractor by profession, who was travelling with his brother-in-law and fellow Canadian, Derek. He had a pleasant light baritone voice and a nice repertoire of witty numbers. The other was an amazingly vibrant American girl, Gloria. Nearly everyone on the trip had some special characteristics but none surpassed flower-powered San Franciscan Gloria. It was she that put stars on her cheek-bones each morning and wore rings on her toes. She was by far the most way-out individual on the trip – perhaps our one authentic hippy.

All our performers had good voices and quite a varied repertoire between them. The Kiwis had already composed a song for the trip and performed it with guitar accompaniment to great acclaim. It was a catchy number and I noted that it neatly advertised their desire for female partners 'to help them through' the journey! I wasn't sure I wanted to be caught up in this personally, but it would be very interesting to watch how they got on.

Encounter Overland to Kathmandu

Well we set out Tuesday morning with some cans and a little bit of cash,
And just in case the action slacks we put our wellies in the bottom of our pack.
And we bought our family bible and Mr. Gossamer his reference we did bring.
But we hope we don't have to resort to all those crazy civilised things...

Chorus: *On the road to Kathmandu*
    Don't know who'll be screwing who,
    So just carry on your wanking
    Or find a friend to help you through.
    'Cause these tents get mighty crowded,
    So under the stars just might suit you,
    'Cause the journey is a long one
    On the road to Kathmandu.

Well this truck she is a beauty; she's got more wheels than my uncle has got balls,
And even Auntie Mary would find it comfortable strapped to the canvas walls.
But the suspension is quite ancient, so they provided us with fancy airline stools.
This Bedford goes most anywhere and along with it goes all this pack of fools...

Chorus: *On the road to Kathmandu*
    Don't know who'll be screwing who,
    So just carry on your wanking
    Or find a friend to help you through.
    'Cause these tents get mighty crowded,
    So under the stars just might suit you,
    'Cause the journey is a long one
    On the road to Kathmandu.

Chapter 3. Meeting with New Customs

Next day we were up at 5am and, moving around rather slower than usual thanks to our late night, only left at 7 o'clock in the direction of Liezen. It was a pleasant morning's drive via Bruck an der Mur and Graz to the Yugoslav border, which we reached by lunchtime. The first town over the border was Maribor, where we shopped and then lunched nearby, rather late in the day. As we drove on towards Zagreb through hilly terrain, we were greeted by a thunderstorm. With less to see through the Perspex panel windows down the sides of the truck, I at last got down to writing a proper letter to my parents. We also soon ground to a halt once more. I wrote:

'At the moment ... we are stuck in a traffic jam due to an accident. We've met one or two on the way, but luckily none involved us! Not that we haven't had the odd break-down already. The most common is having to tow the other truck out first thing in the morning!'

Once we got under way again, we found the road straight and flat. It threatened to be thoroughly boring driving hour after hour towards Kutina, but we had fun in the back. By now drying tea towels decorated the metal struts of the ceiling and bags of shopping were pushed against the kettle on the corner hob. People knew each other well enough to stretch their legs out to rest their bare or sandaled feet on their travel bags in the aisle or even up on the opposite seat, by whoever was sitting there. The atmosphere had relaxed considerably as the miles passed.

The drivers were attempting to make up the time lost yesterday and drove on till nearly 8pm! Then we were hustled through a dark entrance and down to a campsite beyond. It was definitely the worst we had experienced to date. And it suffered from smelly loos, of the parallel-foot-plates-either-side-of-a-hole variety! It was a foretaste of what was to come, when going to the toilet in a natural setting became infinitely preferable to any makeshift facilities we came across.

There were more subtle changes in odour noticeable too. As we moved south the next day, the temperate environment's scents of moist pine trees and lush pasture were giving way to a drier, dustier air mildly scented with herbs. We had come across plenty maize fields already, but I was starting to see crops now that I didn't so readily recognise. There was a much poorer use of land than in Austria though. The road crossed endless plain, the odd sunflower plots dead-looking, the flowers blackened and drooping. I had an excellent view of all this, being once more in the cab, with Ben, normally in the blue truck, driving, accompanied by Ian (who would take over from him in the afternoon). The drivers were obviously making sure they knew both sets of punters, though I wonder in retrospect if James had not negotiated this move, having his eye on Cynthia, an unusually dishy dresser (for this trip at any rate), a magazine editor's secretary from London, who was travelling in the blue truck. She also had the rare attraction of having been a Bunny Girl in her recent past!

My other cab companions that day were the Kiwi duo, Dave and Rob, and Meg, a friendly little lass from California. It was a pleasant laid-back atmosphere, with Dave and Rob generously sharing beer they had bought with us. It briefly struck me that passing the bottle round among us could spread infection, but I reckoned the alcohol would sort any bugs out!

I noted flower-wreathed wayside shrines, where there would have been much plainer crucifixes further north, and remembered that this was Sunday. Did people put wreaths up especially for the holy day? There seemed to have been plenty accidents on the main road, the vehicles left to rust by the roadside. Were the wreaths for those injured?

Otherwise life on the road here seemed more agricultural, a man taking his cow for an early morning constitutional reminded me of Fernandel in the film *La Vache et Le Prisonnier*, in which a POW walks out of Germany into Switzerland, perpetually saying he's 'taking the cow to the bull' in the next village. An elderly frail-looking couple were selling fruit from their horse and cart on the muddy, stalk-strewn verge. The fruit (or was it a vegetable?) they were offering was large and green, completely unknown to me then. I was told it was water melon. Those not being sold had been left rotting at the edge of the field, their ruddy innards a rare splash of colour in an otherwise dull green and dun-coloured landscape. I noticed one of the Swiss girls I'd helped to peel potatoes the first night, Hannah, talking, or rather gesturing, to the woman of the fruit-selling couple. The husband sat apathetically back in the trap that had brought them, the droop of his grey moustache accentuating the line of his long thin face, his clothes fitting only where they touched his meagre frame. His wife was the salesperson, and Hannah had made her smile. I was to learn that Hannah had quite a gift for getting along with local people, and also for taking excellent photographs of the characters we met.

Occasional more affluent fruit stalls along the road sold grapes and small packaged goods that helped our shoppers with their plans for dessert in the evening and gave us nibbles for the hours of uneventful straight road ahead. Up narrow side lanes we glimpsed more horse-drawn traffic, and women going about in what looked like some kind of local costume that was their Sabbath dress perhaps.

Travelling via Slavonski Brod, we reached Belgrade at noon, and, without stopping, continued towards Niš. By this time Ian was driving, and James had joined us in the cab, while Ben had taken up his usual position driving in the blue truck. It was then we hit some problems. In the late afternoon the police stopped and fined our trucks: it was difficult to understand why. Soon afterwards Ian noticed the blue truck, which was leading the way, taking the turn for Sofia instead of Skopje! Ben having been quickly re-routed, the trucks drove on in close convoy and found a motel camp site 70 kms past Niš. By now it was after 7pm. We pitched camp in the dark, adjusted to this by now, and enjoyed a particularly good curry for tea. Following pleasant drinks on the motel terrace afterwards, I showered and made it to bed quite late.

***   ***   ***

We set out next day to enjoy more undulating, almost alpine country. At the most dramatic point a river wound below us, as the road passed through two tunnels in the rock. But the land flattened out again before Skopje, where we spent an hour at the market. There was much that was completely new for me here, for I had previously seen nothing of Islam. I noted in my diary:

'Mosques and Muslims were everywhere ... People were wearing wonderful eastern dress. Men were in fur pill-box hats or skull caps, while the women sported scarves, shawls and often voluminous silk trousers.'

These were of delightfully varied patterned materials, in floral reds and blues. Some women were wearing striped red and white aprons, and red boleros appeared to be highly fashionable too. Female headgear could be quite bizarre, cloth drawn tightly round the head but more loosely over the hair behind, almost like an opaque hair-net. People squatted on the ground together chatting in groups around the stalls, some women clutching babies awkwardly as they did so. It was an extremely colourful scene and I took several photographs, but was careful to indicate to any women that I needed their permission, and indeed one woman did refuse to be photographed, though with a pleasant enough smile.

The goods for sale were similarly exotic to my eyes. Among the fruit and vegetables on the market stalls were peppers, squash and aubergines. And then there were the rugs, scarves and strange carvings. It was very distracting, when I really needed to find a post office so that I could send my parents their first long letter. At last I did. It would still be a few days before I received a letter from them, waiting for me, I hoped, in the Istanbul Poste Restante.

The country south of Skopje grew ever more barren, just sparse scrubland and ploughed stubble. Houses had white or ochre walls and red-tiled roofs. Brown sluggish rivers wound through small narrow valleys, the rocks on either side varying from pink through yellow to dazzling white. Sheep gathered in the shade of the biggest tree in sight, and bony cattle grazed about a seated cowherd.

Around midday we stopped for lunch off the road, half an hour from the Greek border. The boys, stripped to the waist, followed the meal with a Frisbee session, while I explored down a dirt track leading to a seemingly deserted and semi-ruined village. One of a few stray white goats had climbed a house's steps and stood looking out from a gap in the balcony above. It was quite surreal! Oranges, pomegranates and other fruit were growing wild. A green lizard flicked through the underbrush. Nature was definitely taking over.

I returned to find Peg and one of the English girls called Abby petting and snapping a donkey, whose owner, an elderly man, gave us fruit. Later his wife came with grapes for us. I wished we could say thank you with a gift of our own for her, and here Hannah and Heidi, the Swiss girls, were ahead of me. I found they had already thought of bringing a few small presents for just such occasions. So after lunch, I joined them in visiting her, with a cake of soap as a gift. A vine-terraced courtyard led to a very simple dwelling. Earth floors were covered with lino and mats. A huge loaf was in the oven and paper-thin bread (or was it filo pastry?) was stretched out on the covers of single beds, presumably those of her now grown youngsters. She showed us photos of the children, and treated us to figs in syrup. We eyed her gift with a certain amount of trepidation. Thanks to the amount of fruit we were eating, we were the reverse of constipated already, and syrup of figs might be the last straw! However, it would be horribly rude to refuse her kindness. We rolled our eyes as we envisaged the probable consequences, took our medicine smilingly and hurried back to the truck. Problems ahead perhaps, but what a delightful lady!

We continued to the Yugoslav/Greek border and put our clocks forward two hours, for we'd missed carrying out the one hour advance on entering Yugoslavia. The wind was getting up, and as we were offered a camp site free not much further on, we stopped early, around 6pm (or 4 o'clock old time). It was not a good night's camping, for gusts of wind meant we had to keep checking that the tent pegs were holding. My dreams saw me rocketing around, hanging on to guy ropes for dear life!

But the next morning (September 9th – we'd been travelling a whole week already!) was bright and warmer, and I wore my shorts for the first time. It was our cooking day once more, so we washed up after a fairly late breakfast, and were off just after 8 o'clock. We were travelling over a dry plane surrounded by distant hills. The differences between the Yugoslav and Greek highways were slight. Wayside shrines were still evident, but were now in the form of colourful miniature Orthodox 'temples', sometimes set high on poles. The real change was the street lighting along one side of the motorway. There had been none in Yugoslavia.

It took us two hours to reach Thessalonica, where our shopping group engaged in busy buying in the market. There were quaint side streets lined with individual shops from which men shouted their wares. It was not easy to understand or be understood. I noted in my diary,

'We had trouble buying a meal. Ian said to only buy 2½ kgs and we got 4 kgs!'

Clearly I had little idea of what 2½ kilograms looked like, despite having lived on the continent and having shopped using metric measures. The problem, as always, was catering for so many, buying in greater bulk than I was used to.

Having stowed the food in the lockers underneath the rear seats of the truck, we enjoyed a stroll along the wider boulevards and the pleasant sea front. This was my first view of the Mediterranean, its bright colours and distinctive scents quite different to those of the North Sea that I knew so well. I kept thinking of my mother's cousin from the Highlands of Scotland, who had spent several months here during the First World War when the Anglo-French forces attempted to provide Serbia with assistance against German and Austrian troops. He must have found it all really strange as well. It had been his one spell abroad and, as he told me later, "I left some good friends behind me in the cemetery in Salonica." Quite apart from combat, he had been lucky not to fall prey to the malaria which had caused some 500,000 non-battle casualties during the campaign. Nowadays the threat was much less, though we were to start taking twice-weekly Nivaquine tablets in Iran in preparation for the countries further east.

On our return we found some excitement at the rear of the blue truck. Our very last companions had joined the bluies, an Australian architect, Mike, and his wife, Lindy, who had been holidaying in Greece prior to meeting up with Encounter here. How bronzed they were! Being fair-skinned I rather doubted I could ever reach this enviable level of tan. Perhaps after eleven weeks though?

I was gradually getting to know more of the bluies, though I had not as yet travelled with them. (We in the orange truck were free to swap at any time with someone of the blue one for the day.) I knew by now though that Lindy and Mike were joining a group with another married couple, Stephen and Helen, and a couple of very good friends, Anne and Roger, all from London. The latter pair's history interested me, for I could not imagine myself in Anne's situation. They were work colleagues, but Roger had tired of his job and wished to travel. Anne told us she'd fancied the idea too and had come along, rather blindly it seemed to me, with no prospect of the relationship going further. It was of course more romantic than she made out: they married at the end of the trip and have been together happily ever since.

***   ***   ***

We drove on to lunch at a dusty, thorny lakeside just outside the city, and then continued to the Aegean shore, where we thoroughly enjoyed a dip in the lovely breakers on a stretch of beach alongside the road. We finally reached Kavala in the late afternoon, meaning to buy ice creams and have a brief look round.

It was intriguing to think that this was the first landing point of St Paul[7], when he brought Christianity to Europe almost 2000 years before. The Acts of the Apostles tells how St Paul travelled straight from Troy to the island of Samothrace and then to Neapolis, the old name for Kavala, en-route for Philippi, further inland. As a practising Christian I had my light-weight New Testament with me (thinking that it would be useful to verify Christian history at sites in western Turkey ... as well as useful on a Sunday when there were no churches around), so now I could remind myself of exactly what happened all that time ago.

But not until that evening, for my bible was in my rucksack in the trailer. I'd have to remember to put it in my travel bag from now on, for this was accessible all day, unlike the contents of the trailer. It was a shame, for there was a chance now to read for half an hour, as it was my turn to guard the cab. When we stopped in towns for a relatively short time, the drivers ensured that there was always someone on guard, both in the back and in the cab, for it took too long to close everything up completely. Today

---

[7] Acts 16: verses 11 & 12.

Geoff was staying in the back while I was in the cab. In fact he wasn't feeling too well and didn't fancy exploring the port. Several people were feeling sick already. Even Ian was 'off colour': mind, I had a feeling that was because of drinking the local ouzo in fair quantities. But I hoped I wouldn't fall prey to any bug. So far the syrup of figs had behaved rather well!

When one of my companions returned, I set out to look round for half an hour. The main town comprised light-coloured buildings of two or three storeys stacked one row above another, covering the sides of a hill topped by a citadel, its extensive crenulations giving it the appearance of a crown. I walked round the harbour below, watching fishermen preparing for their night's work, their boats' sails stretched overhead to give them shade. Near them on the quay, I came across employment I had never seen before. Net menders, mainly bespectacled older women, sat cross-legged in the midst of swathes of russet-coloured fishing nets, busily darning any recent tears.

Back on the road again, we hardly travelled any distance before our team got down to cooking the evening meal at a beach campsite near the ferry we were to catch the following morning, to the island of Thassos. We had been driving across Europe for a week and the drivers needed some rest. So did we all in fact. It was going to be luxury to relax by the sea for the best part of two days at a stretch.

***   ***   ***

I felt guilty next morning, as cooks were meant to rise really early, ahead of the others, and it was approaching six when I started helping with breakfast. But soon we were off to catch the 7.30 ferry to Thassos. It was a lovely sea trip, though I was a little worried about a lorry bearing bee skeps which I watched tipping about near our trucks as the ship rolled. Were the skeps empty, or would any bees inside get angry and attack us? Ruefully I acknowledged that the recent horror film *Killer Bees* might have influenced me unduly!

On arrival at the port of Limenas, we had a coffee and a look round the shops. The prices reflected its tourist-attracting location. They were over the top ... so we bought little. I then walked along the front with Virginia and Jan, an Australian girl from the blue truck who'd been working as a secretary in London for the last two years. When they sat to 'soak up the atmosphere', I went on through the shipyards and found a quieter, rocky bay, with a few fishing boats moored in front of low trees, shading pleasant larger houses. I enjoyed a brief paddle, and then returned to explore the other end of the port. Beyond the shipping in this direction, I came on a tiny chapel with the ruins of some Greek pillars in front of it, an ancient religious site perhaps.

Returning to the orange truck I found the day's shoppers proudly displaying their buys to everyone. They had managed to find some really interesting flatbread, quite different to any we'd eaten to date. Ian took one look and wailed, "Oh no. Not already!" We were soon to eat this bread every day. It was lovely when fresh, but 24 hours after cooking, it tended to become as tough as shoe leather. Ian had hoped not to have it any sooner than eastern Turkey. None of the rest of us had met the Naan bread popular in Iran, Afghanistan, Pakistan and India before. By the end of the trip we knew it all too well.

We drove on to camp on the beach at the other side of the hills from the port. The sands were beautiful. After lunch we swam and sun-bathed most of the afternoon. I also did my first wash, using my miniature travel clothes line tied between tent posts. It was great to soak up the sun and thoroughly relax.

In the evening we dressed more smartly and returned to dine in Limenas. Every ten days or so, E.O. treated us to a special night out, and this was our first one. It was a lovely evening watching the Greek men dancing, though I did wonder what had happened to the girls! However, the meal, Doner Kebabs, was rather disappointing, none too large portions and arriving terribly late. I tried the dancing, not very successfully, but it was fun. Then we returned to camp and enjoyed a fire on the beach, drinking the Thassos wine, before going to bed in the small hours.

It was absolute luxury to get up at 9am for a leisurely swim. We had brunch, I packed up the now dry washing and had another swim, after which I sunbathed once more. How decadent! We were packed up and ready to move by 3pm, so Virginia and I took a short walk along the beach before we returned to Limenas at 4pm.

Having visited the post office to send cards to friends and family, I also sent off my first completed camera film for development. It looked as though, at a minimum of a film a week, I was going to be using this service a lot. My parents had been prepared to keep the results for me, and would probably have a peep to see what I was viewing.

We then carried out our last exploration of the old Greek sites. We climbed up past the agora (or market) ruins to a religious shrine and theatre right up the hill. Perhaps this was the Acropolis referred to by Lawrence Durrell who described it as "in a state of smithereens"[8] when he wrote about it a couple of years later. Certainly there didn't look to be a single pillar complete, but it had atmosphere and was beautifully placed, giving a marvellous view over the town as the sun was starting to sink towards the horizon over the harbour.

Once more down on the front, we joined Ian, Geoff, Jim and Sue, Kiwi Rob and Abby, for a chat over a refreshingly long drink of orange. It was a good opportunity to learn more about this group and they were a pretty varied lot. Geoff seemed the humorous, moustachioed bachelor type of *Three Men in a Boat*, in contrast with Jim, a plain-speaking (and hard-swearing) northern Australian. Jim had been away from home for eight years, but was now returning with Sue in order to get married. Sue, it seemed, was several years his senior, being in her mid-thirties, and she didn't appear particularly physically attractive, though I could see she had a fair amount of Cockney common sense in her favour. How would this partnership work out, I wondered?

Nor was Rob particularly good-looking, certainly not as handsome as his compatriot Dave for instance: he worked in a bank in Christchurch and it was his obvious delight in company that made him attractive to others. Lastly, for a well-spoken English girl, Abby was another extremely forthright character. She'd held a position as editor in a publishing firm

---

[8] *The Greek Islands* (1980), page 220.

in London, and I could imagine she would stand no nonsense! What an interesting bunch of characters I was travelling with!

The ferry trip back to Kavala was calmer than the one the day before. We then drove back to the original camp site. There was an initial problem with an Australian girl, Lynn, on our arrival, for she was quite ill with sun stroke *and* the dreaded tummy bug that seemed to be going the rounds! After that, Virginia and I made sure we had an early night, and I certainly slept like the proverbial log. A rest on the beach and plenty sea air had suited me fine.

***   ***   ***

So much so that I slept till six! It was a rush to get up, ours one of the last tents to be packed. But we got off at 7am, after drying the washing up a little to atone for our lateness. We swung up over the tailpin (real experts in this manoeuvre by now) and I took an end seat in the truck and watched the poker dice play.

We had a late morning stop at Alexandroupolis for the shoppers. Not only was it Friday, the Muslim holy day, but we were in Ramadan (fasting during daylight hours the routine now for believers), so shopping needed to be done before we entered Turkey. Some of us went to a nice little café, to have drinks, yes, but as always these days, to use the toilet facilities as well. We found them to be excellent here, but for a good reason. They were approached by a spiral staircase into the cellar and unlocked for us by the Patron himself!

We reached the border bridge in time for lunch in the Turkish sector. Exiting Europe proper proved to be an unsettling experience, for the army were everywhere with fixed bayonets. A look-out tower and camouflaged tanks were up the hill over the bridge too. Greece and Turkey had only just concluded hostilities in Cyprus, which had led to a political splitting of the island between the two countries earlier that year. It's amazing to consider this decades later, but that was the worst sign of aggression across borders that we came across during the whole of our Asian Odyssey in 1975.

Chapter 4. The Sights and Sounds of Istanbul

It was after lunch that we came across our first camels! A really straight road, which seemed obviously Roman in origin, led towards Istanbul. Only the camels could thoroughly interest us however, for we were in our own world in the back of the truck, playing poker dice and listening through earphones to the cab music. To this day whenever I hear Elton John's *Bennie and the Jets* (my favourite) or other numbers from the *Goodbye Yellow Brick Road* album, or Mike Oldfield's *Tubular Bells*, I'm transported back to the journey overland.

But as we approached Istanbul the behaviour of the traffic around us immediately drew our attention. I wrote in my diary:

> 'I never heard so many horns blowing as I did from vehicles on these roads, and the driving is SHOCKING!'

The cacophony of car and lorry horns was to accompany us through most of Asia and was utterly alien to me at the time. At home horns were only sounded if something dire had to be warned, and they consisted of simple loud hoots of alarm. Here in Istanbul there was an amazing orchestral medley of sharp North American train-like blasts, persistent bugle calls and three or four-tone honkings.

We reached our camp-site on the outskirts of Istanbul after dark. It was a pleasant and well-used site, with good facilities. We settled down for a two-night stay and were well organised by the time tea was served. This was followed by drinks in the café on site before bed.

The local muezzin's call to prayer at dawn made a brilliant wake-up call next morning! It also gave me a real feeling of being far from home already. I couldn't wait to explore this land of otherworldly sounds! After breakfast the trucks took us into town, the first visit for most of us being to the Poste Restante, Galatasaray, to collect the mail, which in my case had started out before I left Britain! It was lovely to find my parents' letter, and to hear details of the little everyday things that meant 'home' to me. I could see that others felt similarly. It was not the only time that I blessed the Poste Restante system. In a time before mobile phones, receiving mail from family and friends was one of the experiences of worldwide travel I treasured most.

We all then set off on our different itineraries through the city, I with Sarah and Virginia. Sarah invited Scott to come with us and act as chaperone. Ian had advised us that this was necessary in the Bazaar, and indeed I was very glad to have him along. This was especially the case because I saw we were near the Galata tower, a 5th century watchtower and one-time prison, and the tallest building in Istanbul in 1975. (Today some 70 high-rise buildings in the city are at least twice its height.) Scott and I both wanted to visit it, to see the reputedly spectacular view from the top. The others were less keen, so we split up and Scott became my very own personal chaperone. We were out of luck though, as to climb the tower meant paying twice as much for our cameras as for ourselves!

Instead we crossed the Golden Horn by the Atatürk Bridge and started up the hill through the back streets, which, picturesque in the extreme, caused us to meander back and forward in anything but a straight path. Wooden tenements, often so dilapidated that it was a wonder they were still upright, jutted this way and that across the track to impede our progress. The occasional bright white plaster of their lower storeys set off the rich brown panelling of the first floor bay windows overhanging the alleyway. Sacks of rubbish, or perhaps they were work shavings, were stacked everywhere and there was a musty, spicy tang in the air. Much as I enjoyed its atmosphere, I was afraid I could well imagine the area being a delicious haven for rats after dark!

Venturing out on the more open ground above, we came on the Suleiman the Magnificent mosque. What a contrast with the houses we had just passed! Arches and domes arose before us to form an amazing structure, fronted by a gardened area at each corner of which was a slender minaret. We took our shoes off, washed our feet under the taps provided alongside the garden walk, and went to sit in the beautifully carpeted, cool interior, our eyes drawn upward towards the superb ceiling decoration. The mosque was the work of Mimar Sinan, the Turkish 'Michelangelo', a military engineer who became an architect extraordinaire. In some 98 years of life (though mostly from the age of 50 onwards, as chief royal architect) he wasted no time. He built 81 large mosques, 50 small mosques, 55 medresas (educational institutions), 33 palaces, 16 caravanserais (travellers' lodgings), 8 bridges, 19 mausoleums, 7 dams, 32 baths, 3 hospitals and 14 fountains. He served 5 sultans before his death in 1588.

Rested and refreshed, we left and asked our way to the Bazaar. I enquired in Beyazit Square, by the main gates to Istanbul University, and had to buy an ice-cream in payment for the information! Lemon squash sellers were out in their stalls and, more strangely I thought, so were middle-aged men selling bird seed. There were plenty pigeons around pecking vigorously at the seed thrown them by tourists. But what if no tourists turned up? Surely the birds would mob these poor men, who sat, shoulders hunched, over trays covered with neat bowls of seed. It became incumbent to buy their seed and save them from assault, didn't it?

Once reached, we found the open market was bustling with men: very few women were to be seen, but I was interested to note how different they appeared to the Muslim women I'd seen in Skopje. These ladies were in western knee-length skirts with the kind of headscarf our Queen Elizabeth might wear at a breezy race meeting. Kemal Atatürk's secularisation had freed women considerably in their dress. They were rarely walking without a male escort however. I could see Ian had been right about having a chaperone.

And the Grand Bazaar lived up to every other rumour we had heard about it too. It was fascinating. Clothes and pots and pans hung from rafters while smaller goods were displayed around the feet of metal pillars supporting the interior building, a dark and rather forbidding place. In this covered older market, once the site for the Sultan's stables the guide books told, we found ourselves the target of every salesman, especially in the carpet section. We kept saying "No money", but it had little effect. I was very glad to have Scott with me, but he was a bit too nice with them really. However he found a good line when he said he was Australian. "Ah, Australia long way to take carpet!" they agreed. But less polite salesmen grabbed us by the arm, telling of distant Australian and British friends who had loved their buys, and exhorting us to view their wares. We had a quick sandwich for lunch, and escaped hurriedly.

I wanted to see the Blue Mosque, so named because of its blue-tiled interior. Built in the early seventeenth century by Sultan Ahmed, who had worked on it as a labourer himself, it was given six minarets, which caused protests from Mecca not to imitate the six minarets they had there. Thus it was Sultan Ahmed who added a seventh minaret to the great mosque at Mecca, so that the mosque he had constructed in Istanbul no longer rivalled Islam's holiest shrine.

As we neared the Blue Mosque we came across the Swiss girls, Heidi and Hannah. They had had trouble with the local men and had even been accused of being lesbians. But they had met a Turk who explained Islam to them a little. The minaret-shaped tower inside the mosque gave the direction of Mecca. Then there were three presenters, the first at the minaret, the second on the high platform and the third on the far end microphone in the mosque. We found there was a service on (we had heard the first presenter crying from one of the minarets) and we sat in on the end of it. It was good to be in a holy place, but what bowing and scraping there seemed to be!

On we went from here to St Sophia, or Haghia Sophia to call it by its ancient name, dedicated as it was to Holy Wisdom. It certainly had an interesting history, starting as a Christian basilica in 325 AD, becoming a mosque some thousand years later and finally, in 1935, a museum. Nevertheless I found it overly huge and bare. Still it had collected some interesting stories over the centuries. I particularly liked what I'd read about the first organ in the church, elaborately decorated with gold, silver and precious stones and operated by clockwork as well as manually: it was a gift from Elizabeth I of England to the then Sultan, Mehmet III. In 1599 she had sent her organist, Lancashire-born Thomas Dallam, to install the instrument and it had been damaged during the voyage, so took some weeks to reassemble, the Topkapi Palace court watching with great interest. When the instrument was finally played, they and the Sultan loved Thomas' work so much he was offered two wives if he'd stay. He evidently enjoyed the peep he was given of the harem to tempt him, but declined the offer, presumably preferring the ladies of his home town of Warrington to those of Istanbul!

I wasn't brave enough to try out the other information I'd received about St Sophia. "Try clapping your hands under the dome", I'd been told. "You'll be amazed at the echo!" There was enough echo without doing that, so instead I tried the St Sophia toilets, and they were not at all bad. A very helpful lady even showed me a tap near the floor to use when the sink taps wouldn't work for me.

The Topkapi Palace, the former home of the sultans, was next on our list of tourist 'musts'. There we found several of our E.O. companions. We had a good look at the Chinese and Japanese porcelain in the kitchens, as Scott was keen on this. Then we spent some time in the treasury. Here there were items extraordinarily richly decorated with jewels. Fantastic emeralds were set in short sword hilts, adorned headdresses and sultan's thrones, and a pair of candlesticks had been encrusted with 6,666 diamonds, one for each verse in the Koran.

On our way to change money to buy tickets specifically to view the Harem, we ran into Sarah and Virginia again. From the money-changers we had a wonderful view over the Bosphorus, where we could see a Russian ship moored. I wished I had my camera with me, but we'd had to leave them at the gate, as, yet again, it cost twice as much as our entry fee to bring them in. This was becoming an established proviso to Istanbul sight-seeing.

We returned to the Palace harem, which I knew to have quite a reputation. But we were shown round by an extraordinarily uninterested woman guide, equally monotonous in Turkish, English and French. The material she told us hardly needed spicing up though. We started by looking at the cells of the black eunuchs, sent the Sultan by the Ottoman governor of Egypt. It was they who waited on the women of the harem. "Greek women were hired to castrate these men", intoned our guide. There followed a suite for the Sultan's mother (known as the Queen, and the acknowledged controller of the Seraglio), another suite for the Sultan himself and one for the heir apparent. The Sultan's firstborn son might be safe enough, but "Younger brothers of the Sultan were usually strangled with a bow string", droned our guide smothering a yawn.

The concubines' rooms upstairs were not on view, but we were shown the Baghdad Kiosk, a blue tiled room with four couches. Here the Sultan 'took his pleasure'. "A concubine would approach the Sultan under the bed clothes from the foot of the bed", murmured the guide soporifically. "If she was not satisfactory, he would push her out again with his foot." How could this woman be so uninspired, when the subject matter was this riveting? Life in the harem could be very lively I was sure. Hadn't I read that one Sultan actually had 40 women pregnant at once?

My favourite room was the plush amusement room for the Sultan, with high seats for the four legitimate wives (according to Islamic law this was the number the Sultan was allowed), then those for the favourites and concubines, and a dancing area beyond. It would have been the icing on the cake if a group of houris could have entertained us with the Dance of the Seven Veils at this point. Sadly it was not to be.

On leaving the Palace we found our American singer, Gloria, being accosted by some Turks. Scott took her arm, so she thought battery was being added to assault and nearly lashed out! But she was very grateful to be free of the pestering men, and regarded Scott as her knight in shining armour from then on.

By now we had a large group of our travelling companions gathered together, and we all started for the camp-site. This proved quite an adventure. We got on what we thought to be the appropriate bus, but got off too early and soon became lost. Some Turkish women then gave us detailed instructions, though one confused us further by pointing left when she said right. Luckily some of us caught sight of another bus with the correct sign on it and we ran to catch it.

Tea was followed by drinks in the bar, where Ian told me off for writing my diary up in a corner away from the group. But there was a lot to write about and a solid table to write on for once, I argued. It was a struggle to remain faithful to my plans of keeping a record of the trip, but I've been extremely grateful that I did. The most dramatic and bizarre events remain in the memory, but others, ones that are delightful too, can fade all too soon.

And it was my diary that told me the next day was a Sunday. Outwardly it seemed like any other day. Then I remembered of-course that I was in a Muslim country: Sunday was not a holy day here. It was our cooking spell once more, so our foursome was up fairly early and soon out shopping locally, after washing up. We had problems trying to buy meat, for the butcher wanted to sell us a whole lamb and seemed to have very little cut meat, due to Ramadan presumably. I also recorded that we found the eggs very expensive. Clearly we were becoming proficient in the intricacies of the global price system! Actually it said more for the knowledge Ian had of the local prices, for he was the one who gave us the appropriate money to spend.

Mid-morning I set off for town with Sarah, Virginia, Jane and Liz, the last two being another pair of friends who had worked together like Virginia and me, Australian and American nursing colleagues. The American, Jane, came across as extremely practical; her Australian counterpart, Liz, was quieter but always seemed helpful and kind.

We took a dolmuş (a shared taxi or minibus) to the city wall, and then a proper taxi (rather an expensive option, I felt) to the quays. And who should be there but Scott! So we joined together to take a tourist boat on the Bosphorus. Travelling through the great strait gave wonderful views of palaces, parks and mansions on the slow two hour trip to Yeniköy.

I heard some good yarns too. We had luckily met a very pleasant local man who told us everything we wanted to know of the last stand of Emperor Constantine XI Palaeologus in the spring of 1453, before Constantinople fell to Ottoman invaders under Sultan Mehmet II, and became Istanbul. 21 year old Mehmet II was certainly the aggressor. He had marched his troops to within sight of Constantinople's walls. He then built a castle, Boğaz Kesen (meaning 'Throat Cutter', known now as Rumeli Hisari) at the narrowest point of the Bosphorus and loaded it with the heaviest ordinance ever seen in eastern warfare at that time. We were passing the great towers and fortified walls of this structure on the European bank of the strait as we heard about this. It still looked mighty impressive.

Mehmet II then petitioned Constantine for complete and unconditional surrender, which the latter refused to give, pointing out that Mehmet was breaking agreements between the two empires. Next a Turkish fleet turned up in the Sea of Marmara to support the Sultan. Only a handful of Genoese and Greek vessels had been able to help Constantine, and it was when they arrived that things sound to have got really exciting. Academic, Dionysios Hatzopoulos, retells it today, bringing the whole scene very much alive. The Ottoman naval commander,

"…Baltoghlu, immediately dispatched his fleet to attack and capture the [four] ships. The operation seemed easy and soon the ships were surrounded by the smaller Ottoman vessels ... The Sultan on horseback … rushed to the shore to watch the battle. Excited and unable to restrain himself, screaming orders at Baltoghlu, the young Sultan rode into the shallow water. Fighting, the big ships continued pushing the smaller ones, and helped by the wind they were now close to the south-eastern corner of the city. Then the wind dropped and the current began pushing them towards the coast on which stood the Sultan and his troops. Fighting continued, with the Christian sailors hurling on the enemy crews stones, javelins and all sorts of projectiles. Eventually the four vessels came so close to each other that they became bound together, forming a floating castle. Around sunset the wind rose and [this 'castle' of] ships, pushing their way through the [main fleet], and the wrecks, of the enemy vessels, hailed by thousands of people who were standing on the walls, entered the Golden Horn."

The Sultan was absolutely furious with Admiral Baltoghlu and ordered his immediate beheading. He also became convinced that something drastic must be done to combat the besieged city's naval strength. This 'something' must surely be unique in naval history: the fleet would enter the Golden Horn overland. He had been overseeing the building of a road from the Bosphorus to the shore of the Golden Horn. Now was the time to put it to full use.

"On April 22, to the horror of the besieged, a long procession of ships, sitting on wooden platforms, was pulled by teams of oxen and men, over the road, into the port area."[9]

Some seventy boats entered the Golden Horn in this way. The city fell a week, a very long and arduous week, later, and Mehmet II rode into St Sophia. Thus the Byzantine Empire came to its end.

***   ***   ***

At Yenikōy we soon came on the Gazebo restaurant overlooking the Bosphorus, and took a table on the terrace. Our lunch was excellent. The three hors d'oeuvres served were very tasty: we were learning how good Turkish vegetarian fare could be. It was followed by beautifully presented and cooked fillet of bass, a fish unknown to me at the time. Everyone was really friendly too, one customer offering to photograph us. Extremely satisfied with our afternoon, we wandered through the local street market stalls to the quay once more.

The trip back was quicker, only an hour. I remember passing under the great new Bosphorus Bridge, opened just two years before, on the fiftieth anniversary of the founding of the Turkish Republic. It was noted for having the longest suspension bridge span (1,560 metres) outside the USA. I gazed along it with interest towards the far shore, where we would be travelling next day. This was our gateway into Asia.

Meanwhile I admired the pretty little neo-baroque Ortaköy mosque, set just alongside and rather dwarfed by the bridge, and soon afterwards, the graceful and impressive Dolmabahce Palace, which I had noticed before but now looked at with greater interest. It had been built on the site where the team of oxen had hauled Mehmet's fleet over the hill to the Golden Horn.

Back on dry land, we had better luck getting a bus than we had had the day before and returned to the camp site much refreshed, to prepare tea.

---

[9] Hatzopoulos (2013).

Everyone that evening had stories to tell of their sight-seeing during the day.

After getting up fairly late next day to make breakfast and enjoy it in the sunshine, we had a long time to wait before moving on. Ian had some insurance issues to sort out and spare parts were needed for one of the trucks. I hung around writing my diary, playing a round or two of Frisbee with the others, and otherwise marking time till he returned. When we had lunched, we finally set off for the new bridge, and a new continent.

I was right at the back of the truck and thoroughly enjoyed the sights, driving through the thick of the traffic. First a huge commotion was caused by a horse and cart blocking the way: every male in sight had advice to give and gesticulated wildly. Then a cart with dreadful wheel-wobble confirmed my growing opinion that Turks managed to get by with anything. Next, amidst all the vehicles, and giving rise to a great dim of horns, there sat a dog scratching itself in the middle of the road! Following this a truck, crowded with people, provided colour and variety with windscreens fringed and tasselled, decorations I would soon regard as fairly standard in Asia. Amazingly the next sight to draw my attention was a roman aqueduct. Then more bazaar stalls crowded the pavement ... and THEN we got stuck going the wrong way down a one-way street. There were *such* characters around here. I spent a happy hour or more overlooking the weird little cobbled street 'conversing' (though without language) with the male stall-holders and taking photos of the wonderful goings-on. Nearly all the men had something to say to us, with flashing mahogany eyes and gold-filled teeth! There was a certain amount of physical work too, as we had to un-couple and push back the trailer before the truck could reverse to free itself from this last situation.

We finally made it to the new bridge at almost 4pm and continued to Kartel, where we were supposed to catch the ferry over the eastern end of the Sea of Marmara half an hour later. There was a long queue, so we had a snack and drinks, walked round the sea front, wrote and sent off a few postcards, and then played cards in a café. We finally caught the evening ferry to Yalova at half past eight. It was a good clear night and I remember particularly noticing the position of the stars during the hour and a half sea crossing. I wasn't an expert at reading the night sky, but even I noted that the Great Bear was low on the northern horizon at 9.30pm and the North Star, Polaris, half way down the sky already! I had never been so far south. With a thrill I realised that I, who thought of myself as thoroughly European after working alongside members of so many other different European countries while in Switzerland, was now truly embarking on something quite different. Once on dry land again we pitched camp some twenty minutes up into the hills. It was our first night in Asia!

Chapter 5. Ancient Places

So now we were in Asia the going would undoubtedly get tougher. Virginia reckoned it had been tough enough already, but still she was bearing up pretty well. However, good camping facilities would now be gradually rarer to come by and we were starting to take precautions against infection that had not been necessary before. This was the day that I was initiated in the method of water chlorination we were to use from now on. Ian had suggested I do this for the orange truck. I was supplied with a small cylindrical tin that had originally contained camera film. This held the chlorine salts to be used. I was given a matchstick to use as a spoon. In Turkey and Iran, I was to put one matchstick-load of powder in a jerry can (20 litres) of water. This became two matchstick loads per jerry can in Afghanistan. We were also to soak all fresh fruit and vegetables in chlorinated water for at least half an hour before meals from now on. We found we could only just taste this in tea, but otherwise not at all.

Looking around me as we travelled next day, I wondered where the vegetables would come from. The hilly country over which we were driving was covered with dry grassland scattered with thorn bushes and scrub, only relieved by the occasional line of poplars. It was a landscape of dusty yellows, browns and ochres, through which flocks of sheep wandered finding what they could to graze on. Our general impression was of a poorer country, an impression further strengthened by the rubbishy old lorries, scrap iron, pots, pans, bricks and all manner of debris left mouldering by the side of the road.

We passed the Sea of Marmara inlet at Gemlik and drove on towards Bursa. There were half-built houses on the outskirts, but also more of an attempt at cultivation, sunflowers, some maize still, what seemed to be plantations of trees (these were identified as fig trees later), and also dagger-shaped red peppers, olives and even cotton growing. We spent an hour at Mushaphakemalpaşa during which we had a drink and I bought some Turkish Delight. This proved slightly disappointing. I was used to the icing-sugar-dusted rose-flavoured variety, sometimes coated with chocolate, which was popular in England: this Turkish variety lacked the chocolate and sugar, but did contain chopped dates and pistachio nuts, and so was chewier. It was the authentic version however, and I savoured it for that.

We stopped for lunch on a wide grassy verge to the road, by a small stream. Just along from us gypsies had an encampment, the women reaching for their children, a little unsure of us, as we approached. They wore white cloth tied tightly round their heads but were otherwise very colourfully dressed with modest long-sleeved blouses above long multi-coloured floral skirts. These folk seemed to keep their goods in small handcarts and large prams that were standing about. In the background oxen forded the stream.

We moved on into sandstone countryside with rocky outcrops and dry valleys. The roads were often still in the process of being made, and could be pretty rough. Minarets rose from every village and the women, the few we saw, usually wore black head-dresses and billowing trousers now. This contrasted with the western knee-length skirts of the women in Istanbul, only showing they were Muslim by the wearing of a simple head scarf.

There was no site suitable for camping by the sea in this area, and we finally jolted to a halt 10 kms from Bergama, to pitch our tents in an olive grove, which meant finding as flat an area as possible on a ploughed and bumpy surface. Peg and Mark, the Australian architect and his wife on the orange truck, not for the last time voicing popular opinion very effectively, complained bitterly to Ian about how difficult it was to secure the tent pegs and that pitching camp was slowed badly by a lack of sufficient hammers. "Thank goodness for camp beds", we all agreed, but there was no amending the fact that mine ended up on a slope! It was a rather cooler night though: perhaps the muscle work required to stay steady on my bed would keep me warmer!

*** *** ***

We were off by 8 o'clock next morning, I in the 'hot seat' of the cab once more, and it was indeed quite warm, even at first light. James was driving, with Maddie and her friend Rosie (Ros. for short), Lynn and Abby behind me. Thus I had an excellent view as we drove to Bergama, to visit the ruins of the Asklepion of Pergamon. 'Asklepion' was originally a term used to define a type of temple which acted as a healing centre, devoted to Asklepios, Greco-Roman God of medicine. The Pergamon site was founded in the fourth century BC around a sacred spring that still flows and has been found to possess radioactive properties. My background in medical rehabilitation gave me profound respect for the Asklepion here. Not only had it become one of the best-known healing centres of the ancient world, but it had also produced the world's first psychiatric hospital. When Pergamon became part of the Roman Empire this centre really flourished. The influential physician Galen was born in Pergamon and practiced here in the second century AD, having first made his medical reputation treating warriors in gladiatorial games in the city.

As we trod the ancient paving stones of the colonnaded market street in the ruins of Pergamon, we found ourselves behind young children walking to school, the little girls in black pinafores with white lacy collars over their ordinary trousers, and carrying school cases[10]. I wondered what they thought of their world, strewn with carved plinths and ancient columns, tourists ever coming and going. What kinds of fantastical fables might they dream up? For it was only just down the road in Smyrna (now Izmir) that Homer had lived, that great writer of epic poetry. The ruins might spawn art too, judging by the work of a young man sitting cross-legged on a low wall, his back resting against one of the columns as he sketched the scene.

It was to be a day for viewing ancient sites. There was a well preserved theatre at Pergamon, which along with some of the scenery, reminded me of the sites I had seen in Provence, on another, much briefer, camping holiday only three years before. And now we moved on to the Akropol, a hill fortress site, with magnificent views of the region, a fascinating feature of which was the line of a Roman aqueduct stretching from hill to hill below us a little way off. What feats of engineering were achieved a couple of thousand years ago!

We lunched the far side of Izmir and then, along a tree-lined tunnel of a road, went on to Ephesus. It was only then that I realised I had no more film left in my camera! There was no film for sale here, so I bought some

---

[10] See photograph on page 84.

slides instead and hurried after the others. How envious I was of Lukas as he carefully angled to get the best shots with his impressive camera: he promised to send me the best at the end of the trip, which cheered me up a little.

Maddie knew enough about the site to guide us round. It was far more crowded than the previous places we'd seen, but it exceeded Pergamon in interest in that some parts of the ruins were amazingly intact, particularly the Celsus Library, the curiously empty façade (a two storey terrace of window frames) towering above the surrounding well-worn paving, archways and temple remains. This library, completed in 117 AD, stored more than 12,000 scrolls and is said to have been the richest library in ancient times after those of Alexandria and Pergamon. Sadly most of the library's interior, and all of the scrolls, were destroyed less than 150 years after completion, either by fire during a disastrous earthquake that struck Ephesus in 262 AD, or possibly during a Scythian invasion around the same time. The façade had been reconstructed from the stones lying around the site.

Here was another Greek theatre too, which the Romans had later renovated. You could really imagine what it must have been like in Emperor Augustus' times. The acoustics were great: I wished I might have had the chance to watch a drama here. But I had the dramas of the past, those of the New Testament, to content me. Taking my volume out, sitting there in the theatre with Maddie and a few others, I couldn't resist reading aloud the passage from the Acts of the Apostles where Paul runs into trouble with the silversmiths of Ephesus, who felt that he represented a glorified branch of Judaism, that threatened their livelihood as workers for the cult of Diana.

> "The whole city was in confusion. Paul wanted to appear before the assembly but the other Christians would not let him. Some were shouting one thing, some another. But some of the crowd explained the trouble to Alexander .and he, motioning for silence, attempted to make a defence. But when they recognised that he was a Jew, a single cry rose from them all: for about two hours they kept shouting, 'Great is Diana of the Ephesians!'" (Acts, Chapter 19: verses 29-34).

And it was the brave Ephesus town clerk who finally quieted the crowd. It felt extraordinary to be seeing the actual place in front of me as I read. Abby's reaction as I finished was, "That's an interesting point of view." "Well, it happened right here!" I said, realising that she considered it as just another myth. There was no risk of starting any deeper discussion though, for Abby was already off looking at something else. Two thousand years ago the churches of Ephesus and Pergamon were among the seven criticised in Revelations for their lack of full-blooded commitment. It seemed that the general attitude to religious history was as lukewarm as ever.

It was sad that it was not possible to see the Temple of Diana, famed for being one of the seven wonders of the ancient world, but my reading had prepared me for this. Like the Celsus Library it has been destroyed by fire, this time started by a madman, the night in 356 BC that Alexander the Great was born. The temple priests later explained that the goddess Diana couldn't save her temple as she was presiding over Alexander's birth! And it was Alexander that paid for a new temple to be built, the one St Paul saw. It managed to survive some four centuries, but had been reduced to rubble on swampy ground on the outskirts of Selçuk, the settlement near the Ephesus ruins.

Much of the two hours we spent at Ephesus we were pining for a drink, it was so hot! Our eventual camp site was more pleasant and cooler, once more near an olive grove and the ground still very hard. But Ian had bought more hammers, after Peg and Mark's explosion of yesterday, so we were better off in that respect. We felt rather uneasy though when someone reported killing a scorpion as they put up their tent!

That evening we had a big vote, for we were offered two alternative routes ahead, to go to the hot springs further north with the blue truck or to the south coast with the orange truck. Having heard of Pamukkale, where the hot springs were to be found, I chose the former: Virginia decided on the latter. So I prepared to join the blue truck the next day and wondered who I might be sharing with.

***   ***   ***

So next morning saw me loading my gear into the blue truck, driven by Ben. There were several people I didn't know so well here, and I was rather uneasy that the next day I was to cook once more. Our team had been halved, for Sarah had joined Virginia on the coastal route. Tim and I had been put with Graham from the blue truck, a bespectacled English chap who, though pleasant enough, didn't appear too dynamic. I wondered how we'd get on.

We drove off towards Pamukkale, following the railway. At one point we saw a steam train on the line and everyone jumped as it gave a piercing split-note whistle. Like many countries, Turkey had gradually changed its transport expansion priorities from the rail to the road network. But it seems that under-investment led to extremely slow line modernisation. Steam engines were still regularly in service and remained so until the late 1980s. Brought up as I was in the steam era, I found it a very pleasant reminder of my childhood.

One or two of the blue truck's group knew a lot more about plants and the geography of the region than I'd heard up to now. They told me they'd seen tea, tobacco and lemons growing. I'd missed this, so started looking out for them. Some perfect examples of soil erosion were appearing around us at this point too, showing in seamed gullies. The earth colours changed from white to yellow to pink to rust. In places there was mining. Stephen, a knowledgeable Londoner among the bluies, said the Turks had thought of using oil to improve top soil, but that it was proving too expensive. Topsoil erosion certainly appeared to be a problem in much of the country we had passed through since leaving Istanbul.

We stopped in Denizli for three quarters of an hour to shop for tomorrow's meals. Tim, Graham and I had decided on macaroni cheese with some green vegetables as the main evening meal, but I was extremely frustrated that our shop now took two hours and ten minutes in all! It took twenty minutes to reach the market in the first place, but then Graham seemed intent on finding chocolate for himself, rather than getting food for the journey. I had trouble getting vegetables of any quantity and settled for courgettes in the end. Next there was only fancy pasta for sale rather than macaroni. Well, it would do, I supposed. Then we had a real struggle to find cheese, but were lucky enough in the end to come on a select little specialist shop outside the main market and bought one and a half kilos of the hard cheese they had in their window. Then we had a half hour trail back to the truck. As I expected, we were very unpopular on our return.

We continued to Pamukkale, the name meaning 'cotton wool castle', a description of the wonderful calcium formations that had shaped layered semi-circular pools of warm water down the cliff face. From the truck we could see people wandering between the pools, tiny little figures dipping their fingers in the water of the bright white basins. Perhaps they were leaving vases and other objects there, as I'd read was common practice, to coat them pure white with the calcium deposit. Things had to be left for a week or so, but it made for an unusual and therefore much desired souvenir.

Even the water running along the gutters down the sides of the road was steaming. After viewing the hot springs, I had the luxury of bathing, washing my hair and some clothes. The warmth was so relaxing after a rather fraught day. It was lovely to be on my own in the tent too for once, after some threats of sharing with Lukas or Graham! "May they enjoy each other's company", I thought to myself happily. Also there were some books going the rounds among the bluies, one of them being Tolstoy's *War and Peace* which the owner found too much. So I borrowed it and started reading the chunky little tome. The book had been re-printed in paperback following the television dramatization of the novel in a twenty episode series beginning in September 1972, and was of particular interest to me as it had featured someone I had known at school as a minor character. Along with writing my diary, this book was sure to keep me from being bored in the odd quiet moments.

The weather was threatening a storm, lightning dancing down the sky every now and then. I joined the others and enjoyed drinks till tea, when it started raining just as the main course drew to a close. I ran to get my anorak in the tent, only to find it was in the truck, which had been locked up. So I stayed dozing in the tent till the storm was over. Then as I was making to get to the others once more, Maddie called me to say there was a party indoors.

Thus we sang and danced to Rob's guitar accompaniment and then listened to lovely, unworldly Turkish songs till 2am. We were in a circular, richly carpeted, red-lit room, with low couches and decorated hexagonal stools set round the walls. The Turks were very friendly, the wine was good, and we all let our hair down and enjoyed a thoroughly pleasant evening.

I was up at 7am after a lovely uninterrupted sleep and had a quick dip in the camp site pool before breakfast. After washing up, the start of our cooking duty, we set off. It was a sunny morning, and I noticed the swallows gathering and flying south. We passed through some very dry country, yellow grass backed by green hills, the rusty rock showing through.

Once more we came upon a steam train, almost hit it in fact, at a level crossing. Perhaps this shook Ben, or more likely I was still out of favour from yesterday, for when I buzzed him in the cab at the next village requesting that we stopped for more bread, he refused to. A little later I had to buzz him again so that we could sterilise the water for the vegetables. He was not a happy man, oh dear no!

We had lunch on a sandy stretch not far from Lake Burdur's southern shores. Everyone helped thank goodness, for I and the two boys were very slow, and also short of food. Ben kindly stopped for bread and cakes just afterwards at Burdur itself. Bless him, he could be grumpy, particularly of a morning, but usually came up trumps in the end. And our cooking day turned out to be one to make anyone grumpy!

Again, near Burdur there were definite signs of soil erosion, though an effort had been made to plant out the area with trees. Before long we were back in limestone country, and it was then that we came across a bus half plunged off the road at a bridge. I took a photograph of the accident scene, but was soon stopped by a policeman, perhaps a military one? It was one of those days, for the next thing to happen was that a van followed us, and someone in the vehicle began throwing cucumbers and apples into the open back of our truck, one of the apples hitting me hard on the head! Since Greece this had been happening, and we were generally glad of the fresh fruit. We were to be especially glad of these apples that evening, as it happened.

Nearing Antalya, we caught a glimpse of snow covered mountains peeping up on the horizon far to our left. We turned right instead though and climbed up through dense conifers. Eventually a series of hairpin bends brought us to Termessos. Situated more than 3,000 feet above sea level, this ancient site had a truly imposing setting, known as 'The Eagle's Nest' in Pisidian times. Having the natural defences of height and a narrow approach track up a canyon between steep cliffs, a relatively small force could protect the city for an indefinite period, and this convinced many to bypass it in its days of glory. Even Alexander the Great uncharacteristically decided to leave it alone in the fourth century BC. Thus the site has some very well-preserved ruins, tumbling across the saddle between two mountains.

But there was no room at the camp site up there when we arrived, so we descended in the sunset to the forest once more, and the boys and I set about making tea, while the tents went up in the clearing around us. Very soon some of the girls were trying to lend me a hand. There were several problems. One was that the 'courgettes' I had bought turned out to be large cucumbers, which disintegrated to green slush when I tried to cook them. Worse still, the pasta water wouldn't boil for some reason. Helen, Stephen's wife, who had something of a reputation for her cooking on the blue truck, suggested we might be too high: in desperation I added the fancy pasta to the hot water ... and it turned into a solid glutinous paste. I tried hard to do something with it: "Maybe we could add some sauce, liquefying and flavouring it at one go?" Abby suggested helpfully. But when Tim tried spooning it onto plates, he found he could shake the plate upside down and the pasta remained tenaciously in place. Maddie suggested it as a suitable cure for the 'runs' that some on the trip had been experiencing. One of the men said it could be an excellent substitute for Araldite!

Luckily Tim had been successfully heating up soup from the packets we still had from the initial grocery store on the truck. This at least was tasty and edible. But what to do with all the cheese? I cut a little to see what it was like. What a surprise I got! It was lovely ... but not cheese. It was

51

solid marzipan! Well, this would surely produce a rather special sweet. We chopped the apples that remained in our store, plus ones thrown into the truck during the day, added some sultanas from the store and then mixed these with the marzipan to make a very passable desert. How everyone laughed! And I was not allowed to forget the occasion, gaining the nickname 'Pasta Basher'. I was only too grateful to have got away reasonably lightly with this terrible set of errors. To this day there is probably a tall pile of solid non-biodegradable pasta in the woods of Termessos, for no-one could stomach it!

$$*** \qquad *** \qquad ***$$

Breakfast over next day, we made our way up the hill once more, the side covers down against the dust that lifted off the road. We had the luxury of a guide to show us round the site for two hours. The ancient fortifications were three walls thick. Alexander the Great only reached the first wall in his half-hearted attempt at a siege of the city. Providing a viable water supply had been a problem in Termessos originally, for there was only one natural spring. Hence five huge cisterns of limestone had been built to collect rain and snow, and these could still be clearly seen. Visible too were the gymnasium, a theatre perched on cliffs, temples to Zeus and Diana, palace ruins, and some 1,000 tombs in the hillside, a fire-watch tower stationed above. All had suffered in the great earthquake of 527 AD which had killed half the populace and tumbled the buildings around them.

There was an exceptional view through the mountains over to Antalya and the sea; although it was rather misty, you could catch the glint of sun on glass where the city was. We learnt that Antalya had great potential as a resort, for you could climb into the mountains on a spring morning to ski and return to bathe in the sea that afternoon and indeed Antalya has since become Turkey's busiest coastal resort, a record 12.5 million tourists passing through the city in 2014.[11] The city thus thoroughly fulfilled its potential, as part of the amazing rise in tourist revenue from $7 million in 1963 to $32.3 billion in 2013, a 4,600-fold growth over 50 years. I'm glad I visited when I did though.

---

[11] Cetingulec (2014).

Coming back down from Termessos we met the orange truck going up. There were whoops and shouts of recognition, but we had more to see before getting together again. We shopped on the outskirts of Antalya and then continued to Aspendos where we had lunch. Formerly a city founded by the Greeks in 1000 BC, Aspendos was now only a village. But the Romans added a theatre in the time of Emperor Marcus Aurelius (around 162 AD), that seated 15,000 people. This we visited and found it to be better preserved than any we had seen to date, for even the back wall to the stage and some of the dressing room area was almost complete. The acoustics were excellent too, and it still hosts concerts today.

The orange truck arrived at Aspendos as we left, so we exchanged trip stories a little, and then our truck moved on ahead towards Side, where we aimed to gather together once more in the evening. Leaving towards Mersin we saw a fairytale backdrop of mountains. Nearby there were a lot of flat-topped stone dwellings near the road. White-veiled women were busily employed harvesting cotton in the fields, where I noticed that irrigation channels had been built up about a foot from the ground and tall fronds of grass acted as a wind break round the fields.

We reached the coast at Side, a settlement dating back to the seventh century BC, the name of which actually means 'pomegranate' in Anatolian. There was a thriving pirate trade around the port in those early days and a lively slave market which the Romans eventually subdued. Passing quickly through yet more impressive ancient buildings we made for the beach. Sadly bathing was only moderately pleasant, for there was a lot of weed in the water.

There was no particular need to put up the tents, for most of us decided to sleep out on the beach in this warm weather. This was anything but a commercialised resort and despite being so nice, we had the place to ourselves. So when the others arrived, we all went to the local restaurant and had excellent hors d'oeuvres and, sadly, slightly tough cutlet. Once more I noted that the Turks seemed much more at home with vegetarian cooking. There was a great atmosphere in the restaurant. At first Gloria and Rob played their guitars, but then a disc jockey arrived and set up his gear, and live music was discouraged. I enjoyed a good bop, though I became stuck with a partner with a very boring range of step at one point.

However there were a few relationship issues becoming noticeable by this time among the Encounter crowd. It was clear that Ian had fancied his chances with Abby and was really hurt that during her three days in the other truck she had paired up with Dave. And this was not the only bone of contention. This palaver, including a certain amount of shouting as people had more to drink, rather spoiled things. I settled down comfortably in my sleeping bag and was finally lulled to sleep by the waves, once things calmed down, around 2am. I had company, but not the human variety: a dog lay down beside me and kept me beautifully warm in the wee small hours. I only prayed it hadn't fleas! It did wake me howling briefly before it left at daybreak, but generally sleeping out under the stars was to be one of the pleasantest memories of my time in Turkey. How lucky we were to have seen this coast when we did! The *Rough Guide to Turkey*, published in 2010, reported that a 10 km stretch of the beach at Side is now "lined with expensive hotels, beach clubs and watersports rental outfits." There'd be no sleeping out on the beach today.

Chapter 6. Castles and Caves

Lulled by the sound of gently breaking surf I slept on till I became aware that people were starting to stir. No tent to pack away – lovely! We were soon eating breakfast and the drivers warming up the trucks. It was about now that I remember realising that the smell of diesel fuel was integral to this holiday. For long enough afterwards I only had to get a whiff of a large engine, in a bus station perhaps, to be mentally back with the Encounter crowd on the road. Such is the power of olfactory association.

We did our shopping in Manavgat that day, then drove on to Alanya and the region gifted to Cleopatra by Mark Anthony in the days of the Roman Empire. A thousand years later Alanya fell prey to Seljuk Sultan Alaeddin Keykubat I, thanks, it is said, to an ingenious bit of military trickery, in a similar league to Mehmet II's at the Siege of Constantinople. To give the impression of far larger forces than were actually under his command, the Sultan made use of hundreds of wild goats. He attached a lighted candle to each of their horns and drove them up the cliffs ahead of his army, under cover of darkness. The townsfolk were completely taken in and, thinking themselves to be up against a truly mighty force, surrendered immediately.

We made only a brief visit to Kizil Küle (the Red Tower) at Alanya. This 115 foot sturdy hexagonal structure overlooked the harbour, giving marvellous views of the town and along the coast. The sun was hot now as we climbed up, I in the wide-brimmed Italian sunhat I'd bought the year before in Florence. Fair-skinned as I am, I'd found this essential wear despite the fact that it made me look peculiarly eccentric, for it had sadly developed a concertinaed brim thanks to being folded in my rucksack. Below were minarets and the red tiled roofs of houses and lines of fortification by the sea shore, while ahead across the bay, glimmered the hazy outline of steep mountains. Sue, Jim, Rob and Tim were very adventurous and crept right up to the edge of some crumbling masonry, to gaze down at the beautiful empty beach of the bay. It almost gave me vertigo to watch them! In a few years that shoreline would be heaving with humanity, but in 1975 we could enjoy its natural charms. We took deep breaths of the warm, herb-scented air and enjoyed the somnolent hum of insects and the wild calls of seabirds. Descending once more, we came on more camels moving ponderously along the street.

We lunched on a nearby beach. The sand shelved too steeply for swimming to be an easy option but we enjoyed sitting in the breakers to cool down. There were wonderful unspoilt beaches round this coast, and we continued enjoying this scenery and some lovely country all the hot afternoon. There were herbs growing everywhere, and I saw bananas too. We had the whole roof off in the back of the truck for the first time, so that we could stand, steadying ourselves by holding onto the roof frame, to get the best view as we travelled. It was wonderful to feel the wind in your hair.

We moved on to Mamure Kalesi, a crusader castle at Anamur, for another half hour stop. It had been built by Armenian rulers, on the ruins of a fourth century Roman fortress, to give protection against pirates, but had been rehabilitated for use in the Crusades. It had the strangest atmosphere, especially where a mosque had been built in its ruins, surrounded by burnt grass. The dramatic bright sunlight there was at that moment, against a dark sky, reminded me of a Cocteau film! Then a very fair blue-eyed boy showed us up the tower and onto the ramparts. His blond hair and pallid cheeks gave him a surreal appearance among all these olive-skinned and dark-eyed people: how had he come here? Notions of kidnapping and the white slave trade crept into my imagination. Once out on the ramparts I found myself quite frightened by the height too. The steep crenelated walls gave directly onto the breakers on the rocks below. The whole place would have made a superb setting for a gothic drama, and indeed I've found since that the castle has featured as a backdrop in several Turkish films.

There was a gorgeous sunset, as we continued to a beach camp site some 20 miles on. It was rather difficult to access and we had to use sand platforms twice on the way in. I had noticed and had been puzzled by these strange parallel curved bars carried on the side of the trucks. Now I found they were wedged under the wheels to prevent wheel spin when trying to drive over soft sand.

It was a lovely spot again but we decided to sleep in the tents as there were some rain clouds about. In fact it turned out to be a beautiful night with a full moon. Having learnt of my occupation, one or two people were asking me for a back massage. I started with Stephen from the blue truck, showing his wife, Helen, how best to help his back ache, before going for a relaxing night swim myself. The trouble was I'd moved quite a distance from my towel and had a fair old hunt to find it again, even by the light of the moon!

*** *** ***

Virginia and I were up again soon after 5 o'clock and we left an hour and a half later. Orion was bright over the sea, and a growing warm shade of pink outlined the hills at the far end of the bay. Unlike the night before we had no problem driving over the sand going out to the road. Once in the hills conifers lined the route, a twisting road affording marvellous views of the sea. The road had a good surface though, so we were hardly being jolted about at all. I seized the opportunity of giving myself a quick manicure (my finger nails had been a bit long for the massage last night) before we reached our shopping stop at Silifke. Here I spent the best part of an hour changing a fiver into Turkish lira in the bank! That only left me time to send the post cards I'd written to my friends. We lunched on a pebbly beach. The sand was searingly hot and it was very rocky at the water's edge, but it was going to be our last swim, so we all made the most of it.

From here we cut inland, passing through a brief shower. We stopped for drinks and tried a "lovely" (another's description!) primitive loo with peep-holes everywhere! By then we were on the edge of Mersin, which I'd read was a joy for archaeologists: the remains of as many as 32 civilisations had been excavated in the different layers of ground hereabouts, its history of settlement going right back to 3500 BC.

The next region we were to travel through had quite a reputation as well. Alexander the Great had chased the Persians through the narrow Cilician Gates as the Gülek Pass in the Taurus Mountains was known, and St Paul (whose birthplace was in nearby Tarsus) wrote of being in danger from robbers while traversing this area as well[12]. There was some superbly wild mountain scenery here, great ambush country. I noticed herds of black goats, a bit of a rarity in my experience so far. We pitched camp just before the Nigde turn off, while Lukas waited by the road for the other truck, but it never appeared! We would have to wait for them next day.

I did some sewing in the truck, while the others with me started on the Raki. A close cousin of Greek Ouzo but stronger (45-48% alcohol), this seemed to be regarded as *the* Turkish tipple. But, perhaps luckily for me, I just couldn't take to it: give me wine any day. It had become known that my birthday was tomorrow: Kiwi Dave offered to "make it really special for me if I wanted." I took this as lightly as I imagined it was offered. I had no wish to rock the boat and, from what I had recently heard, thought Abby might just have something to say about any such complications in her relationship with him!

The lads were becoming pretty well oiled when I went to bed at 10.30. Virginia fell into the tent just after midnight and began frantically poking and prodding my legs, as her glasses had fallen off somewhere there as she came in. Of-course I was immediately awake, and it was hard to drift off again. The others were singing away in the truck by then. There was a bit of a commotion at one point, which we learnt later occurred when Tim fell off the tailpin of the truck. Happily he didn't hurt himself too badly. Virginia wasn't so happy though, and in fact was sick for a while, but then things quietened down. "A nice way to bring in my 28th birthday", I thought!

*** *** ***

But the day itself was one of the most interesting I have ever had. It started mundanely enough. Several of my travelling companions, including Virginia, nursed hangovers at first, and Tim some bruises into the bargain, so an enforced leisurely start was fortuitous. We waited at the end of the track for the bluies, whiling away the time playing Frisbee, with Ian's cap even (he was rarely to be seen without it). It had dawned pretty chilly, but gradually the mists lifted, the low light playing over the blue outlines of

---

[12] 2 Corinthians 11, verse 26.

further hills, and there was a lovely sunrise. The other truck eventually turned up at 8am and we descended from the hill country to the plain.

This was an arid land, and when we had a loo stop it was the first where there were no bushes to hide behind. Not that we girls worried about this much by now. Inhibitions had been lost long ago, and the event sometimes became a pleasant cross between a gossip shop and a debating society, with support for any sickies, as ailing companions were labelled, thrown in. I have since read of this occurring on the front line in war time. As Remarque puts it,

"...the natural innocence of the business has returned ...so that the convivial performance of this particular activity is ...highly valued ...It is not for nothing that the phrase 'latrine rumour' has come to mean all kinds of gossip; these places are the army equivalent of the street corner or a favourite bar."[13]

So it became for us, both situations causing people to revert to a more basic group behaviour I suppose.

Before long we started climbing once more towards Göreme in Cappadocia, which was utterly different to anything I'd seen before. We caught sight of weird cone-like pinnacles of stone simply riddled with caves. Three volcanoes had erupted 30 million years before, throwing up tuff deposits, compressed volcanic ash which settled to form very soft rock rich in asbestos (as I learnt at a medical seminar some ten years after I'd been to Göreme: the minor threat here of asbestosis was very far from our minds in 1975). The natural rock formations in the Göreme valley formed 'fairy chimneys', chunks of harder rock balancing precariously on spikes of the soft, easily eroded tuff.[14] Wind and rain had combined to create a strange 'lunar landscape' of peculiar shapes. Originally troglodytes built cities in the rock, often several storeys deep, the entrances to these leaving the myriad of cave holes we saw now.

---

[13] *All Quiet on the Western Front* (2011), page 6.
[14] See photograph on page 84.

We got our lunch at Ürgüp, a picturesque small town, already showing the local inclination to burrow into soft rock. The very name of the place means 'a lot of (kup) rock (ur)'. Bright white houses appeared to be piled on top of each other in a crazy haphazard fashion, the cobbled streets steep between rough stone walls. We'd been told that every female here could weave a carpet and that this was a major home industry. The women I noticed wore the usual white headdresses and were walking their laden mules back from shopping, switch in hand to encourage the animals uphill. Their long dark skirts flicked up the dust at their heels. And we found *our* shopping impressively cheap, a little over 50p for meat, vegetables, yogurt and honey! Then we had almost three hours to look round, while the drivers found diesel fuel for the trucks, a camp site for us and a hair-cut for Ian!

We started with the Christian cave churches and the refectory monasteries. These churches became a UNESCO heritage site in 1985. But ten years earlier we were able to range more freely and take photos of the wonderful frescos painted by the Christian monks, dating mainly from the second half of the ninth to the end of the eleventh century, when the sites were finally abandoned. Most of the angels' and saints' faces portrayed in the murals we saw were roughly scratched, probably by Muslims during the later Ottoman period, for depicting faces in Islamic art is strictly taboo. But it was possible that some damage had already been done during the Iconoclastic Period between 726 and 843 AD too. During this time religious imagery, other than the cross, had been seriously frowned upon in Cappadocia.

But later, creativity was allowed to flourish once more, and I thought the angels' wings and the fall of drapery in the frescoes showed sensitive artistry. In one crucifixion scene we saw, whole faces were almost completely obliterated though. It made me wonder how non-Christians would view such art. To them it must be quite gruesome to have a crucified man hanging in a place of worship. I was soon to find that Islamic art concentrated on the natural world - trees, flowers and water. Here there *were* swirls of leaf-like patterns framing scenes but, in the background, as in many renaissance religious paintings, were buildings, significantly reminiscent of the older parts of Istanbul, gable-ended and domed.

Quietly we crept up and down step treads hollowed out by use over the centuries, moving through the rock from one chapel to another. In some cases there were hair-raisingly high, narrow platforms to balance along and we used our torches to light our way down dark, narrow staircases. It is not an exaggeration to say that we were filled with awe for this strange architecture of faith.

To get a more general view of this weird landscape, we crossed to the other side of the valley for a while. It showed us how suitable the volcanic tuff was for fruit farming. Being near to harvest time, there were lovely grapes and apples ripening, no doubt enjoyed centuries ago by monks and local peasants alike. We then returned to the town of Göreme itself, where, rather like the cave dwellings of the past, there were a myriad of little passages between dark houses built into the soft local rock. It had been first settled in the Roman period, but became a strongly Christian region thanks to the evangelical skills of a gentleman curiously known as Gregory the Illuminator (presumably thanks to all the local frescos). The Cappadocian Fathers who accompanied him had created the cave chapels.

Our camp site was only one kilometre from Göreme, and was the last proper one with showers that we were to encounter until we reached Isfahan in Iran. In a fairly futile effort not to be too dirty by then, I, and in fact most of us, washed clothes, hair and self thoroughly. After tea, I was treated to a birthday drink in the bar, and was delighted to receive presents of chocolate and Turkish Delight from the others.

*** *** ***

Next morning dawned pretty cold, but Ian had warned us to look out for scorpions from now on. Hence when I put on my boots for the first time for long enough, I gave them a good shake first!

It was our group's cooking day again, so, once we'd collected our laundry and packed, we washed up and put the breakfast things away before we set off to visit Kaymakli, the underground city. It was a fascinating place. I had read that its twisting narrow passages climbed and descended through seven storeys in the rock. At one point there had been as many as

60,000 cave dwellers living round here. Kaymakli was complete with wells, food storage space and ventilation shafts. It was constructed by the Hattites (pre-Hittite people) between 2000 and 3000 BC, and was in use until at least the 1st century AD. Constructed with preservation in mind, it could withstand a prolonged siege if necessary.

A book on the area that I bought that day added more:

> "During the days when Christianity was in crisis, and torture and oppression were dominant, the believers searched for places where they could live and worship freely. Some of them came to settle in the town of Kaymakli ... they hollowed a huge underground city out of the rock."[15]

Thus it appeared that the underground system had been deserted for several hundred years and had been revived and developed again when necessary as Islam became dominant in the region.

Our wanderings showed us intriguing narrow passages connecting living areas, a huge ventilation shaft, kitchens, bedrooms and even grave holes. There was a Byzantine church with crosses on the walls and altar. A discotheque where drinks were served was the only commercialised part. Here rich-coloured local carpets covered the stone we rested against and gave an idea of how living quarters might have been decorated from the eleventh century on. The reds and greens of the carpets enhanced the blue-grey of the surrounding stone wonderfully.

My professional services were then requested and I gave Meg a quick massage for her twisted ankle. I felt for her. Back in Greece I had managed to land awkwardly on an ankle when returning hurriedly to the truck, and although it was a very minor sprain, moving around these uneven floors a fortnight later had needed particular care and caused the odd jab of discomfort. I wondered how anyone with disabilities had managed in Kaymakli – by the light of flares and candles too.

---

[15] Güzelgöz, Muammer & Memduh (1975), page 68.

We returned to the camp site to hitch on the trailer, and went back through Ürgüp again, seeing more this time of its colourful carpet and copperware sellers and some lovely onyx vases for sale too. Donkeys were everywhere on the roads, as well as horses and carts, as we moved off towards Kayseri. We reached the town fairly late and stayed one and a half hours shopping and collecting post. The former was badly held up at first because Sarah had the shopping money and was missing for half the time! I was beginning to be quite disenchanted with her, for she always seemed to get out of rough jobs and made sure she saw the sights even if it meant that others did not. This was a case in point, for Virginia, Tim and I had no time left to explore Kayseri. Or indeed to post any letters, the Poste Restante being highly disorganised and slow. I couldn't see any post box, so only managed to hand a postcard to an official in the street and just hope my parents might get it! The post I received from them lifted my feelings of frustration though, being a very nice birthday card and letter.

After being so cold that morning it had now grown warmer, even though we climbed the foothills of the neighbouring mountains before lunching. We ran so late our lunch finished only at 4.45pm! By this time towns, often with poplars lining their roads, had taken on the appearance of oases in a desert plain. On we drove through a dusty landscape against a superb mountain backdrop. Put some green grass, bracken and heather on these hills and you'd have been in Scotland I felt.

We finally camped 10 kms before Pinarbaşi on the Malatya road around 6pm. Normally, whoever finished putting up their tent first then put up the tents of the cooks for the evening. In Virginia and my case it was often the Kiwi lads, Rob and Dave who sorted ours, but tonight I helped Dave put up the tent, for it was too early to start tea. Sarah then made a mince, potato and cheese concoction which was very tasty! I quickly forgave her earlier irritating lapses, and set about boiling the tea towels and dish clothes with Tim's help.

***   ***   ***

Nearly half a century on, I'm aware that I can no longer give an accurately full account of my dealings with my fellow passengers, with only a handful of whom I am still in contact. As a medical professional I was used to communicating with all types of people and this was certainly helpful on a trip where I was mixing with others that I sometimes felt I might have avoided in normal circumstances, disrespectful to them as that sounds. But I was learning a lot from them. Indeed by now I was starting to realise that the effect of my travelling environment would possibly change me more than the ideal of reaching and seeing Kathmandu and Asia generally. It looked as though I might even learn more from my companions and our life together than from the new countries we passed through, fascinating though these new sights were. Our shared activity was certainly going to colour my experience of Asia.

Chapter 7. Things Get Stranger in Eastern Anatolia

We had porridge for breakfast next morning, very suitable for a cold bright start in a pseudo-Scottish landscape. Once we got going I travelled in the cab with Ian driving. Beside me were Sue, Jim and Virginia, with Geoff/'Luigi' in the hot seat in front of us.

We drove along a misty and monotonous, dry dust, half-made road for a while. Then the country took life under the sunshine, looking to me very like the Drumochter Pass on the way up to Inverness from Pitlochry. Small meandering streams wound between fields where mounds of hay stood drying, and bare mountainsides lifted up around. But of-course there were inevitable differences to the 'Scottish' scene. I noticed flocks of fat-tailed, often black, sheep, and that bird of prey taking flight from the road certainly wasn't a golden eagle.

There were differences with western Turkey as well, for marching lines of telegraph poles hereabouts were properly cross-barred, not just straightish tree trunks as we'd seen in some country districts. And in the cemeteries we glimpsed, graves no longer had simple headstones but were bed-shaped, built up at the sides and having both head and foot stones, making them very substantial and impressive.

Weirder now were the flat-topped mud houses, often with hay and a couple of sheep grazing on top! I knew nothing of adobe building at this time, regarding these simply as poor dwellings, when they are much the most durable form of home in so many countries, particularly in areas where there are typically hot days and cold nights. Here adobe, a mixture of earth and straw made into bricks and dried in the sun, would actually help maintain a comfortable interior temperature.

We stopped for three quarters of an hour in Gürün, and I tried on the woolly hats for sale, remembering that it was likely to get colder before long! I also enjoyed a coffee and some sweet flaky cake. Then we climbed high into the sun-baked hills, with glimpses down gullies to other valleys with distant trees and houses, green fast-flowing rivers and huge rocky outcrops crowning the ridges above. The road reached 6,000ft. We came up behind some donkeys, one of which was so heavy-laden that I thought there were two alongside each other. Those not so laden were ridden by boys kicking their legs up high, accompanied by sedate side-saddle-riding veiled ladies.

We lunched 60kms west of Malatya, enjoying the view as we munched. Several of us ate standing up, a nice change from all the sitting we were doing on the truck. Then ten minutes after re-starting the truck the fan belt broke and it took two stops to adjust it properly. Ian directed operations each time, while Luigi and Dieter helped him. Two very neatly dressed small boys, in uniform resembling that of the little girls we'd seen going to school through the Pergamon ruins, but presumably on their way home from school this time, came and squatted nearby. They watched proceedings with intent interest and we gave them sweets for their trouble.

We continued on through Malatya towards Elâziğ, crossing the broad grey-green Euphrates river. We were just north of the 'Cradle of Civilisation', the fertile crescent of Mesopotamia. Malatya is famed for its Apricot Festival in July, but I remember it because at the tea stop, the earth closet some of us used had a resident frog hopping around down there. It gave me quite a shock, and I dare say we gave him a bit of a jolt too! I told the others that I was beginning to think of writing a book on my return home entitled something like *Toilets I have Known*.

After this I took my turn in the hot seat in the truck (and it *was* hot). Not much later, Ian said he saw a dead snake on the road, which unnerved us a little! We went on, to camp 15 kms west of Elâziğ in a stubble field. We were now in the heart of eastern Turkey, a region that saw relatively few tourists and the facilities, or lack of them, reflected this. There was no shelter around for us when we went to the toilet, so it was going to be a late night or early morning job, we girls reckoned!

We got to bed early that night and were up again around 5am, to a scanty breakfast for Virginia and me, as we ran late! Off at 6am, we climbed into the hills again, past a body of water that I later found to be the biggest artificial lake in Turkey, actually the result of damming the river Euphrates back near Elâziğ only the year before, in 1974. It was as we moved away from the lake, climbing once more, that the truck's engine boiled, so we ended up kicking our heels in a thoroughly lonely spot. Only the occasional large lorry trundled past on that dusty, half-metalled road. One or two of us had taken to wearing scarves across our faces bandit-style against the dust wafted in the sides of the truck on such occasions.

Once on the way again we headed for Bingöl, where we had a quick meal of vegetables and bread. We were drawing real crowds round the trucks whenever we stopped. Gloria from the blue truck commented that the chief amusement for the Turk was to go and stand at the roadside and see what happened. "At least, that's what I'd do, for sure!" she added. But would she? One thing was very noticeable: no women ever joined the throngs we attracted. In fact we saw relatively few of them at all now.

At this point we were at our nearest to the earthquake zone at Lice (pronounced Lidze). There had been, worryingly for us, an earthquake in Turkey on the 6th of September while we were crossing Europe three weeks before. Over 2,000 people had been killed. Ian had told us of this as we approached Istanbul. All went well for us, for we didn't even suffer any after-shocks in eastern Turkey, but it was very different for the people living near the epicentre of the quake, as can be imagined. It gave the whole community a thorough shake-up in every sense and changed life entirely.

The old town of Lice was built on a steep hillside and so was vulnerable to rock falls if the same thing should happen again, and the traditional stone houses had been irreparably damaged. Within five days the government had decided to move the whole settlement 2 kms further south to a safer location, on the plain at the foot of the slope. However, the area earmarked was prime agricultural land. Also the hillside provided better protection from northerly winds than the new exposed site. It was thus a very unpopular decision as far as the residents were concerned, and had been made without their participation. On top of the obvious disadvantages of the new site, they were initially without a water supply. However, the capacity of the Turkish Government to re-build as rapidly as they did must count as an extraordinary achievement. By the 29th October (in 54 days) 1,568 houses, 40 shops, a school, a mosque and a bakery were already complete. It was just a shame that the prefabs built were small and urban in style, not allowing accommodation for animals and several other rural priorities - an all too common story of well-meaning people in power not really listening to the needs of those in trouble.

That this is an area of high Kurdish presence was significant, for the founding congress of the Kurdistan Workers' Party (the PKK) took place in this area just a few years later, in 1978, and the animosity between the Turks and the Kurds has only increased since. Lice's defiant posture made it a frequent target of oppressive measures by the security forces, especially during the turbulent 1990s. Indeed there was a massacre in Lice in 1993, the incident being seen as one of the worst human rights abuses committed by the Turkish Armed Forces during the Turkish-Kurdish conflicts of this period[16]. Is it too simplistic to suggest that that enforced move back in 1975 could have reinforced an already antipathetic attitude to governmental decisions on the part of the Kurds? From such small beginnings do conflicts sometimes arise.

***   ***   ***

But we in the orange truck were soon to experience an upheaval of our own! 40 kms on from Bingöl we came over a pass and, after lunch, had a water stop, a dip and wash down in a stream on the moors, to make up for the lack of any shower facilities now. All very pleasurable. I photographed the drivers sluicing themselves down among the reeds by a muddy bank. Meanwhile Sharon, the designated nurse in our group, recorded some local children singing on a cassette tape recorder she had brought with her. I wished I could have done this: it would be a wonderful memory of the journey.

However, what happened next has remained a lasting memory without aid of sound recording or photograph. As we continued, James at the wheel, I was reading *War and Peace*. Suddenly I feared for my sight, for the print began to dance before my eyes. It took me a moment or two to realise that it was being sprinkled with tiny dots of tar! We had been driven through wet tar on the road at about 25mph (20mph too fast I reckoned): as usual during our travels in Turkey the truck side protection covers were up, so everyone had got nicely showered – to say nothing of the truck! What a

---

[16] Ron, J. (1995).

panic there was as everyone fished out cleansing wipes and handkerchiefs to try to get clean! James was thoroughly in the dog-house, but to be fair there'd been little warning that the road had recently been re-surfaced.

We pulled up and Ian came to the rescue quickly, advocating the use of petrol in the absence of white spirit. As we applied the petrol to ourselves, I told Geoff of the tar-covered patient I'd helped to clean up while I was working on the Head Injury Unit at Leeds General Infirmary. The poor man had fallen headfirst off scaffolding into a bucket of tar below. Ian overheard and quipped, "Know about the Irish expedition to Everest? They only got 60ft off the ground, because they ran out of scaffolding!" We were definitely in need of a joke or two.

Before long we continued on our way, reaching Lake Van at Tatvan. This lake is large enough to be called an inland sea. It's also nearly 6,000ft up in the mountains and has no outlet, the original river having been blocked by lava flow over a million years ago – a curious geographical feature indeed. It was an austerely beautiful area, but one with a history of political unrest. Ian had warned us that we might have trouble with the locals here, but there was very little to complain about. Certainly people seemed none too friendly, but our only trouble was young boys throwing stones in on us twice. In western Turkey they'd thrown in fruit, and, though more enjoyable in the long run, my personal experience of being hit on the head by a flying apple had been no joke – except for my neighbours in the back of the truck!

We camped up a lonely valley, by a stream. It was a chilly evening, so it was quite good to have some physical work to do, cleaning the truck of tar before tea. Thanks to helping with this I nicely cleaned my skin, but I wasn't sure my shirt would ever be the same again, and wondered how long it would take to grow the stains out of my hair!

Poor James was very grateful to have our help, for some of the orange truck folk were giving him a bit of a hard time. When things went a little wrong, as in this incident, teamwork was all-important on the trip, and it was quite enlightening now to notice who did and who didn't join in this cleaning operation. The Kiwi cry of "She'll be right, mate" was expected and soon made its presence felt, but I got some surprises. An example was that glamorous Cynthia, the ex-Bunny girl, was one of the hardest working of our group. And she was not the only bluie to join in either, though they didn't particularly have to, as Ben had been careful enough to negotiate the newly tarred road at a very slow pace. Only the orange truck had suffered.

I got chatting to the Swiss girl, Hannah, while we washed the truck floor, and promised to give her a massage afterwards. This aim was thwarted however, as after tea soldiers turned up, wanting us to move on! From 1936 until the 1960s the southeast of Turkey was made a military zone, closed to foreigners, and it seemed that the situation remained slightly sensitive. Ian persuaded the soldiers to let us stay, but wanted us to have an early night so that the army would have nothing to complain about. He murmured to some of us that it made him thoroughly uneasy to have these men with guns and fixed bayonets around our camp.

*** *** ***

Next morning at 5am was the coldest it had been to date. We were soon off and making for the Başkale pass. It was a lovely valley road, opening out on blue Lake Van to the left for a while. Then we were climbing a quite fertile narrow valley. There were what I was tempted (by their shape) to call 'ziggurats' of hay in the fields, very green terraces and plenty trees now. But soon it began to get drier again and simultaneously the sun came up brightly. It was seven-thirty and we were approaching the lake once more.

We drove right down to the lakeside, for we had the opportunity to take the ferry to Akdamar Island to see the tenth century Armenian church there, or to give it its full title, the Armenian Cathedral of the Holy Cross. The evangelist I had heard of in Cappadocia, Gregory the Illuminator, had done sterling work in this area, for in the third century Armenia became the first nation to adopt Christianity as its official religion. It was the ruler, Gagik Ardzrouni, of the Vaspurakan dynasty in Armenia who had constructed this church on the island, an excellent example of its type. Originally it was part of a complex of buildings surrounding a palace, a place of retreat, and one which the local Turks were unlikely to approach, being much more at home in the saddle than on a boat. The church's ruined form looked rather forlorn now, its conical terracotta-coloured roof standing out alone above the simple harbour of the island.

I knew little of the church's background in 1975 and naively wondered if the local congregation really took the ferry to church every Sunday. Of-course nothing could have been further from the truth. For over 600 years, from 1116, the island had been the stronghold of the Armenian Catholics in the Van region. But the last head of the church had died in 1895, and in April 1915, frightful events occurred that left the church deserted for years. Just as the Nazis were to round up Jews thirty years later, the Turks gathered weaker Armenians for transportation to Syria, while men of fighting age were executed. During this Armenian genocide, the monks on Akdamar were massacred, the cathedral looted, and the monastic buildings destroyed. The church was only just saved from destruction in 1951. It was further restored quite a time after our visit, in 2005/6, electricity being laid on then, so that it could become a major tourist attraction. Only now are the Turks beginning to allow that the Armenian genocide might have happened at all, their restoration of the church a step in this direction.

Half of us wanted to visit the island and its church in 1975, others being put off by the boat trip. I wasn't too surprised by this, for the ferry did look exceedingly basic, in fact the twenty minute trip promised to be positively scary. We had to sit on the flat roof of the ferry, surrounded by just a two foot high rail to stop us sliding off. This was because the engine and the crew, engaged in constant energetic bailing out of gathering water, took up all the space in the body of the vessel! Luckily the waters were calm.

But once we arrived, we all thought the ruined church unusually lovely. Its façade was not in the best state, but many of its low relief sculpture decorations were intact, showing a fascinating conglomeration of animals and birds, along with biblical characters from the Old Testament. For example, the slight figure who seemed to be waving a tennis racket aloft turned out to be David facing Goliath, sling in hand. And there was Jonah's boat and the man himself, being tipped head first over the bows by the sailors, into the mouth of a fish-tailed scaly wolf-headed creature, presumably meant to be the whale.

The interior of the conical roof was domed, lifted on high arches, and on most surfaces you could just make out vaguely defined coloured frescos. Faces had not been scratched out here, but were thin and aesthetic, resembling those of Russian Orthodox icons. The stonework round window arches was alternately terracotta and cream and the views through these great glassless windows, of the lake and the mountains beyond, beneath a deep blue sky, were stunning. I agreed with Liz when she said there was a special feel about the place.

We had some time now for a quick bathe in the strongly alkaline, sodium–salty waters of the lake. Ian had told us that there was no living creature in this lake (though I've learnt since that he was wrong: just one fish, the Pearl Mullet, thrives here). There were tall tales though (similar to those about Loch Ness) of a monster, the Canavari, which appeared from time to time in the lake. Stranger still, a peculiar type of cat liked to swim in its waters. We shared its enthusiasm. It was a chilly dip despite its being a warm day, and the water seemed faintly soapy, but we felt refreshed, and certainly less dust-covered, afterwards.

We then braved the ferry back for a morning cuppa, or 'chai', in a small café near the quay. We were becoming accustomed to the way tea was served in Asia. Chai came in a small glass on a saucer. There was no milk or sugar to add. I had never been a great tea drinker, but I now preferred it to the local coffee. I had experienced strong Swiss coffee, but the Turkish brew, in equally small quantities, was exceptionally thick, leaving a good quarter of a cup's worth of sediment after drinking. No, chai was my beverage.

We were off again before eleven and held our lunch stop by a stream in a very lonely spot, cows grazing placidly on such rough grass as there was across the water. However an old man with an axe, along with some little boys, turned up to watch us eat. There were no habitations in sight: there was no wood for the man to chop, so where did such folk appear from? It made us feel a little like zoo animals must, to be watched so closely! Hannah and Lukas reversed the situation by photographing the man at close range with their fancy cameras. Sitting cross-legged, he fairly wriggled with delight at the attention, his tanned and wrinkled face creasing into a smile under the shade of his cloth cap.

When we moved on again, we got a wonderful surprise just down the road at Güzelsu. We came on the fairytale Hoşap Castle built high on an outcrop of rock above the village, and set amidst a fantastic landscape – quite psychedelic dunes, coloured maroon, green-grey, misty pale blue and cream. There was an immediate call for a photo stop. Built by a Kurdish ruler in the seventeenth century, the castle looked to me like the remnants of a medieval Gormenghast. There was even a tower or two that,

> "arose like a mutilated finger from among the fists of knuckled masonry and pointed blasphemously at heaven"[17]

I wondered if Mervyn Peake had ever been in Anatolia.

Climbing and twisting up further, we reached a rugged, narrow gorge with sheer rock on the left and more sloping on the right. The road was very dusty and the light shut out, which gave it a weird, wild effect. On we went through arid high country to camp in a barren valley, once more by a stream. As we put up our tents the locals appeared. I wrote to my parents...

> 'It's amazing here how everywhere we stop, whether only to eat or to camp for the night, people appear to gaze at us, like moles out of the ground! Last night we were in a very isolated spot, no dwellings in sight, yet I'd hardly started pinning the ground-sheet out when two men were seen running downhill towards us to stand, mouths open, watching us work. A few minutes later and three horsemen galloped across from the opposite side of the valley: with rich woven rugs over their saddles, they carried small decorated switches and were cloaked. One signed to us that he owned the land and appeared to welcome us. They too stopped to watch while we got tea, but at sunset they were off. During Ramadan month you can only eat between sunset and sunrise, so one can imagine that their appetites were keen!'

Hardly had they disappeared when a twin to our orange truck came down the road towards us. It was Encounter Overland coming from Kathmandu! So we all camped together and exchanged travellers' tales. It was a thoroughly enjoyable evening. We had a meal of vegetable soup; meat

---

[17] *Titus Groan* (1989), page 15.

balls, beans, turnip, potato, tomato and onion stew: then fruit (grapes, water melon, apples and pomegranates) and our usual tea, coffee and wine to follow. (This is one of the few full records of our daily diet that I still have, thanks to writing of it in the letter to my parents.) After tea I honoured my professional promises, giving Liz and Jane facial massages, and Maddie one for the neck and shoulders. Then we sang with Gloria in the blue truck. To enhance the drama of the occasion, she was accompanied by thunder at one point, but there was little accompanying rain.

It was our final night in Turkey, a country that had turned out to be quite different, especially in its eastern regions, to what I had imagined. Very near now was Iran, in my mind's eye more famed as that exotic realm, Persia. My idealistic notions came mainly from hearing my parents reciting parts of *The Rubáiyát of Omar Khayyám*, a neat illustrated copy of which was one of their favourites at home. And who could imagine more romantic opening lines?

> *Awake! For Morning in the Bowl of Night*
> *Has flung the Stone that puts the Stars to Flight:*
> *And Lo! The Hunter of the East has caught*
> *The Sultán's Turret in a Noose of Light.*

What an exquisite picture this conjured up! I was thoroughly impatient to experience this land of stars and light, and to luxuriate in such an impressive sunrise. Given the early start we made most days it seemed a distinct possibility.

Chapter 8. Into the Land of the Shah

We should have to get up exceptionally early though to catch the sunrise, for I noticed next morning that it was well past daybreak when we rose at 5.45. At home it would be dark still in late September, and, as we were further south, I had imagined that dawn would be later too. It would seem that there was no arrangement similar to British Summertime here.

I was travelling up in the cab once more, sitting behind Ian, with Rob in the hot seat, and Tim, Maddie and Virginia beside me. We were driving along dirt roads up through really spectacular scenery to the Başkale Pass between Turkey and Iran. We passed flat-topped adobe dwellings of herdsmen and shepherds on the hill. A white hound and a huge turkey were in one back yard, and there was colourful cloth spread over brushwood to dry. We caught glimpses of massive peaks ahead with what looked like snow patches high upon them. I remembered that Mount Ararat was only slightly further north.

A meandering stream wound through pebbles and sparse grass alongside the road in the narrow valley, the hills rising steep to outcrops of rock on either side. There was a flock of goats grazing up here, the billies horned and white-bearded. We stopped briefly to enjoy the fresh mountain air and to cross and photograph a swing bridge over the stream, which was only a trickle of water now below us. Yet again I was reminded of Scotland, where my relatives' Ross-shire home stood only a field's breadth from a similar swing bridge over the river Meig, up Strathconon. I had joined in bouncing around on this bridge with my cousins as a youngster, scaring the living daylights out of ourselves at times.

We stopped for food in the plateau town of Yüksekova and I guarded the cab while curious hordes of men and boys poked, rattled and tried to climb up onto the vehicle[18]. I was glad to be more protected in the cab, unlike those guarding the rear of the truck. And annoyingly the stop turned out to be of little use to the shoppers, as very few shops were open. Could it possibly be because it was a Sunday afternoon? Surely not in this Muslim

---

[18] See photograph on page 85.

country. It had been worth a try, as this was our last reasonably sized town in Turkey. We hoped for better luck over the border in Iran.

I was looking forward to picking up my next batch of mail in Iran too, but this would not be until we reached Shiraz – probably another week away. I'd stopped sending camera film home by now for fear that it'd be X-rayed en-route, so my films were starting to collect in my rucksack along with the mail received thus far. It left less space for mementos and presents I might buy from now on. Perhaps I should be able to lighten my load by sending films and presents home from Australia? Was that post more reliable? General discussion ensued.

But enough pondering, we were getting going once more, and soon we reached the Iranian border. They were a slow lot on the Turkish side, pretty disorganised. There were kids running around in official areas and paperwork like exit forms had run out or gone missing. We got rather fed up, but at last moved through to the Iranian customs and put our watches forward half an hour. The first man to welcome us to Iran was a Turkish lorry-driver going in the opposite direction! We'd been nearly two hours messing about and were delighted to get on our way again.

Queues of Turkish lorries were filling up with Iranian petrol before crossing the border, so presumably the petrol was cheaper here than in Turkey. Then I noticed the Persian number plates: oh my, Arabic numbers and lettering! How would we manage to make out the prices when we were shopping? We should have to learn the meaning of these strange looking squiggles.

There was another marked difference with Turkey. We were driving over a much smoother surface in Iran: there were even lines drawn down the centre of the road again. And there were some rather nice houses with grass and flowers in front! Women around here had on lovely long skirts, while the men now wore turbans.

One thing remained the same however. We still featured as a bit of a freak show, drawing plenty people to our next lunch site, by a stream in lovely hill country. There was no question where they had all come from this time, for one by one they had idled over from a village visible about half a mile away across the plain. Of-course it's being Ramadan perhaps meant that it was an attraction to see strange folk eating during daylight hours. On the other hand it must have been torture to see good food when they knew they had to fast till sundown! But this begged another question. Would these people think cold meats, salad and piccalilli sauce good food? Or would such fare make us seem even weirder in their eyes?

On we drove to Reza'iyeh (now commonly called Urmia), the capital of Iran's West Azerbaijan province, for the bank's opening at 5pm, but now we discovered that it was a public holiday and so, again, everything was closed. We spent half an hour quickly looking round and tried to get a drink, but this proved to be well-nigh impossible, though people tried to be as helpful as they could. Generally strangers seemed to be treated rather more politely here than in Eastern Turkey. I have since read that at that time anyone obviously not Iranian was assumed to be rich, even if dressed in "torn shirt and patched trousers"[19]. Affluence might gain general respect, but it presented difficulties when attempting to barter in a truly Persian manner. Being assumed to be rich never facilitates such business.

In Reza'iyeh there was a definite western influence in the men's dress and they were certainly more neatly attired than our lads. Shirt and trousers were still the fashion, and we saw few turbans now, nor the fezzes seen in some parts of Turkey. What turbans there were seemed more an adaptation of my idea of a sheik's headdress, being scarf-like in form and twisted round a solid crown, often with fringes. However we noted that women's fashions were much more changeable, the townswomen here being enveloped from head to foot in long lengths of dark blue lightly patterned material, the looser folds of which, around their heads, they drew over their faces when confronted with our menfolk. We wondered about the country women we had glimpsed before, dressed in colourful clothes, generally allowing more obvious movement, presumably because they were involved in manual work. Were they of different ethnic origins, Kurdish perhaps, or just lower class? V.S.Naipaul comments that it is the poor that can be colourful and unveiled:

---

[19] Carroll (1960), page 110.

"...here, as everywhere else, to be conservative and correct was the privilege of the rising."[20]

We continued, to camp in a nearby dusty, thorny field site. I got a lot of grit in my eyes and thorns in my fingers (and elsewhere) putting up the tent. And then there was a thunder storm, so Virginia and I got wet into the bargain! We ate in the truck, nice and warm and in good company, which cheered me considerably. Virginia, however, stayed in a bad mood! On our return to our tent she started complaining loudly about the trip as a whole. "Oh Virginia!" I began wearily ... when from an adjacent tent came the voice of Dave, sharing now with Abby. "For God's sake Virginia, shut up!" I could hear Abby chuckling as I too dissolved into giggles. Virginia, of-course, was not amused! I hoped we would be speaking again in the morning.

***　　***　　***

It was cloudy and damp next morning, but Virginia's grudges couldn't be maintained for long when there was work to be done. We *were* on speaking terms OK. Our stint washing up completed, we were off at 7.45, returning to Reza'iyeh. I successfully changed my first Swiss travellers' cheque at the bank for over 4,000 rials (with no difficulty despite Ian's warnings). Then I joined Virginia, Sarah and Tim to shop. We didn't have a lot of luck, and it didn't help that we managed to leave two of the vegetables that we bought in the shop! This meant that we had more tomatoes than anything else at the lunch stop.

It was still slightly spitting with rain when we got going again after lunch, but the weather seemed to be clearing, the far hills blue and tawny-yellow, and the road ahead good and often very straight. We found ourselves to be a risk to others on the road however, purely because we drew their attention away from their driving. Coming out of one town, a horse and cart pulled out once we'd passed, and still gazing after us, nearly got run down by the following blue truck!!

---

[20] *An Area of Darkness* (1995), page 133.

78

By the shores of Lake Urmia, we noted salt deposits on the shore. Then as we moved south we saw camels grazing by salt pans on the far banks. In the country there were small collections of mud houses with hay drying on their flat roofs. What livestock we saw grazing were mainly herds of long-legged, floppy-eared brown sheep, though there were plenty camels around too. There were incredibly green patches of field sometimes, so there must have been a good irrigation system at work. There was a man sowing seed in a wide-flung, broadcast motion in one field we passed, and another crouched under a canopy of grasses contemplating his crop growing, or so it seemed!

After living for a couple of years in a steeply sloped south-facing wine-cultivating region of Switzerland, by Lake Geneva, I was intrigued to see how vines could be grown on flat land instead. Hillocks had been built up and the vines planted on the top of the hillock system, allowing them to trail down the southern sides.

We stopped briefly for a problem with the fan belt again. To make the most of this opportunity, I gestured to some women and girls in the yards of houses nearby to ask if I might take their photographs. One young girl was particularly attractively dressed in a colourful red top and white skirt with an emerald-green patterned cummerbund. Her dark hair showed beneath a brightly patterned green-edged headscarf. These looked like Kurdish people. Certainly they were much more brightly dressed than the townsfolk we'd seen, making them extremely photogenic.

Maddie joined me and we were getting on famously with them all, including the head of the household, a man standing up on his small two-wheeled cart reining in his horse below, with a whip in hand. He made a strong photograph. But he and the women became angry all of a sudden: Lukas had appeared behind us with his camera and was attempting to photograph the women and girls as we had done. It became obvious that he was at risk of being whipped, so we retreated quickly. Perhaps luckily, Ian was just about to move on again, so we swung over the tailpin with agility. Once settled in his seat, Lukas apologised for queering our pitch. It seemed that for once we women had more freedom than the men, when it came to photography at any rate.

It soon started raining once more, so we went well off the road to camp and made the evening meal in the truck. There was a terrific thunderstorm during the night, sounding for all the world like stage effects.

***   ***   ***

I was up next morning before five, lighting the gas and getting the kettles on for tea. We got off two hours later, the day brighter, but still cold in the back of the truck with the sides up. Noting the date in my diary I realised it would be October tomorrow and that we had been on the road for a month already. It was amazing how I'd become accustomed to this way of life. In fact I wondered if it mightn't be very strange returning to normal humdrum activities once more in December.

We drove through undulating hilly scenery that morning, passing villages of flat-roofed adobe housing, where men in turbans and baggy trousers with wide waist sashes stood staring after us. I tried to imagine what they were thinking and James Elroy Flecker's lines came to mind.

THE MERCHANTS *in chorus*:
We take the Golden Road to Samarkand.

AN OLD MAN:
Have you not girls and garlands in your homes,
Eunuchs and Syrian boys at your command?
Seek not excess: God hateth him who roams!

Did it unsettle these locals to see us travelling in this way, reminding them of the narrowness of their life? Or did they see it as altogether against nature to attempt such journeys? Perhaps, like the Old Man above, they felt we should be satisfied with what we had at home (so much more than they had) and not come disturbing them, treating them as though they were animals in a zoo. The Merchant's answer to the Old Man in Flecker's poem suggested a search for something out of the ordinary.

A MERCHANT:

We travel not for trafficking alone:
By hotter winds our fiery hearts are fanned:
For lust of knowing what should not be known
We make the Golden Journey to Samarkand. [21]

I liked that idea of a risky lust for knowledge beyond the everyday. It was in tune with my inclinations and very probably with those of most of my companions. I was not happy to rest all my days in one area: I wanted to see how others lived. But it wasn't like a visit to the zoo: I felt I might learn and improve my own life by comparing it with what I saw.

Soon the roads widened into city boulevards and we came upon Sanandaj, the capital of the province of Kurdistan and our shopping stop for that day. I bought cakes and dates as well as a bottle of Coke, which we were finding to be a universal drink, or so it seemed. It was interesting to note that here if the Coca-Cola bottle was not returned, the price doubled! I remembered getting the odd penny at home for returned pop bottles in the 1950s, but this gave a much greater reward. It presumably helped keep the city clear of litter too.

The streets were busy. We found ourselves surrounded by a crowd of school boys, gathering to show us their very nicely illustrated exercise books. Nearby there were blind beggars and some old women with hennaed hair. Adding a reddish tint to the hair was a very common practice in Iran we discovered, including to grey or white hair. Salesmen were everywhere too. Even beautiful carpets were being sold in the middle of the muddy streets.

We stopped 30 kms from Sanandaj for lunch. There were washing facilities close by, so I washed my top half and from the knees down and, delight of delights, my hair at last. It was extremely dusty. However it only got washed with soap for now, as my proper wash things were in my rucksack in the trailer. I felt it was a start though.

---

[21] *The Golden Journey to Samarkand* (1913).

There was another thunder storm as we left! So much for Ian's confidently telling us a night or two ago that there'd be no rain in Iran. On we continued through a dust-storm, and then it fairly pelted it down with rain. We had the truck sides and back down by now. I read *War and Peace* till it got too dark, going through the pass near Kermanshah. There was an impressive sheer rock face on the left and a narrow valley to the right. The cooks started chopping for tea in the back of the truck before we reached camp.

70 kms west of Hamadan we camped in a dirt field again! There was a howling gale as we put the tents up, but the wind was surprisingly warm. We had lost the blue truck again, but tea and chat in the orange truck was nice and cosy that evening. I gave Maddie a facial massage and promised Ian a back massage should he get too sore driving. I'd noticed that the orange truck's driving seat was not entirely straight, causing a twist to the lumbar spine which could make for discomfort after an hour or two. If I'd been so inclined there could have been a lucrative post in ergonomic advice for me at Encounter Overland, I felt!

***   ***   ***

The first of October dawned cloudy, the dark sky threatening rain, but there was no longer any wind to speak of. We were off at 6.30, turning back up the road to get water and to try to meet with the bluies. We got the water at a well in a village of mud-houses. Some wood had been piled in the open area of earth between the houses along with a couple of oil drums, perhaps the village's fuel at the start of the cold season. Someone commented that had there been grass this area might have been called the village green, but here became the 'village muddy brown'! But where had the branches of wood been gleaned? The hills around looked very bare. Someone had planted a few trees near the well, but these looked stunted, doing their best in very poor conditions. Foraging must have been done far further afield.

I chatted with three little boys 'wearing' sacking protection from the rain, who were fascinated by the sterilisation process I went through with each filled jerry can of water. But no sooner had I finished than there was another thunder storm and the lads ran for cover. The blue truck arrived soon afterwards, by which time it was raining stair-rods once more.

As the rain cleared, we crossed a plain to a village with what looked like radio telescopes (or even an early warning system) situated beyond it: outlined against the hills, two large dishes faced north east and north west. Towards Russia perhaps? During the Cold War our minds tended to leap to these conclusions. The dishes looked so alien in this landscape that I actually sketched them, as there was little chance of a photo stop. We then climbed steeply into the hills once more, till we could see the whole plain encircled by mountains, orange at the base, black and deep blue beyond, and paling into grey and pearly white in the distance.

We had a shopping stop of an hour at Hamadan. This was Iran's most ancient city, becoming the capital of the Medes in the sixth century BC, when it was known as Ecbatana. There is much still to be excavated in this region: it is thought for example that the Jewish wife of King Xerxes, Esther, who gave her name to a book in the Old Testament, is buried somewhere near the centre of the city. The Greek historian Herodotus wrote in the fourth century BC of the many palaces in the city yielding treasures of precious metalwork and jewellery.

Sadly we had too short a time to look round thoroughly, but along with others, I made an effort here to learn about the Arabic numbering system[22], essential to successful shopping from now on. Shopkeepers soon realised what we were after, perhaps having had similar requests in the past, and wrote their numbers down for us ... in the wrong direction, from right to left. I had forgotten that this would be the case and made a mental note to look at books before long and see how they were written from back to front. What a lot we had to learn!

Meanwhile I bought some sweets and, amazingly it seemed to me, TUC biscuits, very commonly sold as biscuits for cheese at home! There were also Polo mints and Smarties on sale. It seemed that western travellers had made their mark and appropriate trade links had been forged.

---

[22] Arabic numbers we learnt:

1 = ١	3 = ٣	5 = ٥	7 = ٧	9 = ٩
2 = ٢	4 = ٤	6 = ٦	8 = ٨	10 = ٠

Schoolchildren cross the Asklepion site, Bergama, Turkey

Fairy chimneys in the Goreme Valley, Turkey

Crowds gather round when we stop in Yüksekova, Anatolia

Baking bread in Isfahan, Iran

I walked a while through some back streets with Maddie noting, among more ordinary brick dwellings, the simple wattle-and-daub, adobe-type houses again. But then it was time for me to take up guard duty in the rear of the truck for the last twenty minutes of our stay. I climbed in and looked down on the usual crowd of men and boys around the rear wheels and trailer. Then this suddenly parted as Michael and Derek, the Canadian bluies (brothers-in-law travelling together), who were on our truck that day, came diving over the tailpin at the double, closely followed by a slim young Iranian. "Save me!" cried Derek, as the youth exclaimed passionately, "I love you!" He had apparently taken a fancy to Derek's blond good looks. In fact he was interested in any man. I was rather amused at this reversal of roles, finding myself fending off a rather nice-looking young man, encouraging him to leave my friend alone. But I was disappointed too: really men were getting more advances than women on this trip!!

Not long after leaving Hamadan we had a loo stop that caused quite a bit of amusement. For a start we girls were on a shale hillside, and into the bargain there was a strong wind blowing. By the time we arrived back at the truck, several of us were in need of a shower having been downwind of our companions. It had also been a test of our balance as we fought to keep our footing on the shale, so we were feeling quite unsteady!

Lunch was accompanied by yet another thunder storm, though it didn't prevent locals turning up to gaze at us as ever. They had a white donkey in tow that we rather took to. Then on we drove into a dust storm once again. We arrived in Borujerd in the middle of the afternoon, but had difficulty finding our way out again. It amused us in the back to find we were being followed by a youth on a bike and his passenger (seated between himself and the handlebars), both with wide flashing smiles, while we made a tour of the town!

On we travelled to a smaller town with a large cement works and from there started climbing on a worse road, which showed signs of subsidence, particularly at bridges we crossed. We went off-road to find a camp site, which was nicely sheltered and had a good stream running by for once. I had a more thorough wash here. After tea we played solo whist, a frequent accompaniment to time off in my student days, so I found myself one of the better players for once.

***   ***   ***

Next morning I was travelling in the cab once more, with Ian driving. My companions were an international set. Heidi from Switzerland was in the hot seat; Rob the New Zealander, Lynn from Australia and Lukas the Austrian accompanied me in the cab seats.

We drove over bone-dry moorland, occasionally passing through towns with brick buildings and shabby pavements lined with stunted trees, or there were villages, the glassless windows of the mud houses packed with bricks for use against the cold weather of winter. Only occasionally were there flowers on show. We caught glimpses of brick works with baking mounds. In the fields men were ploughing with oxen. A very pot-holed road caused everyone to leap in their seats in spite of Ian's careful driving. The writing in my diary zigzagged wildly. I recorded...

> 'weaving about as I write, to avoid the pot-holes! We've just been passed by two lorries on the wrong side of the road!!'

The weather improved as we travelled on, in bright sunshine, via Aligudarz and Najafabad, making non-stop for Isfahan. Scenes that remain in my memory are viewing the surely back-breaking discomfort of the local people engaged in their grape harvest; being amazed at the load (a donkey could have carried little more) that a woman had on her head; and realising that the adobe villages were becoming more ornate and attractive, now seen against a background of hills. This was happening as the plain opened out more and more. We followed a tree-lined avenue leading to Najafabad and found a wide water channel along the side of the road, and women washing clothes. It felt as though we had reached the lushest of oases, and indeed that is exactly the situation of Isfahan. It seems in the middle of nowhere, for there are no high mountains around, just miles of near-desert country. In fact it's at the heart of an oasis formed by the Zayandeh River.

Elliot wrote that,

> "... Iran's most celebrated monarch, the Safavid Shah Abbas I ... made Isfahan his capital in 1598 ... a showpiece to the world, whose

grandeur and beauty hypnotized and beguiled its foreign visitors ..."[23]

And 377 years on we were beginning to sense that charmed difference with the terrain around as we approached our goal. A beautiful square, with (we weren't imagining it, were we?) *green grass* and a *fountain*, opened out before us! After the dry land we'd passed through this was heaven. It was with increasing pleasure that I anticipated seeing the beautiful gardens and historic buildings of the renowned city.

---

[23] *Mirrors of the Unseen: Journeys in Iran* (2006), page 56.

Chapter 9. The Centre of Persian Culture

A little over ten miles further and we were on the outskirts of Isfahan ... and promptly got lost thanks to a complicated one-way street system. I suggested a route and was astounded, first that Ian bothered to take my advice, and then that it actually worked! In the centre of town were great wide boulevards with views, through arcs of fountains, of the exquisitely azure and turquoise tiled domes of mosques and the lustre of metalwork for sale in bazaar stalls beyond.

Ian and Ben parked the vehicles and we all set off to explore the old city. I'd read that Isfahan had escaped devastation by the Mongols and Timur Lang, so there were hardly any 'ruins' to explore, but there were some fascinating historical buildings. We had from 1.30 to 5pm to look round. We soon found Tourist Information, but they didn't really help us much. We were pretty hungry by now and, after some searching, entered the only restaurant that seemed open, Ramadan still being in operation. We were pleased to find that, although in a city, prices were very reasonable. Eight of us had yoghurt, pancake-thin bread, rice and kebabs with a butter pat, plus a soft drink, for only 80 rials each. Thus fortified I spent the rest of the afternoon exploring the bazaar with Sarah and Tim.

Leaving the bright sunlight of the streets for the alleyways of the bazaar was like diving under water. The sounds of outside life became muffled and changed into echoing conversation, against a distant hammering of metal workers and coppersmiths further within the labyrinth of vaulted tunnels. Odours changed too. Gone were the diesel fumes we were so used to, the pollution of the busy streets: now the subtle scents of wool, leather and spices became perceptible. We had entered that magical subterranean world of the east, last met in Istanbul.

The word 'bazaar' though is a Persian one, so we were engaging in a genuinely Iranian activity now. Michael Carroll had written a few years previously of the reputed move away from such old style bazaar-browsing in Isfahan to more modern shopping in the surrounding streets. He had felt "like a ghost returned" on entering the "deserted avenues" of the Isfahan bazaar after experiencing the bustling city shopping centre. He saw only a few merchants sitting forlornly in the midst of their "meagre stocks ... half asleep." [24] I didn't entirely get that impression. However, I was much amused to find the Persian carpet salesman asleep on six of his comfortably folded Antique Kashtana Reds, so perhaps people were indeed buying, their rugs at least, elsewhere. I felt sure an Istanbul merchant would not have been seen dead behaving in this way!

What did strike me was how superbly ornate was the tiled and arched façade and how beautifully cool it was in there, out of the sun. I was also delighted to find it a lot less busy and noisy than the Istanbul bazaar. We were not continually badgered into buying, and even managed some success with bartering, which I was finding to be quite an art form in these countries. I was relatively naive about the niceties involved in the process, and so was pretty pleased with myself for bartering the price of a painted mother of pearl pendant down from 100 rials to 90. Possessions fought for tend to have a special place in the heart I think and this piece is still a favourite of mine. I wondered if I should be able to return here for longer another time during our stay, as I could see they had stones such as lapis lazuli available. Perhaps though I should wait till I was in its natural home in Afghanistan.

We strolled out from the bazaar, under the tall archway that leads onto the north side of the Maidan-i-Shah, or Royal Square. This green space is actually a vast elongated rectangle, twice the size of Moscow's Red Square, the wonderful architecture of the mosques and palace fringing it making it a feast for the eyes. Such a large area for relaxation would adorn any city, and Isfahan's has been used as everything from a market place to a polo ground. Now it was lined with trees, faintly perfumed by roses in its gardens and had a pool at its centre. We thoroughly enjoyed walking here: after days of mainly sitting in the dusty truck we relished being in the fresh air and sun.

Leaving the Maidan we were much impressed by an extremely smart limousine which purred expensively past us. Since crossing into Asia we had not seen much demonstration of wealth, but there would certainly appear to be people with money around here. Beyond the car, a sleek building in an old style was visible. This was the Shah Abbas hotel, named

---

[24] *From a Persian Teahouse* (1960), pages 111-112.

after the founder of the original capital. It had been converted from a caravanserai, that is, accommodation for itinerant traders, each one a day's camel ride apart from the next. To discover more about such places I later read Paine, who describes them as providing,

"...security in a world of plundered wealth. Travellers had lodgings for themselves and their animals free of charge if they stayed for three days and their goods reimbursed if they were stolen. Accommodation was within a fortified enclosure which sheltered a mosque, baths, even a library and in some cases wandering musicians. The walls surrounding the courtyard were galleried with small individual domed rooms, usually with a fireplace, where the traveller rested while his camels and donkeys were safeguarded in the courtyard below or in stabling outside." [25]

Such a set up could be splendidly converted into a luxury hotel.

Walking a little further gave us an excellent view of the Shah Abbas mosque, which had the most magnificent dome. A narrow royal blue base was decorated with intricate calligraphy, while the dome above was tiled in floral swags on a turquoise ground. Islamic art had begun to fascinate me, a kind of soaring unfettered baroque of the east. There was no doubt that Isfahan was living up to the reputation I'd gained of it from my previous reading. I had never seen such unusual artistic opulence.

Returning now to the trucks we drove on to the camp site. I had a shower and washed half my dirty things. I was in a famous, stylish city: perhaps tomorrow I should wear smarter, fresher clothes. The shower was interesting, for the glass in its door was missing, so we girls had fun trying to hang a towel there, and received plenty comments from the passing boys!

We had a great evening singing sitting around the hostel veranda. A Norwegian sitting beside me joined Gloria, Rob and Michael in performing to guitar accompaniment. Michael's song was a particular hit; it had a sniffing chorus - "Honey have a sniff, have a sniff on me. Honey

---

[25] *The Afghan Amulet* (1994), page 142.

have a sniff on me." We were soon all singing it and throughout the rest of the trip it was a much requested number. It was months later that it finally dawned on me that this song might be referring to drug-taking. I had a lot to learn!

***   ***   ***

The next morning we had the opportunity to enjoy a lie-in, but I got Virginia up at seven: she had to get an extension of her visa with a couple of others on the trip. Breakfast was at 8.30, so I spent the intervening time doing more washing. It was good to have the luxury of a proper sink in which to work.

Then it was time to return to town to do some sight-seeing. I was amazed and rather dispirited to find that Dave and Rob, our Kiwi musicians, were quite satisfied to just stay at the camp site and laze in the sun. They weren't at all bothered about seeing round Isfahan. Sure it was pleasant to just relax after travelling continually, but it was sad to have come this far and not show an interest in seeing such an exotic place properly, I thought. I was coming to the conclusion that the girls on this trip had more character than most of the men. Two English chaps among the bluies gave credence to this idea and I had had to be careful to comment on them at the very back of my diary. I wrote:

> 'Daniel, or 'Treeman' as he's become known, is a bit of an odd guy. His mother "let him come on the trip"! Can bore for Britain!'

And:

> 'Howard is very quiet. Evidently he can be fun, but I've yet to see it!'

Perhaps men with more get-up-and-go coming out east tended to travel on their own and not in large groups like ours.

I joined Chloe and Alice, a French teacher and her attractive Lisa-Minelli-look-alike sister from amongst the English bluies, that I'd found good company. It was lovely weather and we were in a city, so we dressed up a bit and wore skirts for once - not mini-skirts mind, but ones that reached the knee or just below. It was this attire that taught us that the Moslems here could be far stricter than in Turkey. That it happened to be a Friday was something we had not reckoned with properly either.

We had set out along the Chahar Bagh, Isfahan's main street, created originally with beautiful gardens and pools, which it had since lost. It had been Shah Abbas's plan to link the maidan-i-shah with the Zayandeh River in this fashion. As we walked along, the extraordinary effect we were having slowly dawned on us, as the passing traffic almost ground to a halt. First a cyclist stopped and gazed at us, frowning and tutting to himself. Then taxis and other vehicles slowed and men craned out to stare at us. We tried not to notice and somehow melt into the background, but it was well-nigh impossible. The local women were well wrapped up in their eight metres of black or navy sprigged cotton, and although the outline of lower limbs occasionally showed through the material, bare legs were not on view anywhere. Venturing into a shop, I found myself refused service on the strength of my dress as well, or so it seemed. Was I becoming paranoid? It was Chloe who very sensibly brought it to our attention at last that perhaps this reaction was aggravated by the fact that it was Friday, the Moslem holy day. It was an important lesson to learn in this part of the world.

Chastened, we made for the river and more touristy areas of town. The old Safavid Si-o-Seh Pol bridge (the name meaning thirty-three in Farsi, after the number of its arches) over the Zayandeh River was lovely. Shah Abbas thought to plan riverside parks for his city in the early seventeenth century, and this bridge dates from that time. Its paving was:

> "...worn smooth by centuries of use ... each side of the gently curved bridge are its eponymous 33 arches. Narrow ledges, along which it's possible to walk high above the water of the Zayandeh, are on the outside ... alcoves are popular trysting places ..."[26]

And indeed its situation was suitably romantic, with the cliffs of Sofeh mountain and its surrounding hills beyond a row of dark trees, forming a grey-blue backdrop on the far side of the Zayandeh.

---

[26] Worrall (2011), page 253.

I needed goodies to share that evening as we were all dining out together, so bought some banana liqueur and chocolate. Then after a light lunch, Chloe and I continued to the English church in the Jolfa district across the Si-o-Seh Pol Bridge. I'm not sure now how we came to know of this church's existence: perhaps Chloe had heard about it from someone. I was used to the concept of an English-speaking church abroad, for I had recently been a regular attendee at one in Lausanne. But Switzerland was a Christian country and I was very interested to learn what life might be like for a minority sect in a Muslim country. We were lucky enough to come across the pastor's wife who took us to visit the Christian Hospital nearby. I was surprised that there should be one in Iran at all. Sadly we were unable to look round properly though, and I felt depressed at the sight of patients lying down the sides of the corridors. They were terribly over-crowded it seemed. I often wonder what happened to those working there four years later on the fall of the Shah in 1979. According to Jon White[27], the Christian hospitals and schools in Iran were expropriated at this time. He adds that,

"There have been martyrs since the Revolution, and the situation can only really be described… as unpredictable [though] the tiny Church persists."

We never envisaged anything like a revolution when we travelled through Iran in 1975. Indeed life was in some ways very ordinary on our trip, and this moment was an example of that. I took a taxi back to the camp site that day, washed my hair, sorted out my laundry and then lent a hand washing the truck. It was a good time for doing odd jobs, sewing and cleaning, after which I succumbed and joined Dave and Rob to sunbathe a while, before being called upon to massage Jim's neck and shoulders.

At 7pm Virginia and I changed and set out with the whole group to dine in a smart restaurant, one of E.O.'s treats again. I enjoyed a tasty local chicken and rice dish. We then moved on to the Shah Abbas hotel (yes, the luxury number we'd seen the day before) and sat in the moonlit garden, with fountains and soft music playing. We tried buying beer at the bar, but found to our horror that it cost the equivalent of £2 a bottle, an

---

[27] *Anglican churches in Iran?* (2016).

exorbitant price in 1975. We were tempted to go to the disco there, but this too was for the rich, the entrance fee a cool 250 rials. Peg and Mark, Tim, Luigi and I returned to camp and chatted for a while, getting to bed quite early. Tim and I were aware that we had a special cooking day tomorrow, the 4th of October, a joint meal with the bluies to celebrate the amazing coincidence of its being both Ben's and Ian's birthdays.

***   ***   ***

After the washing up following breakfast, we loaded our rucksacks and left for town in the trucks and I helped Sarah, from my orange truck cooking group, and Chloe and Alice from the bluies' one, do shared shopping in the Bazaar for our evening's birthday tea. The whole experience was gloriously picturesque. When we came on a truly magnificent spice stall, trays set out in a patchwork of all colours and textures of herb, their wonderful aromas accompanying the display, there were discussions of what seasonings to use. Chloe was for trying tarragon, which she thought she recognised here, a dark green herb to one side. But here our Farsi failed us: we needed to ask if it was indeed what we thought. On pointing to it questioningly, however, we got an interesting response. "Is not for eat", the merchant told us. He then pointed towards the Persian lamb cap that covered his curly dark head: "Is for hair." We were very grateful to him, for we now realised that we had proposed using henna in our cooking! What on earth would that have tasted like?

Further down the dark Bazaar alleyway we found the baker's, and watched engrossed as four men prepared the naan bread for baking in an oven the like of which we had never seen before.[28] There was a strict division of labour in the baking team. One man was kneading dough, which the next man broke and moulded into what looked like small baps. The third baker skilfully spread one after another of these dough balls out on his hands into a thin circular shape, almost a foot in diameter. Finally the fourth man used a long-handled implement, ending in a form of slice or shovel, to slap the circle of dough onto the wall of a hot cylindrical clay oven facing him. It was a hot job, but I was surprised that he had no protection for his hands, constantly approaching the intense heat of the

---

[28] See photograph on page 85.

oven as he was. In minutes the flat cake of bread was baked and lifted aside to cool with others in a pile. They were delighted that we were showing interest in their work and flashed us gleaming smiles as we took their photographs. Their shining white teeth would have graced a dental advert!

The shopping completed, we had a quick drink and a wander in the Maidan-i-Shah gardens. Here I left the others and went to the jewellery section of the bazaar once more. After a little time comparing what was on offer, I succeeded in buying a blue-green lapis lazuli ring in a rather unusual copper setting, for the very reasonable price of 500 rials, but then managed to get lost in the maze of passages I'd traversed.

Thus it was that I found myself in a deserted, rather decrepit-looking courtyard, now used as a storage area at the edge of the bazaar. Even this area was highly decorated though. Arcades supported by slim Corinthian-type pillars topped by blue and yellow mosaic tiling surrounded a deserted fountain. I could imagine the courtyard in past glory days, the fountain playing and doves cooing above the delicate arches, as men reclining on divans were served by graceful veiled women. A world of exotic dreams, for today weeds grew in cracks in the paving, though above, old-style wind chimneys still channelled cool air through the building.

Thankfully at this point a kind Iranian came to my rescue and led me out again, to near the coppersmiths' area. There I came upon Scott, who I had learnt was interested in anything to do with jewellery or pottery. (He was to open a stall for eastern art in the Victoria Market in Melbourne when he returned home.) Now we continued together almost deafened by the noise of metal hammering and engraving going on around us. It was worth it though, for I bought a plate with 'Allah' inscribed on it in Arabic, which hangs on a wall of my house to this day, a poignant memory of a fascinating culture.

We then went together for cakes and a drink, and got chatting to some students sitting on the cafe wall near us. They agreed to teach us some Farsi and wrote the words in their backwards-seeming script for us in my diary. Naturally I transcribed this into what I heard:

Hello!	**Salarm!**
How are you?	**Harley chomah setoray?**
Well, thanks	**Manhu** (with a rolled R sound) **hastam.**
You're welcome	**Hosh amadid**
Goodbye	**Hodar hafez**

And even now I occasionally surprise an Iranian visiting Britain with one of these phrases, so the students did their job well!

Since our journey overland I've read with interest that, because European and Persian merchants traded extensively between their countries in the late fifteenth century, a few Persian words came to be current in the English language then. The word *lajward* for the lapis lazuli colour became the English 'azure', *sagalat* meaning red cloth gave us 'scarlet' and 'shawl' is very near to the original shàl.[29] The kind of words linking the languages gives an idea of the merchandise involved. Renaissance artists valued the rich blue and red pigments the east provided for their paints: indeed the most expensive blue from lapis lazuli was considered suitable for the clothing of the mother of Christ, the Virgin Mary. Fashion too profited from the trade links.

But now I was to learn more about design of another sort from ancient times. Scott and I had returned to the trucks and we set off in the afternoon, soon leaving the Isfahan oasis and driving on into rocky desert country. It was such arid land in fact that I saw my first qanat bore-holes for water supply that afternoon. This is an ancient irrigation technology I had read about, consisting of long sloping underground water channels with regular vertical access shafts. They carry water from aquifers where snow-melt drains at the base of hills and mountains, and provide a reliable supply to the people living in these dry conditions.[30] This underground system preceded the Romans' aboveground aqueducts, and allowed the Persian rulers their wonderful gardens. We saw how useful they might be as we settled for the night on a camp site near some ruined houses. Our jerry cans of water were certainly needed, for we were in a thoroughly arid plain surrounded by distant hills. Nothing grew here but what we

---

[29] Stuart (1926), pages 90-91.
[30] Ahmadi et al. (2010).

came to call 'hedgehog' scrub, thorny low bushes that burnt well on our fires.

The sun set very fast and we got straight on with the birthday tea. Together with Tim I looked after the soup and pasta. (Oh dear! People still remembered the Termessos incident!) Working with the other trucks' cooks went pretty well. We had soup, spaghetti Bolognese and fruit salad, followed by birthday cake. Ben received a bracelet as a present, and Ian a print and some champagne. There was a good sing-song round the 'hedgehog' fire till around midnight, when most of us hit the hay. Ian, Ben and a few others kept it up till 3am however. There would probably be the odd sore head tomorrow! (In a recent comment Ben, forty years on, still remembers this joint birthday celebration with great pleasure, though he admits that he and Ian had perhaps over-indulged so that the next morning's start was later than usual!)

Chapter 10. Memorials to an Empire

Not all that late for the cooks next morning however! We were back to the routine of an early start, putting the kettles on at 5am. It was very chilly and had been a cold night. I found Lynn in the back of the truck, shivering and faint, thanks probably to the alcohol she'd had the previous night. This kind of thing afflicted her more than others though and I did wonder sometimes if she might have tried local drugs. I sure to goodness hoped she never brought any on the truck! We made sure she had a good lie down while we sorted out breakfast, and she seemed better by the time we set off. I hoped I never felt ill on the trip, for I could think of nothing worse than to be tossed about on uneven road surfaces when feeling off-colour.

Not that the road was so bad at the moment. We were off reasonably early, driving towards Shiraz. Across heathland, mainly scrub and rough grasses, we went, finally stopping to shop for an hour in a small neat town, somewhere near Shahreza. Among other things I bought Atrixo hand cream (which I used often in England but hardly expected to find here), dried apricots for snacking and some herbs for the truck kitchen. It seemed a shame to us to miss trying out the local flavours.

We continued through an increasingly alien flat landscape with what appeared to be threatening dust clouds at the horizon above a shimmering watery mirage. It seemed that dust tornadoes sprang up because of a lack of wind breaks. Only the occasional nomad camp of black-striped tents and the odd camel train added any colour to the landscape. Then suddenly we were passing Abadeh and came on a sight from another age, the strange citadel ramparts of Izadkhast Fortress. They towered above the road, dwarfing the tiny black figures of men and donkeys, laden with panniers full of goods, treading the dusty track below. I thought of the walls of Jericho: the stonework here was crumbling at the base of the ramparts in several places. I wasn't sure these could have withstood the braying of Joshua's trumpets for long either.

On and upwards the road wound now, over a high pass to Pasargadae in a much more fertile area, where we stopped for lunch. It gave us the opportunity to also visit Cyrus the Great's tomb. I knew very little about

Cyrus then, but have since come to regard him as something of a hero among Persian Kings. He had begun building the capital of his empire at Pasargadae around 546 BC. Jona Lendering[31] suggests:

"It is best to imagine Pasargadae as a group of garden pavilions in a park: essentially a camp of nomads, but made out of natural stone. Stylistically, the Audience Hall, the Residential Palace [and] the garden pavilions ... belonged to the architectural tradition of the Iranian nomads, who lived in large tents. However, Cyrus used elements from other cultures as well: sculptures from the Assyrian palaces were used as models, work may have been done by stonemasons from Greek Ionia, and a hybrid demon guarded the gate. Perhaps the population of the town had a similar, mixed character."

The tomb of Cyrus the Great was built within the royal park at Pasargadae, and is now nearer the main road than the site of the ancient city, so it was all we saw in 1975. Raised some thirty feet up on a ziggurat of stone, the little gabled temple-like structure appears too small to commemorate such a great ruler, for Cyrus has the rare accolade of being mentioned several times in no less than four books of the Old Testament of the Bible[32] and of being remembered with reverence by the Jews. As suggested above, he was tolerant of many different cultures, and was admired as much for being a liberator as for being a renowned warrior and conqueror. The book of Ezra[33] tells how he allowed 40,000 Jews in Babylon to return to Jerusalem, taking with them the valuable sacred vessels that Nebuchadnezzar had purloined, and supported the rebuilding of their temple, an unusual manner of behaviour towards a conquered people in those days, particularly those of the Jewish race.

This didn't prevent Cyrus from coming to a pretty gruesome end however. His attempts to conquer all peoples in this area led to his downfall even before the building at Pasargadae was completed. Kapuściński notes that, like many power-hungry rulers since, he:

---

[31] *Pasargadae* (2004).
[32] 2nd Chronicles, Ezra, Isaiah and Daniel.
[33] Ezra 1: vv 2-4.

"... transgressed a fundamental Greek principle, the law of moderation: never to want too much, not to desire everything." (p 92)

Thus he attacked the fierce Massagetae tribe in the north-east of the region and was killed in battle. Their Queen Tomyris (according to Herodotus, the Greek historian of the next century) put out a search for Cyrus' body and...

"When she found it, she shoved his head into the wineskin [in which she had been collecting blood from "still fresh wounds"], and in her rage addressed his body ... "I warned you that I would quench your thirst for blood, and so I shall".[34]

Cyrus' son later attacked the Massagetae to recover what remained of his father's body and buried it at Pasargadae in the tomb we saw. It's unclear whether the Persian King's head was laid there with the rest of his body though. I must say I'm glad I knew nothing of this story while I was eating my lunch nearby, two and a half thousand years later.

No, we drove on towards Persepolis with not the slightest queasy thought. I noted in my diary that we were travelling through an interesting valley. For a start it was tree-lined and there was proper agricultural development of the surrounding land. Chequer-board furrowing was supported by perimeter irrigation from the river, pumped from source. There were still some nomads herding goats. I saw a boy, presumably the goat-herd, lying at the side of the road flicking flies away lazily with a switch. Unlike the country the other side of the pass we'd crossed, most people seemed settled in the neighbouring village: few now dwelt in black-striped tents. About 22 miles short of Persepolis, forestation appeared on the hill slopes to one side and I noted strange strata in the local rock formation, drawn into peaks, like stiff cake dough. Soon these rocks stacked together as inland cliffs on either side of the road.

There were water towers visible, and we passed through one narrow village which was a perfect oasis crowded with trees, such a contrast with the dust-bowl country we'd passed through that morning. Walls now enclosed plantations, and I noted a peculiar system of spreading stubble

---

[34] *Travels with Herodotus* (2008), page 97.

(or so it seemed), once cut, over a field with plenty furrows, and then burning it. One of my companions wondered if this was to help build up top soil.

But there were more ancient monuments to visit. Not long before we were due to reach Persepolis we came upon Naghsh-e-Rostam, where we were given some time to view the tombs of Darius II, Artaxerxes I, Darius I and Xerxes I (thus their tombs appeared before us, from left to right) built into the soaring rock face, with well-worn carvings below as decoration. I remembered some of these kings from my school history classes. Darius I was king in the time of Daniel (of lion's den fame): he was also the Persian king whose forces invaded Greece and were defeated by the Athenians at the battle of Marathon in 490 BC. Xerxes (whose favourite queen was Esther) had rather more success when he led his forces against the Spartans at the battle of Thermopylae ten years later. These were more spectacular tombs than Cyrus', a whole towering cliff-face of great Persian Kings. Their tombs, I was surprised to note (for this was long before the cross became a religious symbol), were engraved into the cliff-face in the shape of huge sturdy crosses with very short crosspieces. Small apertures were visible way up at the crossing by which one could evidently enter the tomb, but how you might clamber up to that level was very unclear. Lower detailed carving depicted the kings' exploits. I wondered if the architects of Mount Rushmore got their idea of a cliff of Presidents from visiting Naghsh-e-Rostam.

Continuing on up the valley, we reached Persepolis. From our first glimpse of its 'chimneys' it could almost have been a deserted industrial site and we imagined it to be quite small, but, on entering, we soon saw that it was both unique for its carving and architecture and covered a much larger area than we had thought. Darius had begun the building of Persepolis, the main ceremonial site of his empire, in 520 BC, and for nearly two hundred years it was "the richest place on earth"[35]. The Persians were still a nomadic people, coming from the Eurasian Steppes, and thus they moved from place to place during the year depending on the availability of local produce and seasonal weather conditions. There was little or no history of permanent building in stone in this area before

---

[35] Bragg (2018).

Persepolis, and just as Jona Lendering described Pasargadae (see page 100), so this site can be regarded as a kind of petrified tent. An "immense stone platform occupying over a million square feet"[36] was part-carved out of the hillside, part-extended further from this great terrace, so that the halls and palaces could be constructed upon it, a very solid 'ground sheet'. The 'chimneys' we'd seen were actually tall slender columns that had once supported roofs, 'tent poles' of intricate stonework. Certainly it was unlike anything I had seen before.

Despite being looted and burnt by Alexander the Great only a couple of centuries after its initial construction, its decorative architecture had been remarkably well preserved. The site was fully excavated only last century, after lying hidden under layers of ash since its destruction. Then, less than four years after our visit, Persepolis was in peril again during the Iranian Revolution when a regional commander ordered the whole place to be flattened for good, but local people were so unhappy about this that some of them lay down in front of the bulldozers in protest. Fortunately word came from Tehran that the damage should not be done, and the ruins remain as an amazing open air museum on a par with Pompeii and Herculaneum in Italy.

We rightly guessed that the site was going to take some exploring. Though the shadows were already long at three thirty in the afternoon, it was hot: we began our visit by sipping cooling drinks at the entrance before exploring everything in the lovely early evening light. We gazed up at enormous door pillars evidently set in high walls originally, most of which had vanished into the dust at our feet long ago. But what workmanship was here! On these gateposts and columns were carved great creatures, lions, huge man-bulls and other weird monsters, one of which turned out to be the malign spirit of the Zoroastrian religion, Ahriman, resembling a fierce semi-armour-coated unicorn-like creature. This character stood on his rear hooves ready to batter King Darius, the bearded and crowned Persian hero who faced him bravely, left arm raised as though to strike the beast. These figures were overwhelming, being at least three times a human's height. It must have struck terror into lowly people entering the

---

[36] Elliot (2006), page 342.

palace buildings for the first time two and a half thousand years ago. They were at risk of suffering neck ache too with so much to look up to!

It would have been surely worth it however. As Kapuscinski comments:

> "…if they succeed in leaving here in one piece, what a distinguished rank they will acquire among their people! He is the one who visited the king, others will say ... One secures in this way one's family's standing for generations to come."[37]

Perhaps those who had worked on the huge stone blocks carried here to form and decorate this amazing place (how, and at what human cost?) could also have boasted of their craft. The beauty of their creation had endured for far longer than their rulers' power and influence.

We wandered through to an area of the original flooring and I was fascinated to see a strange large beetle moving across it. It was hardly out of place. We found highly decorated heads of columns intact but laid carefully on this flooring. They resembled two headed horses, lions or a peculiar parrot-beaked creature. One or two of us climbed astride these to be photographed, but I felt uneasy doing this somehow. It almost seemed to show disrespect for them. I chose to be photographed myself stepping up the beautifully crafted shallow stairs leading to one of the palaces. These were negotiable on horseback originally and were decorated with a carved frieze, showing lines of poised tribute-bearers carrying gifts for the king, behind which, inexplicably, were a couple of frightening encounters between tiger or lion-like evil spirits attacking bulls. I wondered the latter didn't frighten the horses that mounted past them in those early days.

We were not alone looking round; visitors included families, the children quite awestruck at times and led rather reluctantly away from the more gruesome friezes and statues by their veiled mothers. Guides were on hand to answer questions, and one asked me if I should like to "view his ruins by moonlight" – easily the best chat-up line I had yet heard! We

---

[37] *Travels with Herodotus* (2008) page 152.

found he was referring to a Son et Lumière performance to be held at 9pm. Intriguing!

We left to pitch our tents nearby and to have our tea before returning for the evening performance. This was wonderfully done, though perhaps slightly over-dramatically. It all sounded too much of a fairy story: I wanted to hear more facts. It was only afterwards that I learnt how short a time Persepolis had been a sacred site to the Persian kings. Jason Elliot suggests that when Alexander finally found himself before this awe-inspiring wonder of the ancient world, "its magnificence, its wealth, and perhaps its sanctity may have awoken a vengeful streak in the young Macedonian." Although advised to leave well alone, he sought revenge for the Persian "invasions of Greece and the burning of the Acropolis in Athens." Thus it was that he slaughtered the Persepolis guards, toppled the statues of the kings and filched all he could from the treasury. "Ten thousand mules and five thousand camels, according to Plutarch, were needed to transport the spoils."[38] Arthur Pope ascribes his motives slightly differently: stressing the importance of Persepolis to the Persian Empire he writes:

> "It was the embodiment of a national consciousness and, as such, Alexander knew that he must destroy it."[39]

Similar thinking has sadly led to this kind of vandalism in the Middle East again today.

A lucky find for archaeologists were several cuneiform tablets, originally only sun-dried, but which had been baked hard in the heat of Alexander's destruction of the site. These survived to reveal rich details of skilled workmen in the city, the dates and finances involved in various craftwork and land transactions to do with Persepolis, and even instructions about the amounts of sacred alcohol to be used at cult services.[40]

---

[38] Elliot (2006), page 142.
[39] *Persian architecture* (1965).
[40] Moghaddam (2002).

After the show we stumbled back to camp in complete darkness, for we had not thought to bring torches. I nearly fell into several ditches on the way! I ended the evening giving Ian the back massage I'd promised him way back soon after our entry into Iran, before joining Virginia in our tent to wonder at the extraordinary sights of the day as we drifted off to sleep.

*** *** ***

At first light next morning I climbed above our camp site and took a photo of Persepolis beyond. Its columns pierced the morning haze enveloping the lower slopes of the blue hills in the distance. The low sun cast long shadows from its platform base and, half closing my eyes, I could get some impression of what it might have been like in the days when it invoked feelings of awe in any Zoroastrian worshipper or stranger visiting the shrine-cum-palace complex. What changes it had seen!

But there was little time to philosophise on the fate of men's great endeavours or the "tormented history of foreign meddling"[41] this country had suffered over generations since Persepolis had been created. I could see our trucks were about to leave for Shiraz. I ran down to join my friends in the orange vehicle and settled down for the hour's drive to the city I knew of as famed for its roses and wine. Better still, it was the day to visit the Poste Restante. What mail would be awaiting us? We were all impatient to hear news from home.

So on our arrival in Shiraz, I went grudgingly to the Tourist Office, which happened to be nearest, and then straight to the Post Office. There were three letters, two from my parents and one from my cousin and godmother! Not only had I all these, but I luckily noticed another in the show-case to one side, addressed to both me and Virginia, from a mutual friend and ex-colleague in Switzerland. What a haul! I glanced quickly through my relatives' letters and looked forward to reading them thoroughly as we travelled. The one addressed to Virginia and myself needed reading and discussing now: it would be bound to have all the juicy up-to-date gossip from our hospital friends in Lausanne. We sought somewhere to have a drink while we looked through it properly.

---

[41] Molavi (2005), page 33.

Chapter 11. Roses and Wine, Salt and Sand

Virginia and I were lucky in our search for a tea-house. With the help of a kind Iranian, we were directed to a delightfully cool spot with elaborately and luxuriously upholstered couches located by a central pool. The waiters wore colourful hats and sashes. They brought us tea and faloodeh, a cold Iranian dessert of thin corn starch noodles mixed in an iced syrup and served with lemon juice. It was really lovely on a hot day, and I'm not sorry I tried it, though I was to regret the results! We read our joint letter as we sipped our sweet, thoroughly enjoying the calm relaxing interlude and sharing happy memories of our mutual friends.

Then we wandered through the bazaar, which I remember particularly for the fabulous carpets on display. It's been said that Shiraz is the "city of gardens and carpets"[42]: we were to see both at their best. I also noted the number of colourful nomad women around, babies perched at the hip. Their costume was almost early Victorian in style, the blouse and apron of the same cloth and a many-frilled skirt contrasting with these, often in material with a distinct golden thread running through it. Their coloured veil or scarf didn't hide the face.

But I had set myself the task of finding my own copy of the Rubaiyat of Omar Khayyam while I was in Shiraz. The guide books suggested that it was a city as noted for poets and literature as for its rose gardens. I had by now learnt something most unusual however, that:

"Omar Khayyām, most commonly thought of in the West as a poet, was one of the great mathematicians of all time".[43]

The same author wrote of all the extraordinary things that had started in Persia, and it was a long list, with mathematics featuring highly. The foundations of Algebra and Trigonometry were first used here, as were decimal fractions. Hence it was not too surprising that our numbering system developed from the one used in this region as well.

---

[42] Kapuściński (2008), page 148.
[43] Elliott (2006), page 6.

But poetry and mathematics - this was the weirdest mixture of gifts to my mind. It made me all the keener to attain my desire, but I would have done better to wait until we reached Mashhad which is far nearer Omar Khayyam's birthplace. As it was I found a copy at the Vakil Mosque, which we now visited, but it wasn't particularly special and had a binding that lasted for only a few years in fact.

The mosque was another matter, its architecture and tiling beautifully ornate and ready to last for hundreds of years. We gazed admiringly as we wandered in the precincts where we had found the book stall and then noticed that people were entering a side courtyard, perhaps for a service. It was Monday so not the Moslem holy day: were these just daily prayers? Virginia and I conferred. She was a Catholic and I a Protestant, but we were both rather missing our church services. We wondered if we could join to some extent with what was going on here, to say our prayers to God along with other theists, even if of another religion and in a language foreign to us.

We saw it as a risky venture and were fairly sure that we would be turned away, but decided we would at least prepare as well as we could, so we washed our hands and feet and covered our heads. As we entered the courtyard we saw that men were on the area spread with prayer rugs in front and women were sitting cross-legged on the carpet behind them. Beyond that was a paved area, so we made for that and sat down as demurely as possible, feeling it was better not to share the carpet with Muslim believers. This quite disturbed the women in front of us, who kept turning to gaze at these two strangers who had gate-crashed their prayers.

Then a young man, in his late teens or early twenties, came towards us and seemed to be gesturing for us to leave. He had no English, nor had any other person there that we met, but the intention was clear enough. This is what we were prepared for, so we started to get up straight away. What happened next I have told many people since, including a surprised Muslim or two. It's something I shall not forget. A middle-aged man approached, stopped the younger one and gestured for us to sit down again. In doing so he made us feel much more welcome and we were very grateful and bowed our thanks accordingly. I'm sure it wasn't a normal occurrence for two foreign non-Muslims to join them and it showed a tolerance and acceptance of us which would surely have been lacking a few years later when the Shah fell in 1979 and Ayatollah Khomeini came to power.

We watched the rest of the service with interest. A reading from the Koran was followed by the entrance of an elderly priest, who was obviously greatly revered for he was greeted with much hand kissing and obeisance. Then followed intoning of (presumably) prayers. The women changed into white veils at this point and the men took off their top trousers to display what looked like pyjamas beneath! Virginia and I weren't quite sure what to make of this, and found it hard not to stare. But we managed to just keep quiet and bow our heads. No one interfered with us in our prayerful attitude, and indeed our overland journey onward got thoroughly prayed for!

Once the service was over we slipped out and almost directly came across James. We took him through the bazaar to a restaurant we'd seen near the tea-house. Ramadan being over, more restaurants were now open at noon and wine might be bought. We all treated ourselves to chelo kebab, the national dish of Iran, consisting of steamed, saffroned basmati rice and kebab, with doogh to drink. The latter was watered-down yoghurt and not particularly nice. We had tea to follow, and then walked through the market area and down to the Narenjestan or 'place of oranges'. I noted that all the pavements in the market area were tiled in different patterns, as we'd found in Isfahan as well. It was very hot by this time and it was lovely to reach a little shade in the orange orchard, where we admired a beautiful mirror-tiled terrace overlooking roses that, along with the local variety of grape, have made Shiraz world famous. These gardens had been created in the 1870s and the terrace had been the quarters for the men working here. I had never seen anything like this mirror-work before, the tiny glass pieces in the ceiling of the covered porch forming a mosaic reflecting the colours of the blooms in the decorative avenues leading away among the adjacent date palms.

James suggested we should see the Khalili garden. I believe he'd been there when he came through as a passenger with Encounter the last time, before he took up driving. So we hailed an expensive taxi (25 rials, not the flat rate 5 rials) to go out there. But we had little time to see the gardens properly for we had been told to return to the truck for 4.30 and it was almost that already. James got us a lift in to the centre again though.

Once everyone was back to the truck we set off once more to camp on a dust field site not too far away. I had found that my tummy was at last reacting negatively to what I had eaten that day, so had a light tea of soup and something to drink. But I was not feeling particularly sick, so I was happy to dance and fool around with Maddie and the others, wrote a couple of post cards, and chatted to Dieter, Scott, Mark and Tim. The only slightly sour note that evening was that Jim and Sue had argued, and Jim asked me to reconcile the situation with Sue which made me feel quite awkward! This was to happen more than once, and made me wonder how they would manage as a couple when they reached their Australian destination.

***   ***   ***

We were up early next morning and I made for the cab once more, but found myself last one in and so in the 'hot seat' - great views but very stuffy travelling in this heat. James was driving and Rob, Lynn, Tim and Sarah were in the seats behind me, a motley selection of characters. Rob was easy to talk to, the extrovert performer; Lynn more introverted and very straight-talking when she had a strong opinion; Tim, quiet and better with his hands than with small talk; and Sarah, the practical, organising type. Such groupings might have led to strained conversations back home, but on this trip at least we had our experiences to compare notes on - today, what we had seen of Shiraz.

I remember we also discussed our mail and some of the difficulties of people writing to us before they'd received our next letters. In the letter I'd got from my father the day before, he'd said, "I have a feeling that I have written to you about this but can't be sure. When you are engaged in a correspondence which is not alternate but overlapping, it makes it difficult." We all felt this to some extent.

Our journey now was to take us into more desert regions and we needed to stock up with water, so we drove the short distance to Maharlu Lake. This was quite a large stretch of water and there was plenty salt panning taking place, for the lakes in this area are rich in salt. Everyone in our truck took the opportunity to wash thoroughly as we loaded on the water we required and this fascinated those salt panning as well as others travelling through. We drew a fantastic crowd, no car passing without stopping to gaze at our eccentric activities! In fact the same might have happened at home, for we had little modesty by this time and quickly stripped down to our bare essentials when the rare opportunity came to get really cool and clean. We had not showered since Isfahan, four days before, and were very hot and dusty.

Driving on again, James missed the turn north to Estahban and went on to Fasa, further south, where we stopped for drinks and a snack. Then on we went, but I was feeling terribly hot and not so good by this time, so changed places with Rob. He managed no better however, only sticking it for a quarter of an hour. After that he joined us on the back seat, which was a bit of a crush. I wondered how the drivers coped in these conditions: James had no choice but to stay where he was!

We had turned north again to join the proper route that ran onwards from Estahban. This road climbed fairly steeply through rocky and dusty terrain, and once on the correct route we went over a pass, eventually sighting Bakhtegan salt lake to the north, looking like a sea of cloud below. Everyone got out to take photographs, it was so spectacular. Then we went over a terrific drop to reach the town of Neyriz and I saw my first proper mirage of the trip at this point, the buildings shimmering as though appearing from an extension of the nearby lake. This had to be our shopping stop of the day, having missed Estahban, but the cooks hadn't much success. Lunch was straight after leaving town. I dozed in the cab feeling rather unwell: I vowed never to risk food or drink with added ice in a hot country again! Ian had warned us it was unsafe: this was to be thoroughly confirmed a few years later, when I saw great blocks of ice being carved up on a dirty pavement in a back street in Bali, before being put in tourists' drinks! Well, now I was learning my lesson. However I was brought a cup of tea at this point and began to feel much better.

Continuing onward, we climbed a breathtaking hairpin-bending narrow road to the plateau beyond. James was now having trouble with the orange truck's steering wheel, which came loose four times in all, on a dreadfully dusty and potholed dirt track of a road. So we gave up on the idea of catching up with Ian, who was with the bluies for the day, and camped at 5.30. I took it easy, still having some tummy trouble, and ate just the sauce of the main dish and some custard.

My last venture out of the tent before getting an early night was magical though. The stars were brilliant, there being no light pollution whatsoever. The 'great bear' stars were now nearing the horizon at 8.30pm, even earlier than I had noted in Turkey. We were gradually moving ever further south. This was something to report to my father who enjoyed anything to do with navigation, after years at sea during the Second World War.

And it was almost as though we were at war next morning, for we were woken around 4am by a strange siren-cum-hunting-bray-type noise. Virginia and I got up a little later, and at breakfast it turned out that most people thought the noise had been wolves!! I agreed with James that it was much more likely to be caused by wild dogs baying at dawn. We were on our way by 6am, nicely cooler in the rear of the truck, though it was very dusty from yesterday's drive. We had the back cover down but the sides up so we could see any villages we went through. There seemed to be precious few.

Someone called for a photo stop only half an hour into our journey for we were passing a rather wonderfully fortified village, where people were just getting going, several men on their way to work the fields. Inside the walls of the settlement we glimpsed crenulated towers and ramparts, resembling the remains of a Norman castle. I've tried hard to discover this village on today's maps but without success. The area, just into Kerman province, is rather unexpectedly shown on satellite maps these days as a protected bird-spotting area. I can imagine large birds of prey swooping down the steeps of the crags around, but can't say that we noticed any in 1975. I did get a photograph of a pleasantly smiling farmer though, a small rucksack on his back and a long-handled shovel over his shoulder.

One thing was clear; James was thoroughly lost. We definitely got the impression that we were not on our original route. We were leaping about on ghastly roads, the truck vibrating insanely. I'd suffered from sea-sickness in the past, but reckoned I never would again! We jolted rhythmically over 'corrugation' ruts, we vibrated over stones, we were tossed into the air, tipped up and flung about clutching each other. Peg, in the centre of the side seating, complained she had almost received a head injury on the metal of the roof frame during one toss skyward: personally I was hanging on to the rope over the tail-pin for dear life. Meanwhile the dust rose in clouds around us! Our eyes felt gritty with it. Our bathing of the day before had been rendered a waste of time for we were all of us covered in dust once more. As well as hats to protect us from the sun and our hair from more grime, we decided to 'scarf up' as we had in Anatolia, looking as though we were ready to rob the local bank. Geoff was best prepared for the situation, dressed in the Arab headgear he'd bought on holiday in Jordan the year before. Only his eyes showed.

Time and again we stopped to try and ask the way. It was not easy. "Sirjan?" one of the lads would ask anyone we met walking by the roadside. "This way?" pointing left, "Or this way?" pointing right. Invariably the folk they asked simply repeated the questions (and gestures) back to them, smiling broadly the while. It may have been a joke to them, but we found it pretty aggravating. The road signs we came on were no help either, for they were all in Farsi and so completely incomprehensible to us. We finally reached Sirjan, our shopping for lunch spot and the nearest town on the map, well after noon. I guarded the cab while the shopping went on, as this allowed me to rest a little. Lunch was straight afterwards and I just had a cup of tea with some codeine phosphate and dozed well during the afternoon, when we were on tarmac again at last.

As soon as we could see the lights of Kerman, we stopped to camp. I tried eating tea and felt somewhat better. I reckoned another early night was in order. I ventured out to go to the toilet last thing as usual. In this area there was no cover, but it was very dark. I reckoned without the stars though: my figure was blocking them out to anyone watching from the truck's cab, and some of the group were drinking up there. Next thing I knew, I was spot lit as though on stage. The orange truck wasn't a converted fire engine with a searchlight over the cab for nothing. "Turn that thing off!" I shouted, but next minute had to join in the laughter. This form of travelling was such a leveller. Another lesson learned.

***   ***   ***

Next day was our group's cooking day again. Virginia and I were up just after 5am and as soon as we were dressed, she made for the stove and I had the bright idea of waking everyone very efficiently by marching around the tents, pounding a kettle lid with a metal spoon. Each cooking team had its own methods of awakening us, with yells, whistles and so on. This one proved extremely effective, though there were groans from all sides of-course!

We got off around 7am and drove into Kerman to shop. We had barely arrived and parked when the blue truck came past. They had camped down the road from us and watched us go by in the morning! It was a relief to be together once more. In a time before mobile phones, the drivers really had to look out for one another and it must have been a strain at times, especially in this instance, when Ian would have been fairly sure that his trainee driver had got lost somewhere.

When Virginia, Sarah, Tim and I set about shopping, we found the Kerman bazaar a bit of a nightmare. Fruit and vegetables, such as melons, aubergines and courgettes, were cheap and mostly very good, and the local dates and nuts were excellent. That eggs were sold by weight rather than number necessitated some recalculation. But buying meat meant a lot of haggling. We were trying to keep to the money we'd been given to spend by Ian and this proved hard work. The Arabic numerals we'd learnt were really coming into their own, and we worked out that mince was more expensive than we'd become used to, at 220 rials a kilo, when it was generally more like 150 rials. We were offered some ghastly-looking meat for the price too, and later felt sure we'd been 'done' on half the rice we bought as well. We couldn't help wondering at another thing we kept seeing too. In a land which had produced the first calculating machine hundreds of years before, it was very curious to find every shop-keeper still using an abacus to tot up costs!

And then Virginia and Tim got side-tracked (or, Sarah and I suspected, grew tired of wrangling and gesturing) so we two were left to it, feeling tired out by the whole thing. There was no doubt about it, shopping in these situations was anything but restful 'retail therapy'! We must have looked ready to spit when we got back to the truck.

We didn't travel far before we stopped for lunch though, near an irrigation stream. The others bathed before cooking and eating. Having started setting out the meal first, I had a good drink and then washed my hair and extremities while the others lunched. I was hoping that sticking to a liquid diet would correct my digestive troubles.

Then we were away again, into the desert. We drove up a steep pass on a dirt road: it was very hot and there were spectacular reddish coloured slopes of soil and rock on either side. At the top we looked across at a horizon of quite high mountains. We knew we were not alone on the road by the twists and clouds of dust rising from other vehicles travelling further down the slopes below us, mainly lorries transporting goods between Kerman and Mashhad, the second city of Iran and the last one we would come to before entering Afghanistan.

There was an oasis in the valley ahead and we stopped there to take photographs. We were already accustoming ourselves to the desert and this greenery was quite a shock. It was only there because of a narrow water course, and naturally enough the local people had built their domed-roofed adobe houses nearby. They must have welcomed water so near their dwellings. We found them ready for the tourists travelling through too. Pepsi cola was available at roadside stalls.

We went on to camp earlier than usual, by a stream, on dry, wind-smoothed red dunes. We were already well into the Dasht-e-lut, a 300 mile-long strip of desert, which was to be designated a UNESCO world heritage site in July 2016. I was surprised to find the sand crunchy underfoot and the whole environment quite extraordinarily beautiful. It wasn't the sea of sand dunes I'd expected. For a start it was mountainous and hilly, with these fabulous rock formations in greyish-brown and rust-red. The sand didn't appear thoroughly yellow as in my childhood story books either, more ochre, occasionally shot with orange. And now the sun was low and seemed to be sinking very fast, casting a glowing bronze light on the varied terrain around us. The blue truck arrived only five minutes after us and the sun had almost sunk below the horizon in just those few moments.

We got on with the cooking straight away and had a good tea. I looked after the curry, which was pronounced a success, despite the questionable meat. Things were looking up; and there was an amusing moment during the washing-up afterwards. Lukas came and helped, cleaning the large pan we'd used with a handful of sand from the desert floor. "What are you doing?" cried Meg, the American girl on our truck: "That's filthy." "No, I'm cleaning off the grease", replied Lukas calmly. He proceeded to tell us how he'd camped across the Kalahari in Namibia and South Africa. This was the best way to clean frying pans of a morning, he assured us. "The sand is nice and gritty, like a pan scrubber, and really quite clean." Meg was only partially reassured, but it's a tip I've remembered ever since.

We made a fire within the circle of an old lorry tyre that Ian had found lying around. It was good to have its warmth, for now the sun had gone it was decidedly cold. The fire didn't last very long however, and soon, shivering a little, we gazed at those wonderful stars overhead once more. I found it curious that although it might only be a crescent moon shining in the sky above us, we could nearly always just see the dark part of its shape as well these nights. How light-polluted our skies at home must be to cut this out!

***   ***   ***

I was up at 4.30 next morning, bathing in the stream, which was more like an irrigation ditch. I rather relished this time to myself and well remember the strangeness of sitting naked in the ditch and, by the light of my torch, sloshing water over myself, as in a shallow bath. The stream was quite warm, although it was a cold morning.

I put the kettles on, on my return, but we were jinxed. For some reason it took one and a half hours for the kettles to boil! Rather the same jinx as with the pasta in Termessos then. Of-course everyone was fed up with it taking so long. We only just got in our drinks before we finally got off just after the sun came up at 6.30.

Our journey was now through superb, and very varied, sandstone scenery. There were bumpy hillocks and smoother mounds on one side of the truck and coloured rock the other. Before long we entered a more level sandy region, but it was there that we found, at one of our stops, that we had lost two of our four jerry cans of water during our jolting around on the slopes! This couldn't have happened at a worse time - in the desert! It meant rationing water. Ian decreed that from now on only the cooks could wash their hands before meals, and the truck's tank was padlocked between meals to preserve our most valuable resource. I was still doing my sterilising work and all fresh fruit and vegetables continued to be soaked in chlorinated water for at least half an hour before meals. You could hardly taste this, but Ian warned us again that once we entered Afghanistan we should be doubling the dose and that this was going to be more noticeable.

Soon we had another Coke stop! There was a small huddle of houses behind which was an oasis with beautiful warm blue pools amid exotic palm trees. I was amused at the antics of the Swiss girls. Hannah donned a bandana and her shades, and, in her short shorts, lounged sexily against a tree trunk for Heidi to photo her 'à la film star'. It could indeed have been a Hollywood set. There were even some camels nearby: really it only lacked Peter O'Toole and Omar Sharif! The trouble was that we spent so much time enjoying this scene from *Lawrence of Arabia* that the shop was out of Pepsi cola by the time we got there, and I for one was very thirsty!

At the lunch stop people started off irritable, but soon cheered up when some pineapple drink was brought out. It was lovely, and I felt hungrier than I had for a few days, so attempted the meal itself. During lunch though there was a to-do in the back of the orange truck that brought us girls promptly to our knees around Rosie, commonly known to us now as Ros. This was Maddie's one-time next door neighbour in Balham, South London, but a Geordie in origin. She was more subdued than Maddie in temperament and usually made little fuss over difficulties, but now she'd dropped one of her contact lenses on the dirty truck floor and she couldn't see to find it. And it took some finding, but we retrieved it for her at last.

117

It wasn't the last time this happened, and I must say I was glad on this trip that I wore glasses rather than contact lenses. There was regular brushing out of the interior of the truck by the cooks after meals, but the floor inevitably had some degree of grime ingrained in its rough surface. Not a clean place to drop something that would then be touching your eyeball, I felt!

We passed the rest of the hot afternoon in the dusty, vibrating truck, eventually coming on more oases, where we had yet another Coke stop, and I was luckier this time! How lovely a cool drink can be in the desert!

We camped just before 5pm. I spent the last remnants of daylight writing to my cousin's children. I included sketches of myself dressed in jumper and woolly hat in the early morning and in a bikini an hour later, to show the extremes of temperature out here. It was proving difficult to dress appropriately. This had really surprised me. I never thought it could be so cold at night in a desert, known to me up till then as a thoroughly warm environment.

Chapter 12. Inequality in a Holy City

Next morning we set off early, for we hoped to reach Mashhad that day. From the orange truck, Meg needed to have a new visa for Afghanistan, as the original was wrongly dated. Luckily we could get a bit of speed up quite soon, as we came upon a tarmac road (such luxury we felt) at a small town, where at a roundabout, a statue of the Shah stood above a lovely pool. Ah, a return to civilisation!

This was short-lived however. When we drove on, it was to climb up over a narrow rocky pass and it became very bumpy once more. I was trying to write a longer letter to my parents at this point, a letter I still have. I wrote...

'As we've been told that Afghanistan is dreadful for its post – both speed-wise and in reliability, I'm writing now to post this in Mashhad before crossing the frontier out of Iran. At present, we are travelling along dirt tracks ... (hence the bad writing!)'

This was no over-statement: my handwriting had really suffered, the crazy wobble of my pen every now and then in writing a word showing where we had hit a pot-hole or sudden ramp.

Ian had expected to arrive at Mashhad next, but his map was wrong. The large town we now reached gloried in the name of Torbat-e-Heydariyeh. (Torbat is the Farsi for a burial place, and Heydar was a Sufi mystic whose tomb was here.) The area is known for its saffron production, a spice we'd seen on shopping expeditions in several bazaars. We had our lunch there, which was pleasant as it was not so hot now we had left the desert.

We quickly went on and reached Mashhad around 4pm. Ian drove us to the camp site before quickly taking Meg to get her visa sorted out. I found the shower, and had a bit of dirty work to do, for when I washed my filthy hair I blocked the drain! My next task was to scour my comb and then of course wash my clothes. How nice it was to feel fairly clean at last!

But I wasn't going to make the same mistake that I had in Isfahan. There would be no dressing up in a skirt here. At the gate to the camp site we girls had been rather shaken to read a sign which warned that, 'Women who do not cover their arms and legs when leaving this site risk being stoned by the locals!' We had heard that 'infidel' women were tolerated less in Mashhad, the holy city: here was verification of that. And indeed Islamic law seems stricter in this region than elsewhere in Iran to this day: only recently I found a short video of a public flogging in Torbat-e-Heydariyeh on social media; the crime - insulting Islam.

The reason for this strictness is that Mashhad has long been…

> "accustomed to the fervour of pilgrims gathered there from every corner of the Shi'ite world to kiss the tomb of the martyred Imam Reza…" [44]

This direct descendant of the Prophet Mohammed, and the eighth Imam of so-called Twelver Shiites, was born in Medina around 766 AD, and was widely known as a person of both extraordinary scholarship and saintly qualities. Apparently poisoned by a jealous Caliph in 818 AD, he was buried in the then village of Sanabad, which would later become Mashhad, this name meaning 'the place of martyrdom'. The major site to visit in the city is his shrine, the largest mosque by dimension in the world, which we were to see next day.

In the meantime we relaxed after the ordeals of our desert crossing and I even indulged in a rum and marzipan chocolate feast with Virginia before bed! Perhaps not the best treatment for a sensitive digestive system, but far too tempting to be missed.

Next morning Virginia, Sarah and I set off for Mashhad town centre. We went straight to Tourist Information for a map and fixed up a tour of the Holy Shrine: it cost all of my rials. I believe we were very lucky to be able to visit the shrine though, for Barbara Lamplugh[45] who made the same trip, I think perhaps the year before me, writes of non-Muslims being forbidden entry to the shrine. Wrapped in the Iranian women's habitual garb of eight metres or so of dark cloth, we were allowed into the courtyard and saw a fair amount of the shrine (which however covers a huge area), before moving on to the

---

[44] Carroll (1960), page 115.
[45] *Kathmandu by Truck* (1976).

museum and the bazaar. I obviously hadn't the knack of adjusting the veil correctly for I was reprimanded for showing my 'fair curls' as I entered the building!

The tour was then slightly marred by some haggling over money and then by Sarah's weirdly simplistic religious queries. I was interested in the Shia sect of Islam and wanted to have its difference from Sunni Islam explained to me, but Sarah seemed to be asking such basic questions as "Do Muslims believe in God?" It made us sound terribly ignorant, I felt.

There was a wonderful great gold dome over the mosque, and the main door in from the courtyard pool was decorated with glorious azure tiling. The walls were of various colours, rust-red and gold along with white and lighter blues. Fountains were playing out here. The interior featured that beautifully graceful calligraphy we had become accustomed to seeing, inscriptions from the Koran. I noted the elaborate holy keys on display, the sumptuous carpets, and the cask at the shrine of Imam Reza, with women wailing at the padlocked gate of the cage. It was not difficult to realise this amazing place as being second only in importance and sanctity to that at Mecca.

Relinquishing our Muslim coverings, we moved on towards the Post Office, noting, as we passed, the shrine bazaar's stone and alabaster cutters, very friendly craftsmen who were only too happy to have us watch them at work. And it continues to this day, for the upkeep and embellishment of this great shrine is still under way.

We wandered from there to the tomb of Nader Shah, the last powerful Iranian emperor, who was assassinated here in 1747. I have since read in *The Soul of Iran* that:

"Nader Shah instigated a short Iranian revival after years of uncertainty following the fall of the Safavid dynasty in the early eighteenth century. Interestingly, Nader, a Sunni Muslim, believed Iranians were sufficiently Shi'atized that he took no steps to "re-educate" them. In fact, he even contributed to the embellishment of the Imam Reza shrine. His claim to fame rests chiefly on his sacking of Delhi and the magnificently jewelled Peacock Throne he brought back as booty."[46]

It seemed curious that even such a tolerant ruler should have been hated enough by some to end up being assassinated. We discussed the fact that famous people all met their ends badly in Mashhad. It did mean there were several unusual shrines of-course. This particular burial spot was marked by a vigorous statue of Nader Shah, axe in hand, on a rearing horse, followed closely by his henchmen on foot. Stirring stuff!

Now it was time for lunch and we decided to try the Amir Hotel, opposite the memorial. We had chosen well, for there were a good variety of dishes on the menu. During our meal the manager approached and asked us where we came from and when he heard that we all worked in different capacities in hospitals in Europe he asked if we would like to see round a hospital in Mashhad. We jumped at the chance, and he went ahead and arranged a 6pm visit for us to the Shah Reza hospital, a modern establishment supported by the Shah. It would be interesting to see how it differed from the Christian hospital we'd seen briefly in Isfahan.

In the meantime he suggested we visit Aryamehr Park. We hadn't funds between us to pay for the expensive taxis in town, but we were lucky enough to be spotted and picked up by a very pleasant young man, Yaghub, who took us there on the bus. The Park with its lake, trees just starting to turn autumnal reds and golds, and broad avenues between beds of colourful roses, was indeed a lovely restful place to visit. And we profited from talking to Yaghub as well. He told us of the yawning gap between the lives of the rich, the Shah in particular, and poor families like his, from the 'small town of Sari' near the Caspian Sea coast. He was the eldest of his family and was in Mashhad trying to earn money to send home so that his younger siblings might get a decent education. I have since learnt to question this information a little, for Sari is not so small, being indeed a one-time capital of Iran.

Meanwhile we enjoyed playing around on the seesaws and the swings in the children's area and eventually went back to town, delighted to find it only cost 3 rials each on the bus, and had a drink and a bun. Yaghub had to go to

---

[46] Molavi (2005), page 79.

prayers at this point and I was sad to be parted from him. He had been quite a hit with me and we had even exchanged addresses. But I was not to hear from him again.

It's possible that Yaghub hoped us 'rich Westerners' might give him money to help in his efforts. But one thing was beyond doubt: he was not happy with the Shah and the country's successful elite class. This was a growing feeling at this point in Iran's history. Not that one would have thought so to read the guidebooks. The pocket guide I had, read:

> "Mohammed Reza Shah Pahlavi Aryamehr ... continued and widened his [father's] work, with the success that is well-known ... after the Second World War, his first objective was to develop the country as speedily as possible. The tool for this veritable revolution was created in 1962 through the Charter of the "Revolution of the Shah and the Nation" ... It is certainly not an exaggeration to speak of an "economic miracle" in connection with Iran. The national income rose by 9.8% per annum between 1968 and 1973 ... and experts the world over predict that Iran will soon become one of the group of highly-industrialised nations."[47]

This was not to be. Ayatollah Khomeini returned from exile four years later and caused a real revolution, religious in nature this time. The leftist Islamic population (perhaps Yaghub among them), who had felt harassed and marginalised, then saw to it that the Shah was deposed and the Islamic Republic came into being. However, there was a voice who spoke out against it in Mashhad. This was a cleric called Ayatollah Hasan Qomi. In 1981, he criticised Khomeini for being un-Islamic, saying

> "The real clergy does not want power ... it does not approve of those clerics who govern us. The real task of the clergy is to advise and enlighten the people. Real Islam is the religion of forgiving and of compassion."[48]

But he was eventually marginalised as were the many other clerics with similar thoughts. The strident voice of the Republic soon held sway.

---

[47] Hureau [ed.] (1974).
[48] Molavi (2005), page 80.

***   ***   ***

Back at the Amir Hotel once more we waited for the manager, who turned up in a superb limousine to take us to the Shah Reza hospital. This only emphasised that we were now seeing how the other half lived. The hospital certainly gave that impression too. Built in the time of the last Shah's father, it was palatial in the extreme and stood in its own ornate gardens. The director of the hospital was at the door to welcome us as we arrived, an extremely formal reception for us three overlanders! We were then shown round by a Number 7 nurse (senior ward sister/junior management level), who Sarah (a Sister in Charing Cross Hospital, London until recently) was fairly appalled to find was only 22 years old. "Smart, but hardly clinical" was the comment I made in my diary.

An official from the entrance desk and a radiographer also did the honours of showing us round. Virginia, being the radiographer of our group, was extremely impressed by their X-ray unit. The equipment shown us was top class, she said. The Coronary Care Unit was equally well equipped, but had only one nurse looking after eight patients. We also went round a more ordinary ward specialising in minor heart surgery. The personnel were most friendly and helpful, but there was no getting away from the fact that there seemed a shortage of thoroughly experienced staff. However, it was stressed to us that the Shah had endowed and supported everything to do with the hospital: the staff we met were clearly very admiring of his work for them.

We then returned to the Amir Hotel for a cup of tea, and were invited to dinner and a dance afterwards. While the other two went on, I decided against this and got a lift back to the camp site and went straight to bed. I was feeling tired and still not entirely well. But it had been a really interesting and enjoyable day. Such contrasting views of Iran, the Shah and his people! The hospital we'd just seen was a hugely different institution to the over-crowded Christian one in Isfahan. The people we'd met couldn't have been more different too, in background and in wealth.

A similar social tension appears to exist today, for Mashhad has rapidly grown in importance since my visit. In January 2018 the Guardian printed an article on unrest in the city.

"An elite – many connected with the ... charitable foundation that manages the shrine – are profiting from the cluster of luxury hotel and retail developments in the ... district surrounding the holy site ... To the rural poor who flock to Mashhad as pilgrims and many of whom provide the workforce building it, such affluence in a sacred place may even seem hypocritical."[49]

The reporting journalist noted that inequalities were very noticeable to those frustratedly attempting to find a permanent job or having to struggle with everyday life. Sick or elderly people fare particularly badly.

"For those in Mashhad's poorest areas, the infrastructure and service provision is miles off the pace: the 800,000 in its 42 "marginal" neighbourhoods have access to a single hospital, and in some places it's 16,000 to a pharmacy."

The hospital I visited has been re-named the Imam Reza Hospital and is not far from the centre and shrine. The one referred to in the Guardian might be the Razavi Hospital, opened in 2005 and further out from the city. It seems to have a good reputation, but must be working hard to cope with such numbers of patients. The Guardian's journalist suggested there was likely to be more unrest to come, thanks to these social inequalities.

$$*** \qquad *** \qquad ***$$

I had a thoroughly long lie-in next morning and had breakfast in bed, for Virginia brought me tea and a marmalade roll. Very nice! The rest of the morning was spent in mundane tasks and packing, except for one important decision. I consulted Sharon, the nurse among the bluies who had been given responsibility for the medications we were carrying. I was very tired of suffering from diarrhoea and people had suggested I might try antibiotics. What did we have on board? Sharon had an antibiotic which was non-specific but ought to help, she told me, and she started me on it.

We packed the tents away, taking our time, for it was very hot. Once on our way I played poker dice with several others in the back corner of the truck. It pleasantly whiled away the three hours we spent driving through none too

---

[49] Hoad (2018).

interesting country. Patrick Marnham described the area rather wittily a few years before we travelled the route.

"If we ever destroy the ozone belt with an accumulation of burnt-out waste gases and the water evaporates with the heat of the sun, the world for a few years may resemble the semi-inhabited dust bowl which lies between Mashhad and Herat. To a westerner the area seems incapable of supporting any life and is one which would never be inhabited if any sensible man had the strength to drag himself out of it."[50]

We finally camped about 50 kms east of Farīmān, not far from the Afghan border, and awaited Ian's eve-of-border-crossing lecture on Afghanistan. He warned us again about tasting the double strength sterilising salts in our tea on the trucks from now on. In cafes, or 'chai stops' as we would get to know them, tea was evidently drunk without milk but with sugar which was not to be stirred in. It was probably not wise to eat meat in the country and butter was out too. Beware the delicious-looking apple pies at tourist haunts in the Bamiyan valley: they had become known as hepatitis pies! It all sounded a little worrying, especially to one already fighting an infection of some sort.

On the other hand he reminded us that he meant to try and take the northern route through the country, following the Russian border, which would be harder going, but very picturesque compared with the option of going on the main road to Kabul through Kandahar. It also gave slightly easier access to Bamiyan, which any overlander of the 1970s had to see, for it was the home of the most westerly signs of Buddhism - the giant statues in the cliffs there. However, travelling this route entailed obtaining a special permit in Herat, the first city we would come to, and this might mean staying there a day longer than scheduled. His plan sounded like a really ground-breaking adventure and I for one was delighted that we had a leader eager and willing to negotiate a different and challenging route like this. I fervently hoped Ian could pull this manoeuvre off.

Among my companions on the orange truck, Liz and Lukas were the most travelled I reckoned. Liz knew the outback of Australia and Lukas had worked in South Africa. I had listened with fascination to their travel yarns,

---

[50] *Road to Katmandu* (1971), page 92.

especially wanting to hear about Australia, seeing I would be there before long. So now I joined them to discuss what we had heard about Afghanistan and what we might see there. We were keen to experience the wild and savage terrain that featured in writing on the country. We were sure it would be quite different to what we had seen so far ... perhaps most like Anatolia or the Dasht-e-Lut? But we were also climbing higher, into the Hindu Kush - making our way at last towards the 'roof of the world'. A very exciting prospect!

Chapter 13. Return to the Middle Ages

Ian had provided a new burner for our stove which was a great asset at breakfast next morning, for it cooked so much faster. Without this hold-up we soon got to the washing up and were ready to get under way in record time.

Two and a half hours later, at nine o'clock, we arrived at the frontier. Ian came round the truck with the Iranian official collecting passports. The poor man suffered from a severe stammer, but still insisted on saying "T-t-t-t-tank you" to each person, which made the process a little slow. It was made a whole lot slower very soon however, for it turned out that twenty or so of us had visas that had expired yesterday and had to return to Torbat-e-Jam to extend them. That was a town not far from where we had camped last night! Those of us unaffected read and chatted during our enforced wait and had our lunch before the visa renewers returned. Thus we only left Iran at 2pm.

Those who had travelled back into Iran briefly enjoyed a quick lunch in no man's land, and we reached the Afghan border at a quarter to three. A smart little official, of Mongol ethnicity perhaps (my first experience of a person that reminded me of pictures I'd seen of Genghis Khan), hopped in and was half way through checking our passports, when Ian drove off! Panic ensued, but we stopped the truck and 'Officer G. Khan' hurriedly finished his inspection and marched off in a dignified manner ... only gathering speed into a run once we were almost out of sight.

Ian had in fact been told to drive to the Customs, Police and Health checking area. The latter procedure seemed to take forever, involving as it did a great deal of needless red tape. When it was my turn, the official concluded with, "You got camera?" I showed him my trusty Kodak Instamatic. "Oh, very cheap job!" was the response. I was glad to have it berated for once as I could see out of the corner of my eye that James was having quite a time explaining all the lenses in his Pentax camera case to one of the other staff. At last we had the final exit check at 6.30 Afghan-time (having moved our watches one hour forward again). A small boy shouted "Welcome" as we headed off in the direction of Herat, a pleasant moment which cheered us considerably after a pretty tiring day, and we camped soon after leaving the outskirts of Islam Qala, the nearest town to the Iranian border.

The first difference that we noted in Afghanistan was that there were more flies around. Ian had told us a neat story about them the night before. He spoke of the 'raisin market' in Kandahar: approach it and the 'raisins' flew away, leaving a butcher's meat behind on the display slab! We were going to have to be more diligent when purchasing food and cooking it. I'd also been reminded that when sterilising water I now needed to add *two* matchstick loads of chlorine salts, rather than just one, to each jerry can.

The other thing we soon noticed on crossing the border was the decoration of the Afghan lorries, liberally covered with little paintings. Paine describes Pakistani trucks as being "dolled up like tarts in evening dress ..."[51], and the Afghan ones we saw seemed to be attempting something similar in a rather more decorous manner, for they lacked the fringes, the extra colourful calligraphy and the garish pom-poms we saw later. We were to get used to some weird and flamboyant transport on the roads from this time forward.

∗∗∗   ∗∗∗   ∗∗∗

It was the end of our group's turn to cook next morning, and so we were up at 5am to put the kettles on and woke everyone at 5.30, just as we'd got used to doing. We'd reckoned without the new super-fast burner on the stove however. Only five minutes later we had to call that breakfast was ready, which made us thoroughly unpopular! Everyone had to rush about to get to their food before it cooled. It worked well for us cooks of-course, for we had already washed and were on the spot to enjoy our breakfast. In fact, unusually, Virginia and I had time to take our tent down - normally a job Dave or Rob did for us on cooking mornings. It was while doing this that we saw our first scorpion. Only a baby one, thank goodness.

---

[51] *The Afghan Amulet* (1994), page 187.

Women shopping for clothes in Herat, Afghanistan

Nomads' camel train east of Herat

Band-e Amir, Afghanistan

The Young Good Luck houseboat and one of the houseboys

We set off at 6am through dry flat country, with only sparse tussocks of a very hardy form of grass growing - definitely not grazing land. But we were soon buzzing our request for a photo stop. Coming towards the road across this waste land was a wonderfully picturesque vision, the likes of which we had not come upon before, a nomad family travelling by camel. I had heard of the autumn migration of tribes in this area, people in search of better living conditions for the coming winter. It was certain that no-one travelled for pleasure like this round here: there had to be a good reason. That was why the locals reacted as they did to us as we passed. Every overlander had noticed this.

> "In the old days when a caravan appeared from over the skyline, and now, when a bus [or E.O. truck] in a cloud of dust rumbles into the streets, the children run out to stare, the lounger sunning himself against the wall straightens up to gaze at the strangers dropped in for a moment from the outside world."[52]

We were weird intruders from an alien environment, actually travelling for fun, and in not too comfortable a style to boot. But to us it was these nomads in their caravan of camels that were the strange creatures of another world.

As ever the men and boys were to the fore. They lead the camels while the women cared for the loads they carried as well as the children. The men before us wore wide white trousers and tunics under dark western jackets or coats against the colder weather. We were impressed by their turbans which were pristine white. Where had they been laundered? Was it really only slapping against rocks in a stream that bleached them so effectively?

Each camel bore a heavy burden, which from a distance was of triangular shape. It comprised one of the family's women at its apex, small children and great bundles of possessions surrounding her. These women were in dark dress, heads veiled. They tended to cover themselves completely on seeing us and our menfolk. When they had the chance, as now when the whole caravan slowed to gaze at us, the camels turned to nibble at any odd clump of dry grass near their feet.

---

[52] Carroll (1960), pages 173-4.

Driving on and approaching the outskirts of Herat we found that women in the streets wore chaderis, an enveloping column of black cloth hanging from a tight-fitting head cap, the back frilled for easier arm movement. This covered their bodies more completely than any female costume we'd met so far. As I commented in a letter to my parents:

Often Iranian ladies show their ankles, but the Afghan lady is very modest indeed.

There was only a grill for these chaderi-wearing women to see through, so you couldn't even glimpse their lovely dark eyes. It severely limited non-verbal communication and I felt they must feel isolated from society in this characterless dress. I was of course viewing it from a western perspective though: women here undoubtedly felt at ease in a garb they'd worn since puberty.

On across the flat dry plain we drove. As we approached Herat, we took a quick look at the first of the solitary minarets, the remains of the site I'd read had been destroyed by the British during the Afghan campaigns. According to the editor in chief of RadioFreeEurope's English-language website …

"The minarets were once part of a larger musalla complex - or place of worship - built under the direction of Queen Gawhar Shad in 1417. The complex included more minarets, a religious school, and other buildings. Most of the buildings were brought down by the British in the late 19th century. What war has not destroyed, nature has. Three of the nine minarets that still stood at the turn of the 20th century collapsed in earthquakes in 1931 and 1951. A fourth minaret was toppled during the Soviet occupation of Afghanistan in the 1980s and is now only a sad-looking stub." [53]

The Soviets had used this last minaret for target practice. We saw it and the other five remaining Gawhar Shad minarets in 1975 and even then they looked somewhat unloved and undervalued. The decorative, though much plundered, tiling found on the minarets is now of interest to

---

[53] Podelco (2002).

UNESCO, so today the passing road we approached on has been closed to traffic so that there's less damage from vibration.

***　　　***　　　***

The town of Herat seemed a pleasant trading centre with wide boulevard-type streets. It had emerged at the junction between the western and eastern halves of the Persian Empire originally, at a point where the roads to Balkh, Bamiyan, Khiva, Bokhara and the Bolan Pass, the ancient spice and silk routes to north western India, converged: it thus became one of Central Asia's leading centres of trade, or so I had heard. It was thus something of a surprise to encounter a few organisational quirks that would seem to make trade less easy in these more modern times.

Take for example the first place we visited, the 'Tourist Agency'. Really nowhere could have been less ready for the tourist: it was quite the quaintest and most shambolic information centre I had come across to date. The two 'officials' were barefoot, one sitting disconsolately on the floor. We nearly didn't go in at all, as there was a sign marked 'Closed' at the door; and when we did get in, we could only obtain information on Kabul, the capital, some 500 miles away - nothing on Herat itself! However we did manage to learn that the local Bank *was* closed – until Saturday so the story went, and it was now Wednesday. By the weekend we should have left, so no-one could change their travellers' cheques. Everyone we met was changing money on the Black Market. There were plenty chaps offering this service out on the street (as they were also freely offering hashish to passers-by) so we followed suit to get some Afghanis, changing what cash we had. I had no Iranian rials left. Nor did I have a great deal of English currency to change, so hoped to have more luck changing travellers' cheques at a bank in some town further on.

Ian had allowed us another couple of hours to explore the town, so several of us tried a horse and cart ride round town for 25 Afghanis (24p) each. It was extremely good value. We made but slow progress for the 'driver' walked alongside the horse, steering the way by means of a yoke bar above the shoulders of the animal. But it would have been impossible to go any faster. There were extraordinary crowds and happenings on view in front of the trap! We gazed in fascination over our horse's red-bobble-decorated mane as we entered a wide market area, thronged with men, their features varying from Aryan to Mongolian and so full of character, very much alive as they gestured and bartered with each other. The few women around were identifiable as pillars of black among a sea of white turbans.

Cloth covered stalls displayed every kind of item from bed linen to vegetables. There were heavy-laden donkeys, and the odd dog wandering alongside and under the sale counters. The cries of salesmen, the braying of asses and mules, the jangling of harness made for an amazing din and the air was rich with the strangest mixture of odours from spices to ordure. I imagined this was a scene and situation that could have been common in Europe during the Middle Ages.

On the broader streets gesticulating policemen were generally ignored, for bicycles and donkeys often travelled straight through any traffic lights ... and even on the wrong side of the road. There were very few cars in evidence. Meagre trees lined the route beside the water-filled gutters. When we later started to walk to the local mosque we passed our first chai shops, where men slipped off their shoes to sit cross-legged on the raised bed-table/dais affairs I got to know as charpoys, set out by this gutter, sipping black tea brought them from shiny great samovars visible at the dark shop window. Other men were perched high back here enjoying hubble-bubble pipes, their way of vaporising and smoking cannabis or tobacco. (I *had* met a tame version of the hubble-bubble pipe before, for the caterpillar in *Alice in Wonderland* smoked a hookah, another name for it.) The shop windows had no glass and were shut of an evening with large coach-house type wooden doors, before which during the day, as now, young boys were selling fruit. Elsewhere bunches of grapes and pomegranates hung round the opening to greengrocers like Christmas decorations.

We returned to the orange truck after our look round and drove out of town to lunch overlooking Herat. Nomads came to chat and I was interested to notice that people generally had more extensive English vocabularies here than in Iran. Three young lads looking after a herd of goats had quite a conversation with Dave, much aided by gesture. Unsurprisingly the work clothes they wore (tunic and baggy pants with a bolero top) had seen a good deal of wear, but they were well shod. I noticed too that they had very neat haircuts, contrasting with Dave's by now rather shaggy red beard. But he was getting along with them famously and they were all smiling and laughing at their funny language problems. I had to take a photograph, and it's one of my favourites of our getting to know people in the places through which we passed. It's poignant too though, for I often wonder what happened to these boys, whose country has had such a rough time since the 1970s.

After lunch we re-entered Herat and I guarded the truck for a while, after which I helped Tim buy a hat - the decorated skull-fitting cap that we'd started to see here occasionally in the absence of a turban. What a palaver this was, for we were learning to barter effectively by now. As I wrote my parents:

> You really have to bargain ... start walking out of the shop half way through the business – to be dragged back in again by the shop-keeper, offering a lower price. If, after purchasing something, the seller has an angelic smile on his face when he bids you good-bye, you can be sure you've been 'done'. He should be silently swearing!

Tim ended up with a hat that had ear covers and tied under his chin. He was to be very glad of it as the weather got colder. Meanwhile the local 'milliners' were, as ever, fascinated by my sunhat: its concertinaed wide-brim was becoming more eye-catching with every week more that it travelled stored in my rucksack!

Ian returned us to the camp site at 5.30. A storm seemed to threaten as we had tea, with some distant lightning and then mild drizzle, but it came to nothing very much. Virginia and I were, as ever, glad to avoid having to fold away the moistly clinging canvas of a wet tent.

***　　　***　　　***

We had a bit of a lie-in next morning, only getting up at 7am to be off at 8am. I took a photograph of first light over the low hills in which we were camping. Dawn brought alive the terracotta tints of the dry slopes: there was hardly any green to be seen. Even the scrubby meagre clumps of grass by the track glowed yellow and ochre in the pale sun. There seemed a few ruins around - maybe one-time shepherds' mud huts? But there was little grazing for sheep or goats that I could see.

We set off, but soon had to return to the camp site, for Abby had forgotten her shoes! I rather wondered how she'd managed that. Where had she left them if not in her tent ready to wear or pack? By now we were mostly extremely adept at quickly unpacking and repacking our belongings for the day ahead, and we were due to move on today.

We re-entered Herat and I joined Meg in searching for and buying some biscuits. The glucose from biscuits I felt would be a good sugar burst for energy if I was not eating as much as normal. We were in the shopping district of Herat today that was directly below the Castle of Pai Hesar, said to be built on Alexander the Great's fortress. How that man got around! But it reinforced the importance of Herat at a cross roads of trading routes between west and east, a position that had its drawbacks over the centuries. Genghis Khan, in 1222, and Timur Lang, in 1383, both demolished it effectively. Each time though it was rebuilt and some of the ancient buildings remained among the more modern-style streets. Decades of conflict since my visit have brought about yet more change as people from other districts of Afghanistan converge on Herat as a more prosperous and safe place to live: E.O. clients might well find themselves camping among hordes of displaced folks' tents were they to travel this way in the 21st century.

In our shopping we again came upon women dressed in chaderis. They were examining clothing in a stall located right down by the roadside drain, squatting to search for what they needed.[54] One was even managing to balance a small child on her hip - all this in a restricting tube of material and with her eyes covered with net! I couldn't understand how they could be happy to work like this. The salesman (and even the baby) had much more liberty of movement than the women had. They could both kick out their unshod feet and wave their hands freely. But the chaderi-dressed women showed not an inch of skin. Yet they were used to such a life and obviously never questioned it. I wondered what they thought on seeing us.

---

[54] See photograph on page 130.

Did we seem extraordinarily louche and disreputable in their eyes to be showing so much of ourselves and to be moving with such facility?

But it was time for me to do another stint of guard duty. This time I guarded the truck while Ian visited the police station in an effort to obtain the permit for the northern route to Kabul. I imagine he had already done quite a bit of negotiation prior to this and hoped to complete operations now. However he was the first to know "…How swiftly the beanstalk of procrastination grows in the soil of Asia."[55] as Peter Fleming put it. It meant a continual badgering of officialdom was entailed in accomplishing anything out of the ordinary. We were all to learn this at various points during our journey overland.

The police station was conveniently close to the Friday mosque, a beautiful blue and white example of Islamic architecture. This had a blue-domed minaret either side of a taller central prayer area, while smaller towers were set at the corners of a much extended courtyard space to either side. If the building itself was spectacular though, the land around it was dreadfully pitted and uncared for. I watched men carefully circumnavigating pools of dirty water and rutted ground to reach the mosque's main entrance and wondered that more had not been done to smarten up the surroundings of such a lovely place of worship.

My reveries were broken in upon by Ian's return. He was in rebellious mood, for the police still hadn't provided him with a permit to go north. "We're going anyway", he growled. He seemed pretty sure that we could get away with this. "It just takes them ages to get anything done round here", he complained. "It'll sort itself out though."

Joined by several others, we then made for a chai house with a very relaxing atmosphere, where we sat cross-legged on comfortable carpets. The Canadian lads, Derek and Michael, even managed to order egg and chips. Lovely! Sadly I didn't quite feel up to risking this myself as yet.

At 10.30, once everyone was back from their shopping and sight-seeing, we set off in a north-easterly direction on the road to Maimana. We were

---

[55] *News from Tartary* (1936), page 51.

quickly off tarmac and back to jolting along a dirt track. After we'd gone a few miles we lunched and washed up, watching another camel train as it went by.[56] Once it had passed, we girls from the orange truck joined the bluie lasses at a loo stop and were delighted to be treated to a fashion show! Gloria had bought a dress in Herat, not a chaderi but a brilliant maroon number with a richly embroidered bodice, cuffs and hem. It was a real treat to see such a lovely garment and she was complimented all round.

As we boarded our vehicles once more, chattering happily, we noted some men making poor headway trying to get an over-laden mule to advance. They were much amused, as were my fellow travellers, when I tried to help urge it on, as I might get a patient to walk for me. But there's nothing so stubborn as a mule: they had to unload it in the end. "Good for the mule", I thought, somewhat illogically!

On we went to a village, where we were stopped. The police chiefs there insisted on seeing all our passports and having a look at us all individually. A little unsettling! We were given an armed escort on the way to their headquarters: we left with the chief up front with Ian and a soldier in the back with us and another with the bluies. It was a shame that we were in lovely hill country at this point. The village had beautiful trees and flowers, with views of distant hills, but we didn't dare photo anything until we were finally clear. Ian had been right though, or at least he knew how to argue our case: the problem with following the northern route through the country had indeed sorted itself out. Before long we were on our way again.

The terrain now became more rugged. The road often ran alongside a river that we would eventually cross, almost ford sometimes, to link up with the next valley on our route. The rough road was all twists and turns, sometimes quite high above the water. This gave rise to some hair-raising moments passing other trucks going in the opposite direction. We were certainly moving into wilder country.

---

[56] See photograph on page 130.

This geography has led historians to comment that, "Afghanistan is easy to enter or to cross but much more difficult to hold, let alone unite ..."[57] It had been invaded many a time, by the British among others, and it always lead to difficulties for everyone concerned. The Afghans had the reputation of being a proud people: in 1809 one of them told Mountstuart Elphinstone, the British East India Company administrator,

"We are content with discord, we are content with alarms, we are content with blood, we will never be content with a master."[58]

And it was discord and blood among themselves that they were starting to suffer at the time we were travelling the country, though I understood little of it then. I heard from Ian and the better informed of my fellow travellers that Afghanistan had been relying on Russian and other foreign aid, Iranian, Indian and even American, in an unguarded way. I had not realised how close the country was coming to really serious issues. Simpson writes that a couple of years before our journey from Herat to Kabul,

"Mohammed Daoud declared himself president while King Zahir was abroad, but he [Daoud] and his family were later murdered and a new revolutionary Marxist regime was installed under Mohammed Taraki ... in 1978. The previous over-reliance on foreign aid had created an economic crisis when aid began to slow down, and employment prospects could not keep up with the growing aspirations of the educated urban classes ... Rural revolts broke out in protest at proposed socialist land reform ... An army division mutinied in Herat but was crushed by force. Taraki was replaced by his deputy Hafizullah Amin, who subsequently had Taraki smothered to death, but Moscow distrusted Amin. The Soviet Army began pouring over the border on Christmas Eve 1979 ... On 27 December 1979 Soviet Special forces killed Hafizullah Amin ... The situation soon spiralled out of control. The Soviets held the cities but lost the country ..."[59]

---

[57] Simpson (2012), page 11.
[58] Simpson (2012), page 135.
[59] «   «   , page 149.

Such was the background to our trip. Thankfully all this was something I would never have dreamed of. I found Afghans to be extremely pleasant and polite men: I hardly met any women. They did not seem likely to stir up revolt, as I had felt might be a future possibility in Iran. However, as we left Herat behind, I was starting to note the difference between people's standard of living in the rural areas as opposed to the towns. The local agriculture now was still mainly sheep and goat herding, but I was fascinated at one point to see men, in barely two acres of ground by a river, threshing corn in a circle with two teams of oxen. It looked rather a meagre crop, but it was good to find some arable farming again, though the methods were so old-fashioned. It would have been difficult to reach this area with decent machinery though, and pointless really with so small a result. However there was no doubt that the people hereabouts were anything but well off.

By now we had become attuned to a daily life of comprehensible abnormality. This was to shift a notch further on the weirdness dial as we travelled north in Afghanistan. For a start there was over a week without tarmac roads to be endured, and then we were climbing into the Hindu Kush, the weather getting colder all the time. How would we cope?

Chapter 14. A Long Stretch without Tarmac

The next day, Friday 17th October, did not augur well. For one thing Virginia and I had had a poor night. It was Virginia's turn to feel sick. We'd camped at 5pm and I'd put up the tent and a bed for her, as her temperature seemed to be up. What with this, her frequent exits from the tent with the 'runs' and the fact that it really had got a lot colder weather, we spent a wakeful time. It was also memorable as the night when at last I started using the blanket I'd been carrying all this time. There was real need: in spite of going to bed in my thicker socks I could hardly feel my feet, especially my right big toe. I even wondered if I could be suffering from frostbite!

The situation wasn't *that* dire though of course. We got up at five to be off at six, almost as usual. However we had to make decisions regarding where it would be best for Virginia to sit in the truck and what she wanted to have as food and drink that day. I was kept busy getting her tea and dealing with her bed and the tent. Meanwhile there was vehicle trouble. The blue truck had to be towed along to start its cold diesel engine, and then it was discovered that the orange truck was in need of a tyre change. It was definitely one of those days when everything went awry! Hence it was almost 7 o'clock by the time we set off.

Virginia and I travelled in the cab, alongside Dave and Abby, with James driving and Lukas in the 'hot seat' - definitely a misnomer today. Lukas had donned his warmer clothes to sit there. But it was a good day to be up in the cab, as we climbed the Sabzak Pass (7,500 ft) - which would become notorious in 2009 for a battle between NATO's Spanish and Italian forces and the local Taliban. On our trip though it gave us a wonderful view of a kind of small version of the Grand Canyon below us on the far side. The colours of the hills about us were unbelievable; the grey and ochre of sandstone in the lower slopes was topped with layers of blue-purple, pinks and even green in the rocks above the canyon sides. Behind us, sharp teeth of rock towered above. Sadly the cloud was low, but it was still an impressive sight. The dirt road wound down the abrupt slope towards the river beneath.

James pulled clear of the road when he could and we had a photo stop on the zigzags down the steep gorge side. There were some stunted trees nearby that had suffered wind damage so that a few branches lay around on the ground. It was extremely cold and Ian suggested that it would be useful to gather up these dry branches as fire wood, so we set about collecting what we could. Several of us didn't like to look when Liz, Lukas, Greg and Tim (in his new Afghan hat) went very near the cliff edge in an effort to gather up the largest branch hanging over there, but, after much tugging, a good concerted heave got it clear and all was well. We had enough for a grand camp fire that evening.

Decorated lorries climbed past us, half the passengers trudging up after the vehicles on foot. It struck me that this is what would have happened with horse-drawn coaches in the old days, but I rather wondered that it should be necessary now. Did these passengers not trust their driver? James thought it more likely that the vehicles' brakes were none too good. Certainly even I could see that these Afghan trucks had suspension problems and their front wheel wobble looked quite unnerving. My respect for the drivers grew, for this was a very narrow stony track we were following, resembling the worst farm track imaginable. It wasn't easy for James: he even had to watch that low overhangs of rock above didn't scrape the top of our truck. How much worse must it be if you couldn't entirely trust your vehicle?

We were all a little relieved when we finally descended to a level balcony road parallel with the snaking river bed below. Here were odd patches of bright green meadow and every now and then an oasis, trees thrusting up from alongside the water course. The river down there was anything but full and swift-flowing, only small streams forking channels like a stringy network across the valley floor.

We drove on along the canyon to where there were some dwellings visible. On top of the flatter-roofed houses in the straggling town we saw red peppers, nuts, cotton and even melons laid out to dry. Most of the adobe houses had domed roofs however, similar to those we'd seen in Anatolia. We forded one or two wider streams flowing down to the main waterway, and veered briefly to avoid a couple of men chasing a hobbled horse towards the settlement. We'd seen a lot of magpies on the outskirts of Herat and there were plenty hereabouts too, circling us and chattering as we drove on. Virginia and I took to counting them according to the old rhyme. There was rarely 'One for sorrow' or 'Two for joy' but quite often 'Seven for a secret never to be told'!

Continuing along the river bed from the canyon town we found ourselves beginning to climb once more. There was an unusual problem at that point though, as we found ourselves facing a wire stretched across the road at waist height. James was lucky to see it. Dave was for holding it down and driving over it, but Lukas and James thought it looked like an electric cable: it might be unsafe to handle it. "Perhaps what we need then", suggested Abby, "is someone with a broom or something to raise it above the level of our truck." But we only had hand brushes and there was no-one so tall that they could reach that high safely. So the consensus was to push it down with the aid of a couple of the branches we'd collected as firewood. We held it down for the bluies too and this worked.

Only a few moments later we came across a heavily bearded farmer riding towards us on one camel, while leading a second laden with goods. A small boy, perhaps his son, was leading a donkey foal in the rear. The man flashed us a smile and we had to stop and photograph the group. He was obviously delighted to be the centre of attention and adjusted his cloak with care. The camels lifted their heads proudly on their long necks, barely deigning to glance at this weird caravan of vehicles in their path, while the tiny donkey peeped between them, the small boy trying to get in on the act too, but with little success.

Our next encounter on the road was still further from the town. We were brought to a halt by a trumped up road block of a couple of crossed logs. Ian had warned us that this could happen on the northern route and indeed elsewhere in Afghanistan. My map of the area even showed likely points on the road where so-called 'tolls' might be extorted. This one was manned by a fake official in a peaked cap. He looked unusually westernised in dress. His sports jacket was emblazoned with a kangaroo and the words *Wentworth District Football Club* on the chest pocket, an obvious 'gift' from New South Wales, according to our Ozzie expert, Jim! He was given cigarettes to satisfy him and the logs were removed for our two trucks to pass.

We drove on towards another village and called a photo stop on seeing tents in the style of Mongolian yurts that Genghis Khan would have recognised. Our presence was soon broadcast and a man, in his thirties perhaps, soon arrived to watch us, accompanied by seven turbaned small boys. Their dress interested me. They uniformly wore calf-length chemises over baggy trousers that looked pretty flimsy in the present autumnal temperatures. Though reasonably shod, none wore socks. One child actually sported a jumper and another a rather worn coat, while the man himself wore a western-type jacket, but the others were not so affluent. A couple of children were hugging themselves, or hiding their hands in their long sleeves, looking cold. Two had that slightly Mongolian look I'd noticed before, the rounder cheeks and narrower eyes that their ancestors, the one-time invaders from the east might have had in fact. One little boy had a facial palsy so his smile was crazily lopsided, showing the odd missing milk tooth to boot.

These boys were not all the same age, so at first we guessed them to be the man's children, but soon we thought better of this, as they didn't have a family likeness. Might he be a school master with his assorted pupils, in which case perhaps they were learning what westerners looked and sounded like? We might be the first they had seen on this northern road, so rarely travelled by tourists.

This impression was soon reinforced by the arrival of yet more young boys, and also a cigarette-smoking older gentleman, who definitely wielded some power in the village. That he had money seemed without doubt for he flaunted a cloak of a fine striped weave and flashed a gold ring as he smoked; his turban cloth was longer than the norm, acting as a scarf over his shoulders, and his shoes were of better quality. In the England of a hundred years before he might have been the local squire. Was he perhaps a landowner here too – or a village leader of some sort? Of-course he could just be the main master at the school if there was one. There were no institutional-type buildings around though.

As ever it was good to really look around from the cab. Moving away from the village, various different things caught my eye. First I noted dung drying up in the guttering of some dwellings: it would make good fuel for fires on an autumn night, so long as it kept dry. Then there seemed to be packs of dogs around, running wild. Did they get fed by the villagers? Further on I noticed small clumps of wild flowers, marguerite and bird's eye speedwell by the looks of it, growing nearer the river channel. I remember thinking how apt it was that I should see a plant of that name during this rather dodgy point in our journey. Deeper still into the countryside my attention was drawn to the wind-weathered hillsides, criss-crossed by sheep tracks.

It was these little details of local life and the meeting, however brief, with people as we travelled that we would have missed entirely had we flown across Asia, and in the cab now Abby and James discussed how some back home had reacted to their future trip. To travel this slowly for so long, and camping for heaven's sake, meant to them that you were either 'short of the ready' or eccentric to the point of being a bit daft! We were seeing the world in a more intimate way though and I, for one, felt rather proud to be almost "travelling Asia at Asia's pace"[60].

I was now to view Asia far too intimately however. Our shopping stop was Qala-e-Naw, where I spent most of the time with Virginia, at the local midden – a ghastly fly-blown dung heap. It was my first experience of such a place and I hoped it would be my last. The diseases that must be spread here! Virginia was embarrassed at suffering from diarrhoea in front of the other girls at our loo stops and had hoped to find a public lavatory, or what she thought of as one - this was not that palatial provision, but certainly 'public' enough! Personally I thought public toilets so far on this journey had proved to be far worse than going with others into an open field in the fresh air, and my ideas on this score were to become still more entrenched by experiences yet to come.

We lunched further on in a moulded hill region reminding me of painted landscapes by Edward Burra, his late work like *Valley and River, Northumberland 1972* in the Tate. I changed to sitting in the back of the truck for the afternoon. It was cold and dusty, but I was next to Ben, who normally drove the bluies' truck: Ian had changed places with him to give him a rest and Ben was enjoying it. He was in a distinctly frisky mood and had us laughing a lot at the antics he got up to in his floppy-eared hat!

---

[60] Fleming (1936) pages 166-7.

We camped quite late in a narrow stream valley where, fairly sheltered from the wind, it promised to be less cold overnight. We had a lovely hot curry - yes, I risked some - and the camp-fire we made with our gathered branches and logs was a great success. We huddled round and got thoroughly warm before bed.

***   ***   ***

Virginia and I enjoyed a good sleep and were up at 5.30 for a nice mug of drinking chocolate and some of Ian's pancakes. This was Ian's cooking speciality, produced I suspect when life was a shade difficult for the punters. We really appreciated this little luxury when he went to the trouble.

We got off at 6.45, and I sat in the back of the truck next to Maddie, who, being a keen amateur geologist as well as an excellent teacher, gave me lots of information about the effects of glacial action, in particular glaciers and their moraines – my 'Edward Burra' country of yesterday. Following a river in its gorge, we were still in this type of country, interspersed, I learnt, with fluvial overspills and hanging valleys. It was overcast and chilly, but not as cold as the day before.

The dirt road was often really narrow as it twisted between hillsides and we had some difficulty passing oncoming traffic, comprising the odd bus or delivery van. We would all dismount, bar a few passengers leaning out the far side of each vehicle, trying to ensure and maintain an upright position, rather as the crew of a dinghy does in a good wind. Both drivers then slowly moved forward, passengers shouting steering adjustment advice, and would creep past each other, tilting over towards the oncoming vehicle so that they almost touched. Afghan bus passengers obviously saw this as part of the excitement of a trip out!

The shopping stop of the day was at a fascinating small town, Qala Vali. The local market was on a tree-lined road. Having no food shopping to do that day I and some of the other girls made for the colourful material selling stalls first. Men sat in huddled groups or wandered through the area, while women stretched up or squatted to look at the textiles on show. Lengths of these hung from bars above and to the sides of the shops' awnings or were laid upon sheets on the ground, often slipping and becoming quite dirty on the dusty road surface. Clothes lines draped more material under the trees, where I guess it inevitably suffered from bird droppings. It all looked pretty primitive, but plenty commerce was going on, women bartering and haggling with the stallholders. For a westerner it was fascinating to watch.

In the food market we noticed that the flat bread now came in rounds with a pierced pattern in the centre, rather than being oblong as we'd seen in Herat. Bearded men sat on the road leaning against the mud walls of their shops and gazed at us with interested smiles as we passed. The butcher's shop displayed some rather fly-blown cuts of meat, lying unprotected in the sun. I was not too sure my digestion would improve in this country!

However, I found I had an appetite and ate nearly everything offered at our lunch stop a little later. We were in a dusty U-shaped valley in the moraine, so after we'd eaten I explored a camel trail up the hill with Liz, to end up by a threshing area on the upper slopes. We recognised that we were very near Russia now and wondered if we could see to the border from up here.

The afternoon proved to be fairly energetic for us. At one point we had to get out and push the truck when it almost got bogged down in mud, and twice bridges only just failed to collapse beneath us. It didn't help that James, once more at the wheel, stopped in the middle of one rickety bridge to decide what to do! We finally camped two miles from a village, in a ploughed field - never the best surface for camping. We'd travelled 80 miles that day though, which was very good going: our average daily mileage in Northern Afghanistan was to be about 65 miles.

That evening I was called upon to give Jane a back massage, which I hope eased her muscle tensions. It certainly relaxed me a little. This I needed, for Virginia and I were both feeling irritable. It was a colder night and I was now being bothered by a cough. I really was tired of being less than fully fit.

Next morning I felt the better for my rest and had the tent packed away by six o'clock. I set about stowing the crockery from breakfast, but the truck was moved without warning and I was showered with plates. They landed on the seats though, so there were no breakages. James still had to learn to warn us that he was moving the truck! When he heard the clatter he came to apologise and when he found it was me in the back he also asked if he could borrow my hat, to keep the sun out of his eyes. I fetched it from my rucksack before it got packed in the trailer. He looked extremely eccentric in it, concertina-brimmed as it was!

It was a sunny day and more crisply cold. Autumnal colours were appearing among the trees everywhere, vines now tipped with scarlet and orange. We were crossing an undulating plain, with a view of distant mountains rising above the clouds to the right, the forerunners of the Hindu Kush range, emerging from the central higher region of Afghanistan in the east. The next high range east would be the Himalayas which was a thrilling thought.

In one village we came on an unusual sight. At a distance, through a crowd of men, we could just make out a group of girls dancing in a circle to an accompaniment of shrill singing and tambourine rhythms. I almost fell out of the truck in my haste to photo them and found myself facing a solid flank of the local men, intent on stopping my progress. They did so very politely though, and of-course I made no fuss. What was going on was special to them and not to be gazed at by foreigners. I could only respect that. Among ourselves we speculated on why this was happening - a coming of age or a wedding perhaps?

Qaisar, where we did our shopping that morning, was a town absolutely buzzing with people. We wondered if it might be because there was a buzkashi event in the offing. This, Ian had told us, was the national sport, a game played on horseback, originally cross-country between villages, but not with mallet and ball as in polo. Nothing so blue-blooded and genteel. Written during a 1969 trip to Afghanistan made by the Chatwins, the sport was described as:

"... the fierciest game in the world, a wild melee during which horsemen struggle and fight to carry the *buz* - a headless goat, but sometimes a calf - to a scoring area. Although the riders apparently have teams, each man is out for himself, and if he wins, his individual victory brings credit to the town he comes from. The men are big and incredibly strong. The horses are stallions taught to fight; they don't play until about seven years old."[61]

There was however no sign of a match being held. This was disappointing as we'd hoped to witness this local bizarre practice in action.

Shopping went very well though: we were finished in a record twenty minutes. The aubergines, turnips, parsnips, and onions were extremely cheap. Rice was the most expensive item at 20 Afs a kilo. Bread was for sale on the street, being carried in large shallow baskets on the heads of the bakers' men. Having been just baked it was still warm, and they kept it so as long as possible by covering the flat roundels of naan with a colourful blanket.

We drove on to a lunch stop by the roadside and moved the tables out from the shadow of the trees into the sunshine, which made a remarkable difference to the temperature. My fellow cooks washed in a stream nearby while I cleared away with help. I reckoned it was a little chilly to be having a dip if I was on the edge of getting a cold.

Once we got going again in the afternoon, there were sightings of some animal like a wolf on the hill. Rather exciting, but perhaps it was just one of the wild dogs we'd noted earlier. We hadn't seen too much wildlife to date, though some believed they'd seen squirrels.

Before long we reached Maimana, a prosperous-looking town with some nice residences set back from the road in park land. There were plenty horses and carts jogging around, as in Herat. We filled up on water at the local well and, as I sterilised the jerry cans, I chatted to some school boys, who were practising what English they knew. When I'd finished the job in hand, they proceeded to dress me, accompanying each move with the appropriate words. "Zip up", "Tie coat" ... "Anorak", I corrected, and so on. I was surprised to find that this gave Scott, who was helping carry the jerry cans back, cause for concern. He appeared to think this was a form of mild attack, but I was happy enough trying to communicate with them.

---

[61] Omrani, Leeming & Chatwin (2011), page 14.

I was also interested to find the lads wanted me to learn their language too: I got told the names of fruit and vegetables in the pictures in their school books.

There was quite a crowd gathering around the truck again as we returned with the water. This even included some beggar women. But unlike the men and boys, they came and sat, pathetically *un*interested in us! It would have been really good to have got into conversation with them, but it seemed that they had only approached the truck because they saw an opportunity to beg from the surrounding men. They weren't there long, for policemen soon came and hustled the crowds away.

We were about to move on when Sarah, kneeling up on her seat to look down at the pavement, saw a couple of men in western dress, and patronisingly started enquiries.

Sarah: "Excuse me. Where do you come from?"
Men: "Maimana."
Sarah: "I beg your pardon."
Abby: "Maimana, you booboob! HERE!"

I have since learnt that Abby's very unusual surname was the same as that of a High Court judge in the south of England. She shared her possible relative's sense of fair play if not the language he might employ! I have to say that I liked her response and again wondered at Sarah's lack of sense. She'd sounded rather as the 'Memsahib' of colonial days in India was said to have done. It was quite possible that younger Afghans in the towns and cities took to wearing more western styled clothing, a sign that they were doing reasonably well in life and had knowledge of the world beyond their country, perhaps.

We camped rather late in a small side valley, the moon just starting to rise, bright and almost full. I looked after the curry sauce for tea, after which some police arrived to enjoy our fire in the late evening. Ian did not appreciate having them with us, with their fixed bayonets!

It promised to be a cold night. I tried putting my blanket inside my sleeping bag for a change, and this worked better, though I still had nightmares of losing a toe or two to frostbite!

We were up at 4.30, helping Tim to get breakfast ready. It was extremely cold. We got off at 6.45 to travel through duller plateau country. Not that I noticed it very much, for I read for a fair time this particular morning. The truck sides were down due to the cold, so there was less to see. It was a pretty awful road as usual, but we hoped to get onto tarmac later that day when we reached Sheberghan.

We had an early morning tea-cum-shopping stop in Daulatabad. Ian led some of us towards a tea shop, but I got waylaid by the sight of a butcher's shop. In an open alcove of shop window was set the table showing off the various cuts of meat, larger pieces hung further into the interior. A wooden awning hung from two ropes above to shade the bloody specimens, and over this had been cast haphazardly some thick bedraggled cloth, marked with dirt and much frayed at the edges: perhaps this was normally the curtain that closed off the scene at night. The whole resembled some Dutch old master painting, only a shade less neat and clean. As usual three local men framed the photo I took, their delighted smiles showing how they liked the idea that I should portray them at their shop. This endeared them to me far more than I was attracted by their goods!

I walked on to join Ian and the others as they mounted a charpoy outside the chai shop. Tea, crystalline sugar and bread cost 6 Afs. We were each served with an individual pot of tea, a glass, into which you heaped the sugar, and a small loaf of bread. Ian showed us to pour the tea into the glass, on the sugar, which was not stirred in: it was simply allowed to permeate the tea as you drank ... so, black, sweet tea, which though a little strange at first was quite palatable. He also showed us to toast our bread over the ashes of a small fire in the centre of the charpoy. This was the best bit for me! It was warm and tasty, though of course we had no butter. I could have done with a hunk of Wensleydale cheese with it, but dairy products were not forthcoming, nor to be trusted from now on.

We continued on our way to lunch near a nomad camp, where some Afghan men, the local big shots by the sound of it, came to chat and ended up sharing our meal, polishing off both the melon and grapes and the bread! It was a good thing some of us had enjoyed bread with our tea earlier.

152

In the afternoon we had an enforced stop on the undulating plain because an injector cylinder change was necessary on the truck. So we decided to play football, women versus men. The men played with their feet, but the women with anything - hands, pieces of wood as bats and feet. This warmed us up thoroughly. There were some shocking fouls though. I'm afraid the worst occurred when Maddie decided to go for the 'big squat', as 'number two's at a loo stop were now called, on the actual field of play! Foul was the word! That this was pretty happily accepted and laughed about was a real sign of how uninhibited we had become in each other's company.

Back on the road again, I found I had started dreaming that the sea was on the other side of the dunes bordering the road! I shared my thoughts and found several of the others were enjoying similar idealised imaginings. Their dreams were often food and drink related though. I remember bacon butties, steak and chips, strawberries and cream, and draught bitter featuring largely. In other words we were becoming fed up with the food on the trucks and this was, as expected, the toughest part of the journey so far. Hardly had we stopped discussing this than suddenly trees and houses appeared in the distance – Sheberghan ... and tarmac!! A cheer went up in the truck.

We filled up with water in this large pleasant town. I noticed it seemed more up-to-date than most places we'd been through: there were a lot of modern houses. Sadly we had to hurry on for the sun was setting, a lovely red sunset. We hit a 'toll' again before we found a camp site in the plain. It was a fine night - a bright new moon and not a cloud in the sky, but it was strangely difficult to see all the stars. Wood smoke pollution perhaps? Indeed we enjoyed a good barbecue fire, after which I did three massages - Jane's neck and shoulders, then bluie Stephen's lower back and finally Maddie got a facial massage. I then joined everyone round the fire, sitting out there till round 10pm.

*** *** ***

I was up next morning at 5am. It was very cold again. I took the truck malaria tablet again, my third. Virginia took ages to get going ... but so did the orange truck! We finally got away at 6.45, but with some difficulty, as we had to tow the truck, after much pushing and pulling to get her to go at all.

It was a long, straight road we were on. I was in the cab, James driving, in my hat again (he'd really taken a fancy to it and the comments it brought him); Liz was in the hot seat; and Meg, Sarah and Lukas behind with me. At 8am we passed a new smart main road turn-off northwards - down which the Russians were to invade four years later. Half an hour later we reached Mazar-i-Sherif. It's interesting to note how the road we had just journeyed was described in a 2011 guide to the country. "The journey to Mazar-i-Sharif from Herat via Maimana takes two days and is safe."[62] It had taken us five days, for the roads had been dreadful, but we never considered our safety - not in the sense these authors meant at any rate. True our trucks could have descended into a river from one of the rickety bridges en-route, but we had never given a thought to a fundamentalist militia like the Taliban as a safety risk.

Mazar-i-Sherif turned out to be a large sprawling town, with some very pleasant suburbs. It was set on a grid system around a central magnificent, turquoise mosque, a shrine to Ali, son-in-law of the prophet Mohammed. It was said that Ali...

> "already had a shrine somewhere else but then someone thought it would be a good idea to find some of his bones here and build another one. Bring pilgrims and trade."[63]

We had chai and then walked in the mosque's park, where there were some beautifully perfumed roses. It would have cost 20 Afs. to enter the mosque's courtyard and we were not allowed to enter the mosque itself, so we put that idea aside, although the building's tiling was obviously worth a closer look. There was a notice of rules in English which included one that only Moslem women were allowed in one part on a Wednesday. Good for you, girls, I thought; a place of your own, a little independence! I did some guard duty on the truck and then went off to try my luck at the Bank. But I didn't stand a chance. I only had half an hour for my transaction, and eight or nine of our party were ahead of me and had been nearly an hour there already. I watched with fascination as people spent time hanging about waiting while copies of forms were being written;

[62] Omrani, Leeming & Chatwin (2011), page 36.
[63] Paine (1994), page 189.

then being ushered, always very politely, from one room, or even building, to another, and so on. How my father, a retired bank official in England, would be amazed to hear of this! In fact I wrote to my parents later, that in Afghanistan...

'... black market money-changing goes on everywhere – in fact this country has little need of banks, and when you do try using one to cash travellers' cheques you have to count at least one hour for the transaction! This is no exaggeration; many spent even more time than this. One chap had the strange experience of his notes being refused because of the Queen's head on them!'

This happened to Graham, my one-time fellow-caterer from the blue truck. He actually tried to change a five pound note and was led from one teller to another for some forty-five minutes until at last the specimen book was brought out. "Oh no, your note lady's head!" was the verdict. Sadly the cashier expected to see King George V on the bank note, for the specimen copy of a pound note had been issued in 1934! So Graham, although he argued his case, failed in his task after spending an hour in the bank.

My father did indeed dine out on this yarn with his ex-colleagues for some time and my mother was reminded of Kipling's lines –

"Now it is not good for the Christian's health to hustle the Aryan brown,
For the Christian riles, and the Aryan smiles and he weareth the Christian down;
And the end of the fight is a tombstone white with the name of the late deceased,
And the epitaph drear: "A Fool lies here who tried to hustle the East."[64]

---

[64] From *The Naulahka: a Story of East and West*, 1892 (2001).

Chapter 15. Afghan Wonders

We left Mazar-i-Sherif via the diesel station, noting with interest the prices of fuel. Diesel was 8 Afs./litre and petrol 8½ Afs./litre. That, we worked out, meant that, rather surprisingly, petrol cost the same here as in Iran - 36p/gallon. We had imagined it would be more expensive here, as Iran surely had oil reserves.

We lunched beside a dead straight road running towards the hills. I was a little off colour once more so didn't eat much. However I did enjoy lying in the sun for a while. Then on we went through an extremely narrow cut into the hills and camped near a stream, which gave most people the opportunity to have a good wash. We got a pleasant fire going after supper, so we enjoyed one of our sing-songs round it.

My chance to have a dip in the stream came at 5 o'clock next morning. The day was bright and clear. We got off at 6.30 and were in Doshi by 8am. We were now some 80 miles north of Kabul, and the spectacularly scenic route to Bamiyan turned off from the main road near here. We called a photo stop and climbed down from the truck to gaze at a very pleasant scene. A twisting road made its way through small villages with neat cultivated fields towards distant hills bathed in early morning light. Not for the first time I was reminded of Scotland, but we were far higher, right up in the Hindu Kush now. It was extraordinary to realise that at over 8,000 feet we were almost twice as high as our destination of Kathmandu at only 4,500 feet.

A little way up the valley the truck's alternator needed attention, so Maddie, Ros and I wandered into scant woodland and explored stones lying around. Maddie cracked some open to look at the type of rock forming them, a new idea to me. The river running by the road at this point was wide and there were noisy rapids nearby. I was astonished to hear from Maddie that she'd learnt that these waters, which we were to follow an amazingly long way into the mountains, never reached the sea. I had never heard the term endorheic watershed before and imagined that all rivers reached the sea sooner or later. But the Hindu Kush is not the only area in the world where waters end in swamps and inland lakes of-course. We had already come across the example of Lake Van in Anatolia.

We stopped by the river later on for our lunch, and several folk, including Ian, indulged in a dip in its freezing water. Good luck to them, I thought to myself. I helped Meg wash her hair and that was cold enough for me.

The Swiss girls, Hannah and Heidi, had wandered a little way off the road to photograph farmer workers in the field. I followed, fascinated to see a man tilling the soil with oxen and a wooden plough. He was simply standing on the wooden crossbeam and seemed to be holding the yoked oxen's tails! Some of the labourers were working barefoot, even in these chill conditions. These had to be really hardy people!

We continued, in sunny but cold weather, to Bamiyan. Unlike Kathmandu, Bamiyan hadn't the temples that we should see in a month's time, but it was famous as the most western extent of Buddhism, where you could view the two statues of Buddha in the cliffs behind the village. There were a couple of reasons for the Buddhas being in this location. Firstly, Bamiyan was close to the series of linked trade routes that connected the East with the West hundreds of years ago, known as the Silk Route, and then, being a fertile area in a harsh environment, this was a favourite spot for merchants and missionaries to take a few days rest from the hardship of their journeys. Many of these people were Buddhists and...

"Buddhism spread, in part, because it was not location specific. Believers did not need to worship at a particular temple or at a particular site as part of their practice. Worship could take place anywhere and at any time. This freedom resulted in the emergence of Buddhist cave architecture throughout Asia."[65]

There were almost one thousand caves carved into the sandstone cliff at Bamiyan, many showing signs, from what remained of their wall decorations, of Buddhist worship. This was naturally reminiscent of Goreme for us. But literally standing out among these small caves were the great domed niches, each two hundred feet tall, containing the gigantic statues of Buddha, one 120 feet high and the taller of the two being 175 feet high.

---

[65] Rod-ari (2015).

"Afghanistan was where Buddhism met the art of Alexander's Greece. There ... it first developed the most distinctive artistic expression of the religion: the portrayal of the Buddha in human form. The giant statues of Bamiyan were the most monumental legacy of this innovation."[66]

It was partly this portrayal in human form that led to the Taliban's destruction of the statues in 2001. As we had also seen in Goreme, Islam has no time for religious art showing human features.

For nearly one and a half thousand years the Buddhas had stood serenely over the lovely little village of Bamiyan and its green and pleasant fields. During that time religious ideas changed and past notions were forgotten. I can't imagine what reasons people gave for the presence of such spectacularly unusual figures in their landscape, but it seems that by the nineteenth century the locals didn't know what the statues represented. Evidently...

"It took the study of Chinese chronicles and related statues for a British team to establish that they had been Buddhas."[67]

I was almost the first in our truck to catch sight of the Buddhas and I could hardly wait to explore them. Time for lunch first though, at one of the chai houses that lined the main street of Bamiyan. We had our chai alongside egg and chips, which everyone agreed was a wonderful change from the truck's fare. This was not something to miss, so I had a little despite my continuing health issues.

Then I accompanied Peg and Mark, and Lynn and Rob up the side of the largest Buddha. First we climbed up dark steps to reach a long corridor about forty feet above the ground. More shadowy tunnels and steps followed. With rising excitement we passed doors and balconies to arrive at last, nearly two hundred feet above the valley floor, on the level of the head of the Buddha. What a view there was from up here, of the green valley and the hills and mountains beyond! It was breath-taking to imagine how the statue was constructed, the rock worked for ages probably, to

---

[66] Stewart (2004), page 281.
[67] Stewart (2004), page 283.

achieve the high relief projected figure in its niche. Sadly it seemed to have already been scarred at the hands of Moslems. The features of its face were gone and the legs were damaged, but it still had an imposing impact on the surrounding countryside, along with its lesser companion nearby. It took some weeks for the Taliban to wreck these giants and decisions still have to be made as to whether or not they might be re-constructed. I'm so glad I went there when I did and saw them fairly intact.

Rather tired by now, I left the others and went to Mustapha's, where we were to sleep that night and read quietly for a while. Others joined me for supper when we enjoyed the luxury of cake in chocolate sauce. Then I went off to bed early. Some were going to sleep round the fire, but I found a small sleeping-room and laid on the bed there. It was a bit chilly till about 11pm when everyone else started piling in. They let me have my bed to myself though!

***   ***   ***

I was up at 6.15, put warm clothes on and went out into a frosty morning. It was sparklingly clear but extremely cold. There was a fair sprinkling of snow on the mountain peaks. Thanks to this freezing start it took us all quite a time to get going properly, but eventually we set off to get a view of the Buddhas from the other side of the valley. There was an excellent vantage point near a small observatory there. We were on a level with the top of the long cliff within which the Buddhas stood, and were thus able to see the whole mountain range beyond. We could now also see how the cliff was riddled with holes, a multitude of caves carved into the rock. The village was visible through its surrounding trees and some farms with courtyards stood further east amid fields and pastures, such a change from a lot of the rough arid landscape we had been through to reach here. Autumn suited Bamiyan too: there was a slight tinge of gold on the trees and the morning sun's light warmed the long stretch of pale brown sandstone cliff with a rosy hue. Altogether it was a very peaceful scene.

We made a brief visit to the nearby observatory, which had the task of measuring hours of sunshine in the region each day. A glass globe localised the sun's rays, which then burnt round a strip of scaled paper on a slowly rotating drum.

From here we left for Band-e-Amir, another must-see for visiting tourists in Afghanistan at that time. This area, some forty seven miles north-west of Bamiyan, high in the Hindu Kush, at nine and a half thousand feet, was being considered for National Park status in the 1970s, but war was to bring such thinking to a halt not long after our visit there. It finally became Afghanistan's first National Park in 2009.

It was when we were only a quarter of an hour into the journey, in really cold conditions, that Sue showed signs of acute left lower lobe chest pain, which could have been the onset of pleurisy following the chesty cold she'd had recently. Seriously useful at last (my professional expertise was to be acute respiratory physiotherapy), I gave her relaxation and breathing exercises and suggested she be taken back in the truck to rest at Mustapha's. The rest of us then walked on in bright, chilly sunshine. It was good to be on the move to warm ourselves up with some exercise.

When the truck caught up with us again, we piled in and continued up a lovely valley and on to the rather grim moorland above, a plateau where the ice of frozen rivulets of water glistened in the sun. I remember thinking that this must be what tundra looks like, the landscape treeless for as far as the eye could see. In the distance were some herdsmen with horses, and on the horizon were the silhouettes of more high peaks. We went a long way over the moors and then dropped down the twisting road to the lakes. [68]

They were simply glorious on this bright autumn day. Truly, as one guidebook suggests,

> "Band-e-Amir still ranks as one of the great natural wonders of the world."[69]

Below us steep sandy cliffs rose from the sides of a deep blue, almost turquoise lake. This amazing colour, I was to learn later, was due to the presence of 'glacial flour' (calcium carbonate particles) in the water. Maddie explained to me that this was one of a chain of six hanging lakes,

---

[68] See photograph on page 131.

[69] Omrani, Leeming & Chatwin (2011), page 106.

so-called because mineral-rich water seeping out of cracks in the local rock had filled the hanging valleys in the surrounding high plateau to form a great lake. The colours were superb, the slopes tinged on a spectrum from terracotta at the crowning steep rock of the canyon to nearing white for the gently sloping ground dipping to the lake shore. Over time the minerals in the water had been deposited to form natural travertine dams separating the large lake into several smaller ones, the term travertine being used for limestone formed by a process of rapid evaporative precipitation of calcium carbonate[70]. We had seen something of the same formation at Pamukkale in Turkey, there forming cascades of small pools.

Ian had told us there was the possibility of hiring ponies up here to ride from lake to lake. He was fairly scathing regarding the quality of these animals, referring to them as 'old nags'. I was no rider, and wondered if I might trust myself to an older, less frisky horse. However, for us it was out of the question, for as they'd arrived here first, the bluies had had time after lunch to hire them all. When they returned they spoke glowingly of their rides. I was in fact fairly happy not to have had the opportunity: I set out to walk instead, climbing the nearest hill to see the extended view of the lakes. Really beautiful in an other-worldly way.

Band-e-Amir didn't seem spoilt with a lot of tourist shops and gimmicky outlets. On my return, I sat in the sun with Liz, the Australian nurse, who like me was not eating much. After a while, as the bluies started to return from their exploration, I decided to check out the local rather draughty toilet, another foot-plate-either-side-of-the-down-pipe job. I thus gathered another droll experience to add to my book on 'Toilets I have Known'. Having used toilet paper and thrown it down the hole, I was amused to find it blew back to me!

We had a warm journey back on the same route, but with the truck sides down against the chill. On our return to Bamiyan everyone rushed to the 'Kabul Bakery' to try their apple pies (despite Ian's 'Hepatitis Pie' warnings), chocolate brownies and ginger biscuits. Tempting, but I went for the unadulterated chai!

---

[70] Higgins (2019).

Then I joined Sue and others at Mustapha's till the trailer had been unpacked. I was just in time to bag a place in the small room again, but this time on the floor. It had obviously gained a significant reputation, for there was very little space in the room already, at 9pm. Bluie driver, Ben, was on top form commenting on the sleeping attire of all, as though we were on a catwalk! It was cosy enough on the floor and all in all I had quite a good night, after an amazingly different day or two. The variety of experiences I was getting on this holiday was certainly living up to expectations.

*** *** ***

We were up at 6am, in freezing temperatures again. It was the start of our cooking day once more and washing up was torture for the hands. We had real problems as the water in our jerry cans was frozen and the chai house's no better, so it took ages! At least we'd had a rest from dealing with the tents. We got off not long after 7am, driving through yet more picturesque country, some rugged wild valleys. At a chai stop Virginia and I succeeded in buying grapes and melon for lunch. Gloria and I also enjoyed petting a rather dirty donkey we found in a pasture nearby. I hoped it hadn't fleas!

Our lunch stop was at a pleasant viewpoint, the sun much hotter by now. When we continued, there was some good chat in the truck about work in hospitals, favourite films people recommended and so on. We were all well rested and ready to discuss subjects together more than usual perhaps, as we knew we were approaching Kabul and hopefully a little more comfort. Just before 3pm we drove out onto tarmac again, but before anyone could cheer an unexpected issue arose. Odd things started to fall off the trailer! It was a mystery why, when it was now a smoother ride. I took a last photo of the Bamiyan valley while the trailer packing was re-sorted. The days driving along dirt track had slowed us down considerably and we should be arriving late in Kabul, but Ian had prepared days spare for this.

The next stretch of road was a scenic downhill run. On we went quickly to reach Kabul, capital of Afghanistan since the seventeen hundreds, when the first real ruler of the country's son, "Timur Shah (c. 1772-93), moved

162

the capital from Kandahar"[71]. My first impression was that, for a fairly long-established capital city, Kabul was not particularly beautiful. I commented in my diary that it was "more like a shanty town." I don't think I'd seen a real shanty town at that stage in my life and Kabul, as I remember it, didn't come close to being as run down as the shanty towns I've seen since, but I think I had expected more from a capital, not these rickety houses at any rate.

The task now was to check in at the Friends' Hotel and things started to look up slightly. This hotel was in a far more affluent area, including several embassies. There were a few rooms on offer, so Sarah, Meg, Virginia and I tried getting one and we were successfully settled into a largish room. What luxury! The others were still having to camp in the grounds.

Virginia and I then got money from Ian to get more shopping. In return he told us of a Buzkashi game taking place next day in the Ghazi Stadium: would we like to go? Would we! This was something most of us were really keen to see. Then with the help of an Indian official at their Embassy down the road we found the bazaar and bought vegetables and eggs. The Indian chap was very friendly and said he would help us look round Kabul if we liked. We agreed to meet him at 11.30 at the Post Office the next day, since we'd be going there to collect our mail anyway.

As he left us we realised we were quite near Chicken Street at this point, the name said to derive from the fact that a chicken shop had been located in the area in the past, but also perhaps because men were still to be seen occasionally driving flocks of chicken and geese down this street. However it now had the reputation for tourists of being the best place to buy Afghan souvenirs. It was indeed very pleasant there in the dusk, all twinkling lights on jewellery, bags, clothes, rugs and furs. We had to return to get tea going but vowed to pay another visit the following day.

This evening was pretty successful all round, for tea went well and later, when I went to wash I luckily hit the moment when a man was heating the water, so indulged in a lovely hot shower. Not for the first time on this

---

[71] Simpson (2012), page 135.

journey I recognised the importance of good warm running water. What luxury it was to enjoy a city's extra pleasures after so long travelling on rough, dusty roads!

But at 7.15 next morning when I went out to start breakfast I was suffering once more. I had a horrible facial neuralgia presumably thanks to my cold! When I returned home to England this gave me proper trouble. My face swelled up and I turned out to have an abscess on a tooth that had to be extracted. How glad I am that this didn't happen in Afghanistan, though there might have been help closer at hand than I realised at the time. Derek, brother-in-law of our bluie Canadian singer Michael, was actually a dentist, but had very wisely kept this quiet!

At any rate after a good cuppa and an aspirin I decided to take things easier while the others went shopping. As the pain eased I set about washing my dirty clothes out in the courtyard at the back of the hotel. I was not the only one there. A French girl from Nantes was doing the same chore and it was nice to chat with her over the task. Once I'd finished I walked to the Mustapha Hotel and was successful at last in changing some money: now I was more ready for a shopping expedition.

I met with Virginia again just after 11am and we set off for the Post Office to meet our Indian friend. Sadly there was no sign of him, but we collected our mail, in my case two letters from my parents which were nice to read. We were now free to fit in with what others were doing for lunch - chicken, a lovely change, at the Spinzar Hotel, after which we piled into taxis to go to the Ghazi Stadium to watch the Buzkashi match. This stadium gained quite a bit of notoriety later under the Taliban regime, when it acted as a soccer pitch but also as an execution site.

When we visited, we found the open air stadium absolutely crowded with men and boys. As ever there was no sign of any women other than foreigners like us. The more agile, usually the young men and boys, were up on the surrounding walls hoping to get a glimpse of what was happening, but others muscled in below, unable to see properly, but definitely able to hear and cheer on their side. We found ourselves alongside a tanned and tough-looking team dressed in khaki. They paraded near us on their proud stallions, whip in mouth, fur-hatted, khaki tunic and trousers gathered in at the waist by a red tie. Looking at the photograph I'd taken of a couple of them afterwards, it astounded me that they wore no gloves when I considered how their hands must have been scarred in this game. Their rivals, a team wearing blue tunics, were visible at the other end of the stadium.

Once we were all in our seats, the horsemen took their appointed positions, some eleven or twelve to each side, and battle commenced. I have to say that although I was watching carefully for the 'entrance' of the poor decapitated goat, I missed it. Somehow a rider had it across his saddle and the whole field became a tumult of pounding hooves, swishing tails and stretching and tugging horsemen. It was amazing to watch. There were tremendous twists and reverses as first one side and then the other tore away with the goat, often only holding it by one leg. The horses were splendid beasts and the horsemanship outstanding. Even though I had no notion of the rules (were there any?), I found the whole atmosphere and action before me extremely exciting. As far as I was concerned it beat football hollow!

Hoarse with cheering and shouting we left at 4pm to take a taxi to the old bazaar. I bought the necessities of life for the overlander, toilet rolls, hand cream, batteries, and a pen, after which we returned to the hotel. We changed briefly and hurried on to do some shopping on Chicken Street. I bought Afghan slippers and socks for my future hostesses in Melbourne and Auckland. Then we moved on to the Steak Restaurant off Chicken Street where we found superb value for money: three courses plus coffee cost the equivalent of 60p! It was only a shame that I wasn't quite up to eating so much.

***   ***   ***

I was awakened next morning by Peg and Mark wanting sterilisation for the new water they were using at breakfast, so I got up a little before the others and, after quite a wait, managed to get a lukewarm shower. Breakfast was unusual, cauliflower cheese, which was a good change I thought. Packing accomplished, Meg, Virginia and I returned to Chicken Street, where I bought baby socks for my godson, a bolero for my goddaughter and a lovely black and gold tunic for myself, the whole lot for less than £2.50! This was certainly *the* place to shop in the east so far.

On our way back to the hotel we passed the courthouse and I was fascinated to see scribes busy by the railings outside, writing letters for people. It had probably been like that in biblical times. There must have been an important person involved in one of the cases that morning, for the paparazzi were there in force too. What surprised me was the kind of photographic equipment they had: it was out of the ark, the kind of camera my Victorian grandparents might have used! The whole scene here could have been from a hundred years ago in Britain.

Once we had moved out of our hotel room, we went to lunch at the Steak House and finally left Kabul just after 2pm. I was in the cab; Ian driving, Liz in the hot seat and Mark, Peg and Jane with me. And a thoroughly spectacular journey we made. The road from Kabul to Jalalabad was completed by the Americans in 1969, so we were delighted to find that it had an excellent surface: indeed it would have been extremely dangerous if it had been without tarmac. In its more worn state today it is a road where accidents are evidently common[72]. It followed the Kabul River for some forty miles as it flowed through a deep gorge and so was situated half way up a cliff face and was uncomfortably narrow and winding. It was dark under the lowering cliffs and the river was barely visible far below. I found it a scenically stunning ride, but I was very glad not to be driving myself!

Once out of the Kabul Gorge we camped on very stony ground, and a baby scorpion was seen again, so I watched out. It was a lovely clear night and I saw a shooting star. Our last night in Afghanistan also turned out to be quite a warm night under canvas.

This country had certainly been very different, and fascinating in many ways. I liked the people ... well, perhaps it would be better to say that I liked the men, for I had not got to speak with any women really. Dervla Murphy put it well:

---

[72] dangerousroads (2020).

"This is the only country [Afghanistan] I was ever in where not one single man of any type has made the slightest attempt to 'get off' with me ... They [can] look as though murder was their favourite hobby (and maybe it is - among themselves) yet they're as gentle as lambs with me."[73]

Yes, I too had found the men here consistently polite and respectful to us western women and far less trouble than some men in the previous countries we had passed through. Their country was wonderful in its variety of spectacular scenery, and their more natural way of life had its allure. I decided that I should like to return to explore Afghanistan more at greater leisure. Sadly of course, this was soon to become really difficult and I have never attained my objective to date. For these people life is anything but easy and heaven only knows what the future holds.

---

[73] *Full Tilt* (1965), page 94.

Chapter 16. From the Khyber to Kashmir

We got up at 5.15 next day to set out an hour and a half later towards the Khyber Pass, another famous, or rather infamous, name to conjure with. This narrow gap in the Hindu Kush mountains between Afghanistan and Pakistan, had all too often been the site of warfare and invasion. It had been the route into India taken by invaders such as Alexander the Great and Genghis Khan. It was in the Victorian era however that the Khyber Pass gained its dreadful reputation with the British for being the site of a massacre of thousands of Anglo-Indian troops in 1842 as they retreated from Kabul.

"Until the First Afghan War, the East India Company had an overwhelming reputation for efficiency and good luck. The British were considered to be unconquerable and omnipotent. The First Afghan War severely undermined this view. The retreat from Kabul in January 1842 and the annihilation of Elphinstone's Kabul garrison dealt a mortal blow to British prestige in the East..."[74]

A place of ill omen then, that most of us were, rather bloodthirstily, eager to see.

We had an early morning short stop in Jalalabad, the last town we were to go through before the frontier with Pakistan. I was feeling out of sorts though so I rested in the truck and saw little of the town. The rest did me good, and once we got going again I found myself discussing Buddhism with Scott. He'd been reading about the religion and showed me the book, pointing out a chapter on the psychology linked to Buddhism. As I remember it had quite a lot to do with what has become popular as 'mindfulness'. I read a little of Scott's book and found it fairly interesting. We then somehow got onto the subject of aeromechanics, which I reckoned was more up Scott's street than mine. It was a strange segue; perhaps we'd arrived at this subject via 'levitation'? It was however a nice example of the weird conversations that happened sometimes in the back of the truck as we travelled.

---

[74] BritishBattles.com (2020).

We reached the Pakistan border and, although Ian had told us that photography at frontiers could be risky, I sneaked a photograph. There seemed to be quite a few people camping or just hanging around here and there were two or three dilapidated-looking stalls selling vegetables and simple goods. Some people had brought an animal with them as well. I was ready for some horses or perhaps camels, but from my vantage point I could see the odd goat, a single sheep and a rather distinctive white cow, presumably to provide milk on the journey. Ah, but was this one of the 'holy' cows I had read wandered the streets in the Indian sub-continent? The likelihood was not, as we were about to enter a Muslim country and it was Hindus that venerated the cow, so this would be more likely in India proper.

We had been assured that to send mail from Afghanistan was extremely slow at best, and unlikely to arrive at its destination at worst, so when I started writing a letter to my parents now, I was breaking an enforced silence of two weeks. I wrote half a letter, but then had to stop, for this border crossing was going more briskly than we had become used to. We were through by noon, the clocks going half an hour forward. We drove over a pleasant no-man's-land into Pakistan ... and onto the left hand side of the road again! Was it really almost two months since we had last been over here, before leaving England? It felt quite peculiar.

We were then immediately set upon by money changers – right outside the Customs House and the Bank. Wasn't this practice frowned upon at all? Well, it was fortunate that Ian had warned us this was the only way to change Afghan currency, as they didn't in the bank! Thus the money changers knew they were on to a very good thing with the tourists and no-one made a fuss that they were so brazen about it. It also allowed us to be rid of our Afghanis straight away and have some small change for drinks and snacks.

On we climbed up the Khyber Pass to lunch late half way up. It was pretty hot: now when did we last experience that? The country was all very brown, mostly rock shale. Below us in the valley ran the railway: to one side it suddenly vanished into an archway, denoting one of the thirty-two tunnels there are on this stretch I supposed. Further below was the river bed, overlooked on the far side by steep crags. The place made an impression all right, but disappointingly it was not half as dramatic as the Kabul Gorge.

I was astounded though by the car loads of men that went past on their way to the Afghan frontier. It seemed to show an extraordinary population explosion in Pakistan, or possibly an extreme wish to leave the country in favour of Afghanistan. One small van I saw was transporting at least fifteen men and their bundles, and I could only see those on top of the van and hanging on to one of the sides and the back! How many were there on the far side and actually in the cab? Amazingly the vehicle's tyres appeared to be coping with this excess weight.

Not long afterwards we drove past a fort on the road that I thought I'd seen in old pictures of the Afghan campaigns. This turned out to be Shagai Fort near Landi Kotal, the headquarters of the Khyber Rifles. This region of the North West Frontier had required an almost constant military presence in the early twentieth century because of local Pathan tribal problems, cattle and gun raids, blood feuds and the like. There was evidently "... this little air of danger, where there was always the chance of a stray bullet"[75], and at Landi Kotal itself there was a notice at the gate warning, "Abandon hope all ye who enter here"[76], as at the gate of hell in Dante's *Inferno*. An uncomfortable and testing billet for any soldier.

Moving onto a poorer road surface, we jolted between trees in the valley. We passed old men riding bicycles, horses and wagons which strangely resembled rickshaws, and yaks (or were they just very hairy oxen?) yoked to carts. As we got lower into the valley somebody recognised fields of sugar cane alongside us. We drove on to a picnic spot by the Indus River, just before Attock. The tents were put up in the dark. It was a good tea that suited me better. I wrote the other half of the letter to my parents, to be posted in Lahore tomorrow I hoped, and then joined the others for Ian's talk on the next few days, followed by the night's entertainment.

After explaining a little of what to expect in Pakistan, Ian told us we should visit Amritsar briefly (depending on how long it took to cross the

---

[75] Allen (1985), page 169.
[76]   "   "   , page 173.

Pakistan - India border) to see the Golden Temple of the Sikhs. Then we would make for the hills and once in Kashmir would stay on houseboats for a week, a very welcome rest for the drivers and quite a change for us, staying in the same place for a while. The houseboats were a relic of the nineteenth century, when the local Maharajah had not allowed the British to buy land or build in his realm. If they still wanted those beautiful cooler days away from the heat of the Indian plain, they would have to be more inventive, so they resorted to living on Lake Dahl instead. It sounded quite exotic and different.

For the moment though we were delighted to be on the plain. It was lovely and warm this evening and Rob strummed and sang, accompanied by crickets, till the early hours. Virginia and I left him to it before midnight, but his music was not an unpleasant background to fall asleep to.

*** *** ***

We were up before five and I went, armed with my camera, to watch dawn coming up over the Indus. It took most of us till 6.30 to get going because of our late night. We stopped briefly to try the roadside snacks for sale. I rather riskily bought potato fritters, which were tasty but quite hot and spicy. The area was crowded for the local cattle market and for the first time I saw water buffalo pulling carts along the tree-lined road.

While we travelled this particular day I dozed a lot. I remember it as the day when I suffered more abdominal pain than at any other time on the trip, and therefore took my codeine medication. I thus only woke up for stops in towns. Rawalpindi was the major city we went through on our way to Lahore and it varied considerably from Afghanistan's cities in that the British influence here was very noticeable. Rawalpindi had been annexed by the British in 1849 and had become Pakistan's capital in the mid twentieth century before neighbouring Islamabad took over. There were larger buildings that suggested Victorian industry to one brought up in the north of England: there was a cricket ground, a church, some smart hotels and a very western-looking embassy. There was also a lot more European dress evident.

Preparing breakfast at the trucks in Delhi

Doing puja by, and in, the Ganges at Benares, India

Pokhara market, Nepal, with a glimpse of Machapuchare in the clouds

The 'Roof of the World' with Everest at its centre

When I awoke next it was 2pm and we had reached Lahore at last. We stopped in Mall Road, known as 'The Mall', a major shopping area but with some rather nice buildings from the time of the British Raj. Before sight-seeing we ate at Lord's, and I commented in my diary - "... good service and food. Afternoon teas for goodness sake!" Yes, there were definite echoes of Empire here that we had not experienced before.

We strolled along looking in the handicraft stores, where there was some lovely stuff - decorated woodwork, materials and pottery. I then went to the Post Office and posted the letter to my parents and postcards to three people I would be staying with 'down under', as well as to other friends. I was rather appalled to find they were only going to be franked: there were no stamps! My parents had some comments to make later too:

"Your letter posted in Lahore reached us yesterday morning. It had taken seven days, and was the dirtiest yet. It had obviously been sliding over some grimy counters in Pakistan."

One or two of us then moved on to visit the English church, but found it shut. I should have liked to explore the city a little more, to find where Rudyard Kipling had lived when here in the 1880s, but by this time I was tired and still feeling pretty unwell, so I decided to go early to bed, missing the meal with the others on reaching camp.

***   ***   ***

I was awoken by the Muezzins' cries from 4am, but up till then had slept well. It was our cooking day once more so we began by washing up after breakfast as usual. We finally got off at 8.30am, into a lovely sunny morning. I travelled in the cab, James and then Ian driving, Lukas, Scott and Maddie my companions, and there was plenty to watch on the crowded road. Two water buffaloes carried amazing loads. More grimly, another, some time since its death by the looks of it, for it was much bloated, was being skinned by the roadside. A strain of dog that looked more like a hyena or jackal to me was ranging around, while a man close by was washing his bike in the river Ravi. And the salesman patter of a passing boy was very enticing: he cried, "Excellent super biscuits ... why not?"

We soon reached the Pakistan border and clocks went forward another half hour. It brought me up with a jolt to realise that I'd hardly registered the country properly. Had we really crossed Pakistan so quickly - in only two days? It's certainly the part of our trip that I remember least now. Of-course it hadn't helped that I'd been unwell.

The Pakistan border procedures weren't too much hassle, but the activity around us was extraordinary. Between Pakistan and India was a long shuffle service of coolies (blue-tunic'd in India and pink-tunic'd in Pakistan (so that they couldn't easily abscond, Ian suggested), carrying Afghan grapes in wooden crates on their heads from one lorry to another, for goods vehicles weren't allowed to cross the border! It was extremely photogenic, but Ian stopped me as I reached for my camera of-course. There was quite a police presence, very smart Sikhs in khaki with black turbans sporting a red pom-pom in the centre. Ian had told us that if we got lost sight-seeing or needed help of any kind on the streets in India the Sikh police were the ones to approach, being the most sensible and intelligent! This is backed up by several sources; for example Habashi suggests that historically,

"The Sikhs were the economic elite and wealthiest in West Punjab."[77]

The "elite" part of this at least appeared to have stuck, so we took notice of their presence. But what a palaver this was, having to carry all the contents of trucks between countries across no-man's-land!

We had a moment of delayed shock as we left Pakistan. One of the officials seeing us through looked straight in the driver's window! A second later it registered with us that he must be extremely tall to do any such thing. We enquired and sure enough, he told us he was 7ft 3ins tall. Quite a giant, especially in Asia!

The Indian border was much more of a hassle, altogether a longer drawn-out affair. First we went to the Passport Office. We all had to sit in rows of chairs in a small hall, and then stand up when named. The officials

---

[77] *Golden Temple in Amritsar, Punjab, India* (2019).

there were quite friendly, giggling happily to themselves. "Who is Daphne? ...Oh very nice!" was the response when I rose to my feet.

Having all checked in, we returned to the truck, and in my case a long hot wait in the cab. The others wandered around chatting to the folks in the back, while I dozed a little. I had of necessity to get out briefly to find the toilets, and soon wished I hadn't. They were filthy and thoroughly unhealthy, reaffirming my opinion by now that relieving oneself in the open field was infinitely preferable to using the institutional facilities.

A little while after my return to the cab Ian took the opportunity to find out how I felt, obviously worried that one of his punters was under par. I said I just felt tired a lot of the time. "Shake", was his response, and indeed some of the driving had been fairly hairy of late. But I managed to reassure him that I was still enjoying the trip ... and I was. At this point I took his advice and left the cab again to get some exercise, and an extraordinary meeting awaited me.

I actually came across the volunteer I'd talked with at Earl's Court Youth Hostel three months back. What an amazing coincidence! We compared notes and found we'd travelled a lot of the same ground, though we were both envious of our slight variations in route. He had travelled through Tehran when crossing Iran and had managed to visit the Caspian Sea, which I felt must have been really interesting, and he was envious of my journey through northern Afghanistan, having taken the usual backpacker's southern route through Kandahar. We wished each other well and I returned to the truck, for I saw a Customs Official approaching it.

This was a weirdly threatening, yet shoulder-patting official whose methods were quite unnerving. He wasn't too worried about how many Pakistani rupees we had as we'd thought he might be. No, he was searching for hash.

"You tell me if you have hashish – is better for you. I your friend, no your enemy. If I find someone with hashish, I kill that person, with my bare bayonet ... so!" (Lunging forward dramatically, while we all took a step back) "You see how I search for hashish – come on, you see."

And he got the trailer unloaded and was extremely thorough, looking methodically in every rucksack. Having completed his task and found nothing of interest, he proceeded to go further than any of us (bar Ian and James) expected. He actually asked for a tip!

The way he approached his task made me wonder if this was how the British had behaved in order to get things done effectively during the Raj. I had the strangest feeling that he was enjoying a bit of play-acting, mimicking what he had experienced or heard of in the past. V.S.Naipaul suggests that what can appear incongruous and slightly absurd in India should be seen in this light, for,

> "...no people, by their varied physical endowments, are as capable of mimicry as the Indians."[78]

And this gentleman's behaviour had certainly seemed to us bordering on the absurd. Several of us discussed it later and someone wondered if people under empirical rule had always attempted to mimic their rulers. I tried to imagine Anglo-Saxons imitating their Roman masters. Mulling this over, the consensus was that, even from the little we had seen so far, Indians might mimic better than the English.

But it led us to wonder if it wasn't because they were so often long-term invaded, by the Arabs and Turks, and then the Mughals, before the British. The Indians hadn't gone out to explore the world themselves as Europeans often had, but had been imposed upon instead. I reckoned there might be something in this but personally needed to learn more about Indian history before coming to any conclusion. It was interesting to realise how often it had been Europeans exploring the world though. American and African native people had been satisfied to stay at home it seemed: the Chinese had made sure of it by building a great long wall against the rest of the known world. And here we were perpetuating the child-like curiosity that had driven the Europeans to journey further!

***   ***   ***

---

[78] *An Area of Darkness* (1995), page 55.

But now to explore India at last. Back to our nomadic routine, we moved on to have a lunch stop just over the border, and I enjoyed a lovely cool drink. Then we got going on the twenty odd miles to Amritsar to reach there before nightfall. This was the famed city of the Sikhs, whose most important pilgrimage site, the Golden Temple, drew many a tourist: some actually stayed on site, being provided a bed and three meals a day free, part of the religious welcoming of strangers, of whatever race or creed, that Sikhs prided themselves on.

Being a popular tourist destination had its effect on the local traffic. The roads were crowded with bicycles long before we reached the city; in fact there was far more traffic on the roads than we'd seen for some time. Again there were oxen being used as beasts of burden and a few dogs wandering around. I witnessed a man actually chased off his bike by a barking dog. By the time we reached the outskirts of Amritsar we found the frightful traffic really claustrophobic.

It was almost dusk by now. We drove straight to the Golden Temple. Entering, we removed our shoes, stepped through a shallow water trough and all the women were given a head square to wear. Impressive paler buildings fronted by a white marble walkway surrounded the central pool on which the glistening golden shrine stood out on a small island. It was one of those fairytale buildings we had been expecting to see in India, golden-domed and with intricate corner decorations each topped by a pinnacle. Its reflection glimmered in the surrounding water, a pool known as Amrita Saras, or Pool of Nectar, from which Amritsar got its name[79]. It is said to have healing qualities, though these may be spiritual rather than physical.

"Pilgrims immerse themselves in the water, a symbolic cleansing of the soul."[80]

We walked round enjoying the rosy glow of the setting sun behind the shrine, accompanied all the time by chanting relayed through loud speakers. Then passing through an ornate gold-leafed portal, we crossed

---

[79] www.britannica.com (2020).

[80] *Golden Temple in Amritsar, Punjab, India* (2019).

the causeway and dared to enter the Temple. It was an old man who was intoning the prayer that we'd heard outside. He stood before what looked like a draped coffin, or was it simply an altar? There were many pilgrims present, including American and European women. I should dearly have liked to ask about the religion and have it explained to me a little, but we had come at the end of the day and no-one was still around to tell us more. After listening for a short while, soaking up the wonderfully foreign, though thoroughly prayerful atmosphere, we returned to wait for the truck near the entrance to the Temple, at which point conversation began to feature the other famous bit of history that most people had heard of to do with the city.

On exiting the shrine we had found ourselves very near the Jallianwala Bagh, the site of the 1919 Amritsar Massacre, where a tall monument reminded people of that dreadful event. To be viewing the site of a massacre for the second time in three days seemed to be surfeiting on gore. This part of the world had surely had its fill of such events. And here once more the British had come off badly, though in a very different way to what had happened on the Khyber. Following local unrest, British troops, having closed off the one exit to this walled area, fired without warning on a large crowd of unarmed Indians killing several hundred people and wounding many hundreds more. What made things even worse was that it was thought that many people gathered there that day were not protesters at all but only celebrating a spring festival. The British could not easily be seen in a good light after this bloodbath. It resulted amongst other things in Mahatma Gandhi's organisation of...

"His first large-scale and sustained nonviolent protest campaign, the non-cooperation movement (1920–22), which thrust him to prominence in the Indian nationalist struggle."[81]

In other words it might be said to have begun the wind-down of the days of Empire in India.

Tensions in this area were fairly common in the twentieth century and have had quite dramatic results for both the Sikh population and India as

---

[81] Pletcher (2020).

a nation. The separatist leader Jarnail Singh Bhindranwale, accused of insurrection in 1983, occupied the Golden Temple complex and made it his headquarters. Prime Minister Indira Gandhi ordered his and his followers' removal by force in the following year and Bhindranwale was killed during this operation. According to Habashi[82],

"The military action led to an uproar amongst Sikhs worldwide and ...led to assaults on members of the Sikh community within India. Four months after the operation, on October 31, 1984, Indira Gandhi was assassinated by two Sikh bodyguards. Subsequently, more than 3,000 Sikhs were killed in the Sikh riots in 1984."

Once again I am, in retrospect, very grateful that we travelled to Amritsar when we did.

But I was feeling very tired by now and was glad when Geoff came to lead us to the Guest House where we were staying the night, and I was relegated with the other 'sickies' (my fellow cook Tim, our nurse, Sharon and Jan from Melbourne) to the front room and had an early night. My last memory of this evening was of Indian music faintly heard out on the street somewhere. It seemed to lead me off into dreams of the 'Roof of the World'. Perhaps we'd glimpse the Himalayas tomorrow on our way to Kashmir.

***   ***   ***

We were up at 6am, awoken by the hawking and spitting of people outside which was to become a fairly regular morning chorus from now on. It seemed that in these areas of denser population, and possibly pollution, clearing the throat and nasal cavities was a common ritual of a morning.

Soon we were on our way north, towards the hills. As was my usual custom at this point I had only had a drink for breakfast, but during the morning we stopped at a rather special place. UNICEF had installed a milk bar at the roadside, selling vanilla–flavoured milk and cheese cake. These healthy foods were free to the local women and children, though we tourists paid for the snack. It was just what I felt I needed, and indeed agreed with my

---

[82] *Golden Temple in Amritsar, Punjab, India* (2019).

digestive system much better than other foods I'd tried. If I am ever asked why it is that I support UNICEF as a charity, I can honestly answer that I thoroughly benefited from their goods in time of need.

It was interesting to note the changes in vegetation around us as we travelled that day. There were paddy fields at first, but surrounded by cactus hedges. These hedges were the first to disappear, though the terraced paddy fields continued a little longer. Then by early afternoon, as we gradually climbed higher, these were replaced by trees. From Jammu I had my first sight of snowy peaks in the distance. Soon we were into a mountain region with tree-covered slopes and a river twisting far below. There was a lovely cloudless sky, and it was becoming ever cooler.

We stopped as night fell at a Guest House in Kud. At about 6,000ft this town is part of the lower Himalayan range of hills. It reminded Virginia and me of Switzerland once more. We shared a very pleasant room with a bathroom attached. The lights didn't work at first, but we had candles which gave an oldie-worldie feel to the place. We had yet to learn that it was common in this area for electricity to fail every two or three days. The others bought me soup and potatoes in bed, so I had a lovely early night. Perhaps the antibiotics Sharon had given me in Mashhad were beginning to work. Certainly I had started eating a little more, which was a real blessing!

Up at half past five, we were soon off over the passes en route for Kashmir. Several of us were extremely excited to actually see monkeys in the trees and even on the road! I was feeling more like taking notice and knelt up over the side of my seat in the truck to gaze down from our winding high road on the river at the bottom of the gorge. There were wonderful tiered paddy fields on the slopes around us, with some irrigation systems incorporated to help growth. From one pass we eventually started up the valley towards the second. Hills stretched to the horizon in shades of blue, from forest-clad Prussian blue to the palest powder blue hints as the most distant peaks met the sky.

We had a tea and biscuit stop at Banihal, where Ian found a young man had been sent to meet us. The houseboat owner's son, Bashir, had arrived from Lake Dahl. His father, Mr Gulam, wished to know why we were late. Bashir was a pleasant lad who walked with a limp (due to long-standing osteomyelitis, I found out later). Taking him on board, we continued on our way, travelling up a beautifully farmed narrow valley at first.

Then we encountered some tricky bits of road, with many a curve and the odd hairpin bend. I was reminded of the twisting heights of the Col des Mosses in the Suisse Romande where I had taken my first ski lessons. The road here had a much worse quality surface than its Swiss counterpart however. There were also the odd signs to read as you slowed to take a corner, with slogans in English such as, 'Remember your wives and children. Drive with care.' Not a common feature in Europe!

In the late morning we reached the almost two-mile-long tunnel at Jawahar (7200ft), created in the 1950s as the only route from Jammu to Srinagar in Kashmir, for the railway ended at Jammu. Traffic hold-ups were well known here and can still be quite a problem in winter when the area is prone to heavy snows and avalanches. We had a straight forward run through the tunnel, and yes, there was a lovely view of the Himalayas as we exited and began to descend into the green Vale of Kashmir beyond. We were soon driving through a flat landscape once more, fringed far off to either side by the hills. Poplars lined the road to Srinagar, reminding me of old master Hobbema paintings I'd seen, such as *The Road to Middelharnis*. But in Kashmir chinar (oriental plane) trees often appeared too, their "sweet shade" thought by Kashmiris to be medicinal[83]. The houses hereabouts appeared to have typical alpine architecture, sturdy, steep-roofed wooden buildings.

We reached Srinagar at two o'clock very hungry; yes, even me. We drove to Lake Dahl and saw that it was lined with timbered houseboats. These had very interesting and sometimes surprising names - *Green Mountain*, *Montreal*, *Kashmir Hilton*, *Egypt* and ours, *Young Good Luck*, all labelled 'special class'. We met Mr Gulam, or more properly Hadji Gulam Nabi Khan, the houseboat owner, a neatly white-bearded and bespectacled Indian gentleman. (The 'Hadji' title he bore, told us that he had been on pilgrimage to Mecca, the 'hajj'.) We then collected our rucksacks and Ian and Ben saw to parking and safe storage of the trucks, while we were

---

[83] Naipaul (1995), page 100.

ferried to our houseboats in groups of seven or eight to each one. Virginia and I were sharing with Sarah of our cooking party; Meg, the orange truck's American lass; Chloe and Alice, the sisters from the bluies; and Jane and Liz, the American and Australian nursing friends.

The houseboats still had an air of Victorian England about them once we got to look round. We arrived by shikara, one of a fleet of local gondola taxis, and entered up steps from the water onto a veranda. [84] This gave entrance to a room with mahogany occasional furniture including a bookcase stocked with some light English reading (Bertie Wooster featured here I noted); there were patterned curtains, decorative china and brassware was on display, and there was wood panelling in the background. It was dated and rather worn, but as I put in my diary, the *Young Good Luck* houseboat was,

> a lovely cosy wee place, though the toilet's not flushing and the lights are giving trouble.

It was not really so 'wee', for our three shared bedrooms had en-suite bathrooms and there was a separate dining room.

It did appear cosy to us though for the lounge we'd entered from the veranda on arrival had a central stove to keep us warm. Its very unimaginative and functional tubular appearance, precariously balanced on a rickety wooden support, was strangely at odds with its surroundings, and particularly with the richly coloured Kashmir carpet on which it rested. This together with the similarly eccentric plumbing and electrics in the houseboat were no real surprise. We'd spent more than two months roughing it across Asia by now and rather enjoyed the weird aspects of the place. But one absolute selling point, to me at any rate, was the outlook from our lovely sunny veranda. In the distance across the lake the snow-capped Himalayas could be glimpsed beyond the surrounding hills. Now that was bliss!

During the light lunch we now had 'on board' we realised that there was also a very new element to our experience here; we had servants. Well, house boys to be precise, who carried our food to table from its preparation in separate kitchens behind the boat. Surely this was luxury indeed!

---

[84] See photograph on page 131.

Chapter 17. A Garden, not a Country

Our first thought as ever in a new spot was collecting mail. Instead of using a Poste Restante in Srinagar our neighbouring houseboat was the place to go. It was bigger and newer than most and it was where Ian was staying: in Kashmir the incoming mail was directed to his houseboat, to *Montreal*. It made it sound as though we were going to Canada for the post!

So we soon got round to visiting next door and received, in my case, two letters, one from my parents and one from a colleague working in Switzerland. I spent the evening writing responses and sorting things out generally. It would be good to get some laundry done here, and there was even a repair or two to be done to my clothes.

We had a nice tea, but afterwards there was some fuss because a few of us wanted to see Srinagar and found Ian had pinched our shikara to sort out some business. Each houseboat was meant to have its own shikara, the romantic covered gondola with decorated cushions and awnings, punted along by the ferryman with a pole, which had been our means of reaching the houseboat originally. It was our main mode of transport between houseboats as well as on visits to town and elsewhere. The folk sharing with Ian had gone off to town in theirs and now he had taken ours in order to complete his work. Sarah for one was pretty upset.

But most of us had other fish to fry. It was Hallowe'en and we made efforts to celebrate the fact. I can't remember for the life of me how, but I managed to dress as a witch! A few years before, I had been a witch in an amateur production of Verdi's *Macbeth* in Scotland. The *Glasgow Herald* had particularly praised the female chorus' ability by writing of us as "splendidly writhing witches"! (Verdi amplifies Shakespeare's three witches to thirty for musical purposes.) So at least I could sing and act the part. It was useful I imagine that some of the clothes I had that needed mending might almost pass for rags, and my hair was certainly unruly enough now! It was such a mop of curls that Gloria had suggested I go 'Afro' from now on. Gathered round the central stove in our houseboat, we had fun trying to remember bits of Burns' *Tam o' Shanter* and other suitable poems and stories to scare each other with.

The treat of a different breakfast awaited us next morning in our dining room: there was an omelette, followed by toast (a shade cool from the trip to us from the kitchens out back), buttered or with jam, and tea or coffee. We'd last had butter in Isfahan and jam too was a rarity to be savoured. An excellent start to the day.

A laundry-man turned up and his boat was soon heaped with the dirty clothes of our houseboat and those of our neighbours. We then set off for town in our returned shikara. We passed some interesting wooden buildings in various states of repair. One old three-storied house on a promontory jutting into the lake looked as though it were being prepared for tourists, workmen renewing decorations to its top storey where there was a long balcony. It had rather a romantic air, a look of Grimm's Fairy Tales perhaps. It was a shame though that the land around it was just well-trodden mud. Rapunzel would surely have scorned to let down her hair from the balcony here.

The shikara took us to look round the show rooms of some factories and mills, where we gazed appreciatively at the beautiful furs and shawls on offer. In the crafts village on the edge of Srinagar Virginia ordered an embroidered shirt and the man selling it her quite tired me out trying to sell me something too. These were well practised salesmen who called for hard bartering! We soon needed a rest and went back to the houseboat for lunch.

I decided to laze in the afternoon and ended up next door with Maddie, Ros and co., receiving salesmen with their wares. There was an almost continuous parade of boats of these folk ready to show us their goods. I bought a very decorative papier-mâché Easter egg shell to be used to contain a present for my cousin. When asked what she would like me to bring her back from my trip she had simply requested "a stone from Kathmandu". Now I'd found the appropriate 'box' to carry it in. I also bought a tiger's eye stone to set as a tie pin for my father.

Ian turned up later on and, complaining of his back, wondered if I might give him a massage. I promised to after my evening meal and returned to the *Young Good Luck* houseboat for a nice mutton curry with the others, who had gone exploring the Srinagar shops further. I rather wondered why, when the shops so pleasantly came to us here. It was going to be a lovely lazy rest staying on Lake Dahl, as long as you could put up with all these salesmen's patter.

Giving Ian his back massage by the fire in *Montreal*'s sitting room that evening gave me a reputation with the houseboys. Ian had been happy to be massaged in front of his punters and fellow travellers: I'm not so sure he was ready for the houseboat staff, but they soon found out what I was up to and they beamed with delight as they watched. Said the sauciest, Nasir, "This is like you get in the ladies' parlour." I began to understand more fully why the Institute of Massage, the forerunner of the Chartered Society of Physiotherapy, had started up 80 years before in England, to distance medical massage from the form known to happen in houses of ill repute!

We had a delightful lie-in next morning till 8am. Virginia, Sarah, Chloe, Liz, Jane and I followed breakfast with an exploration of the lake, with the ultimate goal of visiting the Nishat Mughal Garden, or Nishat Bagh as it was locally known. The Mughal Emperors evidently appreciated the sensory luxuries of a garden, colours, scents and the sound of running water, as had the Moors at the Alhambra, which I was to visit some ten years later. We set off in a couple of shikaras. It would have been very relaxing lying in the sunny boat, but for the salesmen who kept stopping us to advertise and show us their wares.

After a while though we moved beyond their influence and started to notice all the activity that seemed to be going on apart from trading. It was intriguing to watch, and some activities we saw raised serious questions in our minds. I've already mentioned that the flushing of our houseboat toilets was unreliable. I remember, some seven years after my overland trip, talking to the well-travelled son of an up-and-coming New Zealand family about his experiences in Kashmir. He waxed extremely lyrical about the delightful old-world charm of his houseboat and I responded by asking him if the charm he had experienced had, like mine, included a loo that flushed over the back of the toilet pan through the floorboards and thence into the lake! His mother overheard and was suitably appalled, I fear. But it was this kind of plumbing mishap which now made us thoroughly question the advisability of washing clothes in the lake's waters, let alone pots and pans, yet here were women busy at both these tasks. They squatted down at water level on wooden planks projecting from alongside the local houses, dunking and scrubbing their laundry or kitchen ware, their barely clad toes clinging to the ledge they balanced on.

People in this area were moving about on the lake, rowing long narrow boats. I saw a man, sitting cross-legged and leaning forward to gaze along the barrel of an enormously long gun, at least five feet in length I reckoned, held down along the forward half of his boat, trained parallel with, and only inches above, the lake surface towards an area of tall reeds. Our shikara guide informed us that he was shooting wildfowl and that his weapon was a duck gun. It seemed a risky procedure with tourist shikaras around.

Then there were women collecting weed from the lake bottom. You only had to twirl a kinked pole in the water and lift it up, to find you'd hooked a bundle of damp lake weed. I wondered what it would be used for. Naipaul pointed out the many uses of Lake Dahl.

"...the lake was charted and regulated ...such regulations were necessary because the lake ...was rich. It provided for all. It provided weeds and mud for vegetable plots ... It provided fodder for animals. It provided reeds for thatching. It provided fish."[85]

And water fowl too apparently. We tourists were only just discovering how things worked here.

We were passing now from the main lake to smaller stretches of water. Eventually, after passing through the third of these, we reached the Mughal Garden, where we were to have our packed lunch. It was a beautifully planned garden, arranged on a gentle slope around a water course for tumbling pools and fountains, sadly dry at this time. Flowers made a colourful show - scented stocks, chrysanthemums, and plenty roses, attracting large butterflies, striped bumble bees and red dragonflies.

---

[85] *An Area of Darkness* (1995), page 112.

There were some magnificent trees too, the large maples turning autumnal red. All were set against a background of the surrounding hills and more distant mountain crags.

A dark maroon and white painted wooden pavilion, with two long balconies on the first and second floors, stood on the lower slope facing the lake and one of the best views to be had here. Across the water was a low curved bridge in the middle distance, beyond which the Durrani hill fort of Srinagar could be seen on the horizon. There had been fortifications here since 1590, built by the Mughal Emperor Akbar, whose reign coincided with Queen Elizabeth I's in England[86]. The present fort only dated from the early nineteenth century however. It was curious that among the houseboats and on our visit to the trading centres in town we had not been aware of this hill and fortress at all, and it seemed strange to get to know Srinagar better like this at a distance.

We were lucky to visit Nishat Mughal Garden in the seventies during a period of relative stability in Kashmir. Haenraets, Schwann and Hollingsworth (2010) note how at that time such places became a popular attraction for the increased numbers of visitors in Kashmir. We were witness to that, for we saw several Indian families admiring the floral displays while we were there. The women, in their bright saris, added yet more colour to the scene we enjoyed, once we'd gradually climbed the paved ways and steps to the terraces above.

In 1969 the local Department of Floriculture undertook improvements. They created more flower beds and formal rose gardens. Though these were naturally good moves, it did mean that some ... "existing structures and buildings were adapted or even removed ..."[87] A particular case they refer to is the demolition of buildings in the Nishat Mughul Gardens around 1975. This could refer, among other things, to the pavilion we saw in that year. It certainly does not appear in more recent photographs and I tend to agree with the authors that this is a shame and changes the atmosphere of the gardens. The pavilion gave an idea of how Emperors might have relaxed on the balconies there, using the setting as a perfect

---

[86] Finnemore (1915), page 33.
[87] *Paradise in Conflict* (2010), page 5.

summer retreat, much as the British were to use Kashmir in later centuries. Emperor Akbar is evidently credited with saying, "Kashmir is a garden; do not call it a country."

It's interesting to note that, according to Haenraets, Schwann and Hollingsworth, the Nishat Bagh, along with the Shalimar Bagh nearby (made famous by Laurence Hope's poem '*Pale hands I loved beside the Shalimar*' and the love lyric deriving from it), were included in the 2008 World Monument Fund List of 100 Most Endangered Sites. They were at risk because of the context of ongoing conflict in Kashmir, yet another area of the world that I have sadly found it difficult to re-visit.

Refreshed, we left in our shikaras and soon found ourselves drifting slowly through a weird area of narrow canals, tall trees on the banks reflecting linearly into the still clear water below. Then we were passing house backs and twisting between cabbage and cauliflower patches on water green with fallen leaves. We were approaching our end-point, the wood-carving factory. It was fascinating to watch the intricate decoration and finishing work done so expertly here. I bought a small box and a paper knife. I also asked for a carved elephant, which arrived very promptly during tea on our return. After this the evening passed pleasantly playing cards and chatting.

***   ***   ***

I rose at 8 o'clock next morning still a shade concerned about my health. It had been a warmer night but a fairly uncomfortable one as far as my digestive system was concerned. I was unhappy that the antibiotic (Thalozole - considered bad practice in the 21st century) hadn't helped me more by now. I decided to visit a chemist during our shopping expedition that morning.

Otherwise it was to be a day for spending. Before breakfast the shawl salesman appeared and I bought myself a rather lovely embroidered black number. Then the laundry man turned up again, returning work done and receiving more. But after breakfast we set off for the carpet factory, where I made my largest purchase. First we went in a taxi with Mr Gulam's son to the showroom of *Cheap John* Carpets. This name was typical of the ones used by local firms, involving as it did some word play recognisable and seen as amusing by English-speaking visitors. (Another example I heard of that very evening was told me by Jane, who as I was looking at carpets, had been buying a leather jacket from the firm *Honest Injun*.) There were the usual prayer rugs and large carpets on display, but also some medium sized rugs, the colours of which really appealed to me. Eventually I succumbed to buying one with lovely rich red and blue decorations upon a cream ground.

I'm afraid I didn't bargain a lot with the salesman and probably paid too much, just under £200. (For a start Bashir Gulam would probably have got commission on the deal, but I rather naively never thought of that.) I paid 300 Swiss Francs deposit in traveller's cheques and agreed that it should be shipped home to Leeds; I certainly couldn't carry it with me to Australia and New Zealand. I was rather surprised that instead of sending it to my parents' address, *Cheap John* Carpets wanted it sent to my branch of Barclays Bank in Leeds. I supposed that ensured it would be paid for, but I was going to have to warn my parents of this as soon as I could. As my father had worked for Barclays, he would have the manager's telephone number and be able to sort it out I was sure. As it turned out a puzzled manager got in touch with my father, who had not yet received my news. It caused quite a stir in my branch, and much amusement thereafter for all concerned.

It was only then that we visited the factory floor and saw how the carpets were made. If I had seen this first I might not have been tempted to buy, for the main workforce was child labour. Lines of three or four young boys were tying knots on the looms, their smaller fingers being very suitable for this delicate work. In the middle of each line was an adult experienced craftsman, encouraging, advising and keeping them close to the pattern required. The children didn't appear to be unhappy at their work; they showed interest in our visit and one of them waved to me cheerily. But they didn't look particularly well-nourished and they were missing out on their schooling. It made me feel guilty and I often wonder what happened to them in later life, as I view their work, the carpet still my pride and joy in the sitting-room of my home.

I went on from the Carpet Factory to the chemist's, a useful visit as they informed me that I had been taking half the dosage normally prescribed of Thalazole. No wonder it had not been having the desired effect. They suggested I try Streptotriads, which they had in stock. In retrospect I feel sure that all these non-specific antibiotics could have been prolonging my problems, but I was grateful for their advice at the time.

We returned for lunch and I lazed reading most of the afternoon, before playing cards for a while with the girls next door. Then at sunset, about six o'clock, I set off with Virginia to investigate the fireworks in the city centre. It was a Hindu holiday, Diwali I believe, the festival of lights. There were candles on the balconies of houses and along the shop fronts, and plenty explosions of jumping fire crackers everywhere around. This frightened Virginia quite a bit, so it wasn't long before we took a taxi back to the shikara quay and returned to the *Young Good Luck* for the, by now, habitual mutton and potato tea!

The rest of the evening was spent preparing to move onward towards our final destinations in Asia, though we weren't leaving Kashmir till the day after next. Ian called to check our visas: he was going to travel ahead of us to Delhi, to confirm future arrangements and verify everyone's air bookings and onward travel. He also told us of the opportunity to do a pony trip the next day into the surrounding hills to Gulmarg, a holiday settlement 3,000ft above the Vale of Kashmir. Our bluie sisters, Chloe and Alice, were interested in this, but the rest of us weren't riders, so decided to have a more restful day. I was rather envious of those going up there though, for I should have liked to explore the higher regions more.

Then I completed the day by packing the gifts I'd bought myself so that I could avail myself of Bashir Gulam's offer to see them safely to the post. My rucksack was becoming too heavy and this was an obvious way to lighten the load a little. It was just as well that I kept the gifts I'd bought for others with me, for sadly I was not to see those things I sent home again. As my carpet made it successfully to Leeds, I have to suspect that, rather than there being a fault with the postal system, Bashir never posted these other goods and possibly resold them. But I shall never know where they got to for certain.

To ensure that I was warm that night, and because I thought I might have glimpsed fleas in my bed, having experienced this on holidays before, I tucked myself in my sleeping bag when I went to bed. It made for a very nice and comfortable night's sleep.

***   ***   ***

I enjoyed another lazy lie-in next day, reading a Bertie Wooster story in bed before I got up just after 8am. There were nice boiled eggs for breakfast too. I was thoroughly enjoying this restful period in Kashmir.

The laundry arrived: how pleasant to be prepared to set out to explore India in really clean clothes! We then made for town with several chores to complete. Meg wanted to see a doctor and had learnt of one at the chemist's yesterday, so we took her there in a taxi from the shikara quay. Dr Dhar lived in a pleasant residential district; we were all taken into his consulting room, even the messenger too. There was no plinth or bed in the room, only chairs round a table. The European-looking old-school doctor examined Meg's nose and throat and quickly sounded her chest, all for 15 rupees. Then it was back to the chemist's for four lots of pills, which came to just over 18 rupees. Thus the treatment in all cost about £2.

We then continued in the taxi to the Punjabi National Bank, where we changed some travellers' cheques and, as usual these days, had a fair wait before we got our money. We next got a taxi to the post office, but as the taxi driver thought we'd asked for the 'Police HQ', or so he said, this too took a while longer than we'd expected. We were at least getting to see more of Srinagar in the process we supposed! I posted a birthday card to a cousin and postcards to my parents amongst others. On the way back to lunch we bought some real delicacies - satsumas and macaroons.

I followed this with a restful afternoon reading on our veranda. Then I remembered that I had some small debts to pay now I was 'in the money'. These went back to our journey, without being able to visit banks, in Afghanistan. Once these were settled, mostly in *Montreal*, I joined Jane, Liz, and Meg in paddling around between houseboats in a small craft the houseboys gave us, as Chloe and Alice had taken the shikara for their trip to Gulmarg.

I had found myself to be pretty dreadful with oars when living on Lake Geneva in Switzerland and I was no more of a success now. I kept going round in circles! But between us we managed to visit plenty of our friends. We chatted with Tim and Luigi, as well as Sue, Jim and Jan, and saw Mark and Lukas to wave to. The big news we learnt from them was that two of our party (Sabrina and Dieter) were going to stay on in Kashmir rather than continue to the end of the trip in Kathmandu. Apparently Dieter was ill. It was true that we had not seen him here at all, but he and Sabrina tended to keep themselves to themselves and I, for one, had not thought to check how they were doing.

Somehow we hadn't thought of anyone leaving our party and we were all a bit shocked and upset by this news. In discussing Kashmiri houseboat stays, however, Pullman points out that this was a quite common occurrence:

> "...backpackers on the hippie trail would often stay for a month at a time in this nirvana, and it's not hard to see why. A stay on a houseboat offers a wonderful place to relax as you quickly become attuned to the slow pace of life." [88]

We certainly agreed that a spell here had relaxed us and that it should be good for Dieter. But we rather questioned how he and Sabrina would continue their journey to New Zealand. Perhaps Ian was sorting this out amongst other business in Delhi.

We returned to the *Young Good Luck* to find a special final meal in preparation - a duck supper. It was brought in to some acclaim, but when the houseboy tried to carve it there were problems. He was showing off a very decorative carving knife and fork with the touristy papier-mâché handles we'd seen people selling. These looked very attractive, but we were amused to find that they were not good tools for dealing with our duck. Our laughter died a little when we found our exasperated houseboy ended up tearing the fowl apart with his bare hands. As Liz commented, after he had gone back to the kitchen quarters, "I hope he's washed his hands thoroughly since tending the stove earlier on!" It had to be said

---

[88] *The Houseboats of Kashmir* (2017).

though that even if the implements failed to come up to scratch, the duck at least was a success.

In the sitting room after our meal I took a photo of the houseboys round the fire, to their obvious delight. They had been friendly and helpful during our stay and they had also had to put up with a fair amount of 'Memsahib' treatment from Sarah, always embarrassing to the rest of us. "This toast is cold," was a common complaint at breakfast for example, one morning followed by, "And you're standing on my foot!" Our boy, Ahmed, had been reaching across her to place the tea on the table. "Well, pull your foot in out of the way", we muttered to Sarah, as Ahmed jumped back. I felt it couldn't be a very pleasant job dealing with tourists at times.

I then spent some time that evening packing those presents not already sent off with Bashir, by no means an easy task. My rucksack was becoming ever more unwieldy. I blessed the fact that I should be leaving some of the contents with friends in the Antipodes, and wondered if there would be room for any souvenirs bought during the remainder of our trip.

Then it was time for a lovely hot bath. I probably wasn't going to have the chance to enjoy such luxury again till Australia. What a thought! No wonder Dieter and Sabrina were keen to stay on here!

It's worth pointing out here that my thoughts were in direct contravention to Indian custom. I had yet to realise that soaking in a bath was not seen as a luxury in the east. In Britain at that time showers were relatively uncommon, but they were seen as the real way of getting thoroughly clean in India. Their attitude was "How filthy to soak in your own dirt in a bath!" It was necessary to wash away the dust and filth of a hot country. Bathe in a well-flowing river perhaps, but not in a bath. The houseboats were prepared for westerners, not the local population.

Last thing, I signed the visitors' book and noted that a fair number of physios had stayed in the *Young Good Luck*. I can't remember how I knew this. Perhaps there was a column for occupation or maybe they just signed their name with MCSP (Member of the Chartered Society of Physiotherapy) after it. It seems a strange thing to note in this way.

Things were nearly back to normal Encounter Overland routine as we rose at five next morning to breakfast at 6am. Sarah had caught cold and became very irritable with Mr Gulam over breakfast, having lost her voice. Once she was out of the room, I thanked Hadji Gulam and left a tip for him and the boys.

We set off in the shikara across a frosty lake, to the wharf near which our vehicles were parked. They had presumably been driven there the night before, because now it was found that our truck's fuel had frozen in its tank, so we were likely to be badly held up. We were supposed to leave at 7 o'clock but the hours passed slowly by as we hung around on the roadside until at last, the orange truck had to be towed away at 11am to get a complete change of fuel. It was an extremely cold wait, but not without interest.

For a start we discovered the local way of keeping warm when outside. We'd seen men wrapped in blankets around the streets of Srinagar, but hadn't realised that under their blanket might be hidden an excellent source of heat. Here on the quayside were plenty locals waiting for boats and other transport, and their favoured position was squatting, huddled in their blankets over something in their lap. This turned out to be mud-lined wicker charcoal braziers, their embers glowing and providing a pleasant warmth. We were tempted to see the contraption as a bit of a fire hazard but the Kashmiris were happy enough.

The whole scene was a kind of misty winter landscape, the locals gathered in their blankets, the westerners in parkas and scarves or hats, nearby tall trees rimy with frost and the smell of smoke in the foggy air, for in one or two places on the pavement people had actually gathered sticks and lit small fires. Gloria's cigarette lighter was made use of in one instance. It made me think of Bruegel's winter paintings, but without snow. Like those scenes though there were plenty people around. In fact there were probably more than usual on the wharf at the start of that particular day, for eventually a party of six people arrived who were setting off for Mecca on the hajj. They got a big send-off from their families and waiting friends.

When we realised that it would be a long wait, Virginia and I went to a nearby hotel with Alice for coffee and buttered toast, which was nice and warming. Several others had the same idea. Chatting to the Swiss girls I found they'd gone pony trekking to Gulmarg with Gloria: they waxed lyrical about the scenery up there, the snowy mountain peaks above and the view of Srinagar below, hundreds of houseboats jutting out into Lake Dahl. It made me quite envious, but also very excited to soon be seeing those mountains close up.

We returned to lunch off the blue truck, a rather pathetic effort in the circumstances. Some local cows refused to eat offerings of our luncheon meat, wise beasts, though to our surprise they were found to enjoy banana skins. Local women, poor souls, came and tried to buy the crockery before our washing up was done! At two o'clock it was at last decided to go back to the houseboats and we had a sunny, peaceful afternoon on the *Young Good Luck*. The only excitement was that our boy, Ahmed, managed to fall in the water at one point. He hauled himself out dripping to a very unsympathetic chorus from us of "He's fallen in the water!" Spike Milligan's well-known catchphrase from the 1950's *Goon Show*.

We had a pleasant evening receiving guests – first Cynthia and James; then Maddie, Ros and Michael, closely followed by Nazir, *Montreal*'s house boy. I got into conversation with Nazir on the pronunciation of Hindi and Maddie and I helped him read some English he wanted to translate. He was a simple-hearted, bright lad that had never been to school. He told us Ian had phoned. I asked him how Ian was. "Oh, well I think. I hope so - God bless him!"

During the evening I also had an enlightening discussion with Hadji Gulam on the similarities of Islam and Christianity. He believed Christ would return to earth: "How interesting", I said; "We believe that too." "Yes", he said, "He will go to Mecca, circuit the Kaaba the requisite seven times and rule earth for forty years." This was a bit of a conversation stopper as far as I was concerned. To each particular faith its rites and rituals. But I reckoned, and still believe, that we shared a belief in the same God, despite our differences.

*** *** ***

I slept that night in half my clothes as I only had hand luggage, my rucksack being installed in the orange truck's trailer already. We were woken promptly at 5.45 by Mr Gulam, and had boiled eggs for breakfast. Cynthia passed through on her way from *Green Mountain* to *Montreal* and told us that her and James' bed had collapsed during the night. After she'd left, Alice voiced what we were all thinking. "I can't say I'm surprised after what they've probably been up to in it!" General laughter. Camping near James and Cynthia's tent had given them quite a reputation with us all!

We were among the first to reach the quay - about 6.30. It was extremely cold, certainly colder than yesterday morning. And there was trouble with the orange truck once more. The drivers had to tinker with the engine and thaw it out after a false start. Ben helped James try to warm the diesel by lighting a fire under the truck's fuel tank. This gave Meg a dreadful shock: "What the hell are you doing? The whole thing will blow up!" she cried. It took quite an effort on Ben's part to explain and pacify her. I, for one, was all ears too for, like Meg, I'd never realised that this could be done with diesel, when it was so dangerous with a petrol engine. We finally left Lake Dahl at 8.40.

After two hours' ride through the Vale of Kashmir we started to climb. Soon we reached the Jawahar tunnel. We had gone three hundred yards or so into it, with a long queue of traffic behind us, when the orange truck suddenly conked out! There was panic as everyone searched for their torches, horns blared and Rob in the back with us cursed colourfully. I have no doubt that James was doing the same in the cab. Mayhem! It was ten long minutes before we re-started! Sad as I had been to leave Kashmir, I was thoroughly glad to reach the sunshine once more at the other end of that tunnel!

Chapter 18. Kwality India

Safely out of the Jawahar tunnel we set off back down the twisting descent towards the Indian plain. At the sharper corners in the route we were again amused to find roadside slogans prominently displayed. "Start early, drive slowly, arrive safely" and "We love our children. Do you?" were a couple of them. Good though the intention might be, we couldn't help thinking that distracting a driver like this from keeping his eyes on such an awkward road might be a mistake.

Lower down we came on a quite unexpected sight, a pipe band. Those playing the bagpipes and drums marched in time and held themselves very smartly erect. We wondered if perhaps they were Indian Army recruits, but they were not in uniform, nor were kilts or tartan in evidence, although they played Scottish music. Was this music popular in Northern India?

We lunched just off a bridge, while skinny dogs and ragged children scavenged around the tables with us. We wondered if this, a novelty for us, was to become more common in India. There were certainly more people around and more signs of poverty here than we'd seen up to now on our trip.

Then we continued on our way, climbing once more in lovely sunshine to reach a further pass. By the time dusk fell, however, we had had another breakdown or two! Finally arriving in Kud again, we all felt extremely jaded. We packed six into our room at the Guest House – Jane, Liz, Meg, Sarah, Virginia and me. We had a good tea, and then a lovely warm night!

We were up again at six to be off at 7am. When James suggested this, his goal was met with hollow laughter and even he had to prophesy it would be nearer 10am. He was very nearly spot on, for it was in fact 9.50 when we set out. We had again renewed our diesel completely. When our drivers investigated, they found leaves in the inspection tank: we had had very poor quality fuel in there in fact.

And once more the poverty of the locals had been drawn to our attention. The blue truck had gone to collect the requisite cans of diesel and on return Ben and James began emptying the orange truck's fuel into the roadside gutter preparatory to replacing it with the new fuel. This brought the whole neighbourhood out with cans, jam jars, anything in which to collect fuel. They were going to let nothing go to waste and started collecting it from the gutter, but Ben then aimed it into their containers: we had quite a queue.

At last we set off. I was travelling in the cab, James at the wheel. Alice was in the hot seat, and Dave, Abby and Luigi were behind with me. We travelled on for about an hour, getting quite far down the gorge, before we started breaking down again. While James and Ben tinkered with the engine, trying to sort things out, we descended to the road for a bit of exercise. At one point I actually found myself helping men to herd some water buffalo that were tending to go astray, phased by coming upon our vehicles in the track they normally took. Both my grandfathers had been countrymen, a farmer and a game-keeper: surely I had a little of this still in the genes!

When we lunched it was by a marshy pond. I enjoyed watching the frogs and bright red double-winged dragonflies, while I drank my cuppa. I was still having to be careful that I didn't eat much. A real nuisance!

Then we drove on down the valley to Jammu without incident and spent an hour looking round. Crossing the road to set off was already a challenge. There was quite a crush of pony and traps, multitudinous bicycles, and the odd moped or car. I tried to go to the bank, but it was closed to those wishing to change travellers' cheques, so I ended up window-shopping, beginning in the bazaar area. Here mostly clothes, linen and decorative tableware were on display. The vendors were usually men, the shoppers women. The latter, I was interested to find, often wore smart long dresses or fitted blouse and long skirt, as alternative options to the standard sari.

In minor roads we found stranger sights; for example, one chemist displayed a sign offering to test blood, sputum, stool and pretty much any bodily fluid. Then there were white holy cows wandering placidly everywhere, as we'd been told there might be, searching the gutters for titbits. More attractive to me though were quite a few good second-hand book shops. I noticed a copy of the Koran, and glanced through the opening passages. More inviting though was a paperback copy of *The Pass beyond Kashmir*, an adventure yarn by Berkely Mather (the pseudonym of John Evan Weston-Davies). I'd never heard of the author, but the title was promising, considering our recent experiences. I bought it.

We camped not far from Jammu on the common, circling the tents round the trucks, as Maddie commented, "North American pioneers gathered round their wagons packed with valuable goods." This was not too good an analogy though, for of course we had our belongings in our rucksacks in the tents with us.

***   ***   ***

Next morning we were up at five, and finally left at a quarter past six. I hadn't had much help from Virginia and told her off for leaving me to deal with the tent. It was still dark, day-break happening around 7am at that point, and I guess we were both having trouble returning to the routine we'd accepted as normal before our relaxing break in Kashmir.

Gold and crimson daylight spreading across the eastern horizon as the sun rose, we drove through long grass and scrub: it wasn't hard for me to imagine tigers peering out at us from between the tall fronds by the roadside. (I'd been reading the story of a man-eating tiger in a paperback of Tim's.) But my romantic imaginings were brought to earth by the condition of the road. The monsoon rains of a couple of months back had eroded the surface so that it was worn down to just stones in places, making for quite rough and bumpy going.

In the back of the orange truck we waxed philosophical. People were interested in the glimpses we'd had of religions other than Christianity. Scott was as ever keen to discuss Buddhism, while Maddie broadened the topic to general discussion of man's origins. Had our race landed from another planet? She spoke of various thoughts to do with South America and the so-called Nasca Lines in Peru. I had never heard of these and neither had Scott: we chatted happily on this intriguing subject for some time. I know I referred to C.S.Lewis' science fiction novel *Out of the Silent Planet*, in which Earth is viewed as the only planet not communicating with the others in our solar system.

But we were jolted back to earth again as we reached Pathankot in the Punjab. We were still quite near to the Pakistan border, about a third of our way from Srinagar to Delhi and this was a busier city than any we had seen since Iran, with plenty traffic even this early in the morning. Bollywood stars smiled down temptingly from huge posters set high alongside road junctions, and gaudily coloured hotels lined the main thoroughfares, but as our progress slowed in the narrow streets I became fascinated by the sights around us. Outside some old brick houses a man was washing himself at a pump in the street and another was cleaning his teeth. Others cleared their throats noisily and spat the resultant phlegm in the gutter. All life seemed to occur on Indian pavements ... well, life we would have kept to ourselves in the west. Weren't there bathrooms in their houses?

Sikh boys with white top knots and girls in white saris were making their way to school, while a woman shuffled past carrying a huge bundle of straw on her head. There were khaki- coloured army vans in the traffic passing us and avoiding tactics had to be taken to circuit a tricycle cart having its tyre inflated on our side of the road. A nearby shop had by far the filthiest awning I had seen yet, but walking by it were gracefully slim women wearing gloriously colourful green and red saris. And the whole while you couldn't help but note the all-pervading savoury scents of spicy food. It was a rich and varied scene, scents and sights locating us very definitely in the Indian sub-continent.

Then we were out in the countryside once more, passing one of several large river basins we were to see during that morning, branches of the great River Indus. People had set up ramshackle bamboo shelters where they left their things while they bathed in the broad river. The strip of sand we could see was crowded with people and bundles of their possessions here too.

We had a forty minute stop in Jullundur. I found the post office and proceeded to post a letter to my parents. As usual now it seemed, this was not entirely straight forward. The letter had to be weighed at another counter before they would stamp it. Meanwhile I noted the advice given to customers in some very wise signage. "Avoid rumours and loose talk" urged the first notice, set up just along the counter from me, and "A soft answer turns away wrath" stressed a second, hanging above the official serving me. This seemed a very apt saying in a country where officialdom could be so frustrating.

We had our lunch stop by the road, in hot sunshine. I sought the shade of a tree and relaxed there. Before we got going once more, I ventured into a nearby cane crop for my 'big squat' (this being an expression habitually used by James, who turned his trousers up to the length of long shorts, "ready for the big squat" as he put it!) Even this very mundane procedure had an exotic twist now: large insects rustled the cane leaves above me! Might there be snakes here?

We had a milk stop mid-afternoon at another of the UNICEF-aided projects. The milk bar was surrounded by lovely green lawns, with parasols set out over seats. I'd only tried the vanilla-flavoured milk before, but now attempted a little milk cake too, cheesecake almost – sweet, dry, and vanilla-flavoured like the milk on sale. I was fairly confident that these products would do me good.

We passed Ambala in the late afternoon and drew just off the road into the trees to camp. It made for a noisy night, as we were between the road and the railway!

***   ***   ***

We were up again at five o'clock and off just after six. The routine was returning, and on our washing-up day too, when our little cooking group sometimes felt things seemed to go extra slowly. Bluie Gloria put it nicely: "We're actually five minutes ahead of schedule, as we're usually a quarter of an hour late!"

The countryside continued much the same meanwhile. The scenery was flat plain with plentiful jungle grass on either side, interrupted intermittently with small rather seedy townships with wide lorry-parked verges. I began the day reading some of *The Pass beyond Kashmir*, the Berkely Mather novel I'd acquired. It was set in Bombay, with good local touches, an amusing conglomeration of the negative things we had noticed in the country so far. I commented in my diary that the author too had apparently noticed the hawking and spitting chorus in the mornings and after siesta, as well as the smells and filth.

I think it's fair to say that there was general disappointment among us at what we had seen of India since commencing our journey towards Delhi. Cockney Sue commented that streets in India often seemed to resemble the meaner streets of the poorer areas of London and Ros, who knew the north of England better, said they reminded her of dingy parts of Newcastle. Several of our fellow travellers agreed and I certainly recognised what she was talking about. We described these poorer streets as 'grotty'. We had been led to expect an environment that was, idiosyncratic perhaps, but definitely far more exotic, and I have found since that other travellers, such as Naipaul, approaching cities in India for the first time, would have agreed with us:

> "...nothing I had read or heard had prepared me for the red-brick city on the other side of Howrah Bridge [Calcutta] which, if you could ignore the stalls and rickshaws and white-clad hurrying crowds, was at first like another Birmingham."[89]

The question was, had the British caused India to look like this or had the Indians once more somehow mimicked the colonial life-style and left their own behind?

The sun came up, a misty red, seeming to be reflected by the red dust of the bricks edging either side of the long straight roads. James had to veer from time to time onto this verge to avoid oncoming lorries driving over-fast seemingly straight towards him. More unsettling still, after one of these erratic moments of steering those sitting over the tailpin witnessed a pedestrian being knocked down by one of the speeding trucks after it had passed us. We didn't think the man was too dangerously hurt. We had become accustomed by now to the common sight of a man trudging with the aid of a long cane, along the margins of the road to get from one town to another. The truck had caught his cane a glancing blow, causing the man to lose his balance. It worried us that the driving could be this erratic though.

---

[89] *An Area of Darkness* (1995), page 264.

Then the road widened, and there were pavements once more, high walls and pleasant houses. We had reached the outskirts of Delhi. I was impressed by the lovely buildings, the parks, and the beautiful saris of the women we saw now. This was more what I had been expecting of India. We reached New Delhi and our camp site just after 10am, to be greeted by Ian from whom we received our mail, my parents' letter and one from a cousin, a lovely surprise.

But it was our cooking day so there was shopping to be done. This proved to be a problem, as I wrote in my diary:

> Sarah was an absolute PAIN! She complained of having to cook, as the bluies aren't, and left me to go and get what vegetables I could manage to find.

The bluies were going to sight-see and cater for themselves, but our lot still expected lunch. Sarah was unhappy to have her time seeing Delhi curtailed and Virginia tended to side with her. I was thoroughly fed up with the pair of them and stalked off in indignation. I hadn't got far along the road though when I heard feet pounding to catch me up. It was Tim. I was extremely grateful for his help and we got lunch sorted for noon.

By this time it was really hot and Tim and I treated ourselves to a drink and a mango ice cream, from a stall in the camp site area – Kwality's – real luxury, for Ian had told us that Kwality ice cream was the only brand to trust in India! I followed this by doing some washing and then indulged in the second luxury of a shower. There was a bit of a wait for this luxury though, but I whiled the time away watching chipmunks in the surrounding trees!

Returning to the tent I found Virginia had returned repentant, and she came with useful information on a way to explore the major sights in a reasonably short time. Motorcycle taxis, the so-called phut-phuts, could evidently be hired in the locality. She led the way to Connaught Circus, the circular road near our parkland camping area, famed as the shopping and business hub of Delhi. It was thronged with people, but sure enough there were some phut-phuts charging 25 rupees for an hour's worth of sight-seeing. These vehicles, open at the sides but covered above, accommodated two people on the seat behind the motorcyclist driver out front. We clung on for dear life and in this way dodged briskly through the traffic and out into the quiet, wide boulevard of the Rajpath.

It was glorious weather, bright and clear and there was India Gate, Lutyens' great arched memorial to the soldiers of the British Indian Army that died in the First World War, reminding me of the Arc de Triomphe in Paris. Then another circus of a road ran round the more slender arched canopy of the memorial to King George V and the parliament buildings appeared in their elaborate grandeur on either side. There were hardly any vehicles about, making it very different to the busy centre of the city, where vague clouds of smoky haze on the horizon showed the pollution which has since become far more of a problem in Delhi.

Our driver next drove us to a Sikh temple, a rather lovely ornate white building, but with two extra attractions in its grounds. Near the arched entrance to the temple grounds a snake-charmer had staked out his territory. This was a sight we were to see more than once in the next few days, often regarded as part of the Indian street experience. However I have since learnt that the Indian government passed a law in 1972 banning the ownership of snakes. Although I can vouch for this being rarely strongly enforced at first, it appears now that snake-charming is becoming a thing of the past.[90]

The charmer squatted before the snake basket blowing his strange 'pungi', a long woodwind instrument with a globular enlarged section just above the finger holes, traditionally made by hollowing out a small gourd and attaching it to the pipe's reed, we were later told. At its whining tones the snake in its basket rose curvaceously, moving as though to dance to the music it heard. It was not a particularly beautifully patterned creature and almost certainly not venomous, but rather graceful to watch, while still unnervingly reminiscent of pictures I'd seen of a cobra, hood-spread, ready to strike.

The other attraction was more questionable in our eyes, a man making a monkey do a dance in a veil! The poor animal didn't look happy and it

---

[90] Flintoff (2011).

seemed to us a peculiar sight in a temple precinct, something more appropriate in a side-show at a fair or circus. Of course the same thing could have been said of the snake-charmer, but somehow he appeared to show the snake more respect than did the other man his monkey.

I also noted something else as we left the scene; an obviously well off couple went past us leaving the temple. How did we know their financial status? Partly from their clothes, as we would have guessed at home in the West too, the man being smartly dressed in a dark suit and turban: but more significantly the woman was plainly overweight, an absolute rarity as far as we had seen so far in this part of the world. We had exclaimed already a number of times at how skinny and ill-nourished some of the poor folk in towns in India appeared, particularly the children. To see a sturdy, plump woman in such an environment was quite a shock: she had to be wealthy. We were rapidly learning that there was a considerable difference between rich and poor in this country.

On we were then taken to the beautiful Lakshmi Narayan temple, with its tastefully coloured marble décor. Dedicated to the Hindu god Vishnu and his consort, Lakshmi goddess of wealth and prosperity, it boasted three slender towers typical of a Hindu temple, though unusually rich yellow and terracotta in colour. Terraces ran around their bases like cream foam, with the odd decorated wooden balcony added at first floor level. It was perhaps because,

> "The temple was inaugurated by Mahatma Gandhi with the condition that the site would be open to all castes and faiths"[91],

that our phut-phut driver had included it in our trip round, but it was definitely one of the most attractive places we visited in that hour. We removed our shoes and wandered among several Indian families that were also visiting.

I was particularly attracted to a statue of an elephant. Standing on a low dais, the animal was raising a globular vessel above its head with a great curve of its trunk and seemed to be smiling, an effect achieved by carved

---

[91] *The Bold and Beautiful Laxmi Narayan Temple* (2020).

lines across its cheeks. I wasn't the only person to be attracted to the statue. A small child was hugging its leg, strongly resisting any return to his mother, despite her calls. It became a focus for photographs and was added to my collection.

Leaving our driver back in Connaught Circus we walked across Central Park and heard familiar music; another pipe band was playing. This was definitely music the Indians appreciated it seemed (indeed there were "an estimated 300 pipe bands in India" in the 1980s[92]), perhaps because the drone element is common to both the Scottish and Indian traditions. This time though, an unusually syncopated background drum beat was added. For their performance in the capital's main park the members of this band, unlike the one we had seen returning from Kashmir, were in uniform - white, belted tunics over black trousers and very colourful red, yellow and black patterned turbans – an attractive show to watch.

But we needed to get back to the camp site. We stopped at the Kwality stall again for a snack though. Tonight was to be one of our meals out on Encounter and it was going to be later than usual. We were going to the son et lumiére show at the Red Fort at 8pm and would go on to the restaurant from there. Ever a popular venue, we had to queue round the side of the small restaurant Kwality ran, alongside the ice cream stall. A lad behind me in the queue noticed a bit of string hanging down from behind the poster advertising the various ices for sale. "What's that?" he asked his mate, and pulled the string. To his, and our, horror a rat shot off skittering over the roof: he had just pulled its tail! It did make us question for a moment what we were doing, but I'm afraid it didn't stop us buying our Kwality products in the end! We enjoyed an extremely nice ice cream milk shake each, and then returned to the camp to change and collect money for our evening out. It was a surprise to be told that it only cost 7 rupees for the show at the Red Fort.

We arrived late though, as it started at 7.30 not 8pm as we'd thought. Quickly we crept in the half-dark to our seats. It turned out to be an interesting show, telling us a lot about the history of the Mughal dynasty. On the other hand it worried me considerably, for it seemed pretty biased

---

[92] *Bagpipes in India* (1987).

against the British. Up to then I had rather thought of England's role in India as being mainly a force for good, introducing useful law and order to the country. I had thoughtlessly supposed that the Indians would be grateful to be the 'Jewel in the Crown' of our Empire. It was obvious I had plenty to learn on that score.

We went on to the Moti Mahal restaurant, and found ourselves the only non-Indians in the place, a good sign of authenticity in a tourist area. They had lovely chicken dishes – half tandoori, half pokhara chicken (fried in batter) along with warm bread, onions and other vegetables and hot spicy sauce. I had lemon soda to drink. We ate with our fingers and finished by rinsing them in lemon water. Liquorice seeds (very tasty as a sweet titbit after the main course) and also tooth picks were provided. On returning to the camping, I indulged in a wonderful pineapple Kwality ice cream. I had eaten more today than I had in weeks. Things were looking up.

***   ***   ***

I awoke to the cries of parakeets and got up at 6.45 to get started on a huge 'Last breakfast in Delhi' – fried bread, a slice of ham, two fried eggs and two tomato halves per person! [93] Restricting myself to an egg and a cuppa as I served, I enjoyed a Kwality choco-nut ice later. Ian was late, so we made his separately. He got a real telling off from Sarah for not staying longer in Delhi and this caused factions to form. I really disliked this sort of thing and hurried away to our tent.

Virginia and I packed, stowed the tent and rucksacks, and then, sun-lotioned and be-hatted as it was fairly hot, joined those ready to leave in the blue truck around 9.15. We were to be picked up again after lunch to travel on. We had coffee in Connaught Circus and I then went to Iraqi Airlines with Virginia to try to sort out her ongoing flights after Kathmandu. She was not particularly satisfied though. Next we went to Qantas in the Janpath Hotel, where I booked provisionally for flights between Melbourne, Tasmania and Auckland. This went well, but as we left we were neatly caught out by a shoe shine boy, who threw polish on to Virginia's sandal so that he could clean it and then tore the sandal

---

[93] See photograph on page 172.

taking it off! It was still wearable, but not surprisingly Virginia was thoroughly fed up. The boy certainly got no money from us!

We went on to Cook's in the Imperial Hotel, where I tried to change my Swiss travellers' cheques. The cashier told me he really liked my sun hat (the Florentine concertinaed job) but refused to cash the cheques! I hadn't expected to find any resistance to changing cheques in a currency which at the time was definitely stronger than the pound. To comfort ourselves a little we visited the Imperial Hotel's ladies' room – magnificent luxury! We prayed fervently that no-one would come in and, I'm sorry to have to confess that we quickly washed our hair with some of their very nice free shampoo. We hadn't smelt so good in weeks! I was glad of my hat which covered my wet hair nicely and Virginia had a comb in her money belt, so we were able to look reasonably neat, if a shade damp, as we smartly exited the premises.

We went to and fro then between Connaught Circus and Iraqi airlines again, bartering hard with taxis to make sure they charged us the regulation 2 rupees Ian had told us to expect and not the 5 rupees a couple of drivers tried to overcharge us. All this was to organise Virginia's travel, which she found took some argument.

But there was still the issue of the travellers' cheques, so next we went to the State Bank of India. Here they pocketed my camera at the door ("Is forbidden take photos in bank"), and it seemed a poor sign when the Indian gentleman ahead of me in the queue was clearly dissatisfied with the cashier's dealings with him. I listened in awe as he verbalised his frustrations (in English – one of India's 5% Brahmin elite perhaps), glancing in my direction every now and then as though I would surely agree with him. Eventually he left looking exceedingly aggrieved - "Oh, there is no getting any sense out of you people!" and I moved into the firing line ... to be complimented on my sunhat once more! The cashier solidly refused to change Swiss travellers' cheques however. I began to thoroughly agree with the previous customer. What was wrong with these banks?

Virginia left me in order to fix her flights properly and I continued to Grindley's Bank which I saw just down the road. This was providential, for I had found that Grindley's was actually named in the folder carrying my Swiss travellers' cheques as one of the banks that was bound to cash them. However, it still seemed difficult. "Why?" I asked. "Oh", was the response, "Is having to go over the sea and then mountains - big botheration!" the man sighed deeply. Then with a winning smile, "I am liking your hat, memsahib." Enough of this, I thought, and showed him the information in the cheque folder. To my relief he then ruefully accepted the 'botheration' and I even got a good rate. It was then that I remembered that I had left my camera at the State Bank and had to return to collect it from the doorman. What a palaver!

By this time it was 1.30. I went to Kwality and joined some of the others for grilled sandwiches and a chocolate sundae before 2pm, when we met the truck in Connaught Place and were soon on our way again. I quenched my thirst with one of some oranges Virginia had bought (strangely still looking unripe, green in fact, but very juicy). She was still worried about her later travel arrangements, but I have to say I was feeling good, the 'botherations' done away with. It was a lovely sunny day and we had the exciting prospect of some really important places to see in the next day or two.

Chapter 19. Mausolea and Erotica

As we travelled on though, we became aware that all might not be so good with Ian. He seemed to be driving rather faster than usual: surely Sarah hadn't put him in that much ill humour. We whisked past an elephant and, as we were all gazing fascinated at its rump, the trailer ran over a water buffalo's leg! It was horrible for Peg in the end seat, sitting there because she wasn't feeling well, to see this incident so close up. But the water buffalo was up again in two seconds, so it was hopefully OK. The conversation then ran on what might have happened if the animal had been a holy cow!

We drove on to visit the tomb of Akbar the Great, an important Mughal architectural gem, but reached it as dusk fell. Sadly it was too late to explore the site properly, the place now being closed to visitors: perhaps Ian had been driving fast to try and beat this deadline. However the arched gateway was impressive enough. It had the look of a triumphal arch again, with two-storey wings on each side, and a minaret at each corner of the structure. We could just see that the marble decoration was extremely intricate. It was our first tantalising glimpse of the rich examples of Islamic art that we were to see in the next few days, more than one linked to Emperor Akbar, probably greatest of the Mughal emperors.

We had a drink and continued to the camp site, Drive Inn, just past Agra. It wasn't until the tent was up that we noticed the blocked sewer smell! I then washed and to my surprise found galvanic current flowed with the water from the tap. It gave a nice little shock!

And we of the orange truck received another shock over tea. Sharon had left the trip that day. I didn't know bluie Sharon well, except as the person who had advocated the antibiotics that I had taken, but what little I did know of her made me less surprised by her absence. A Londoner, she had appeared a thoroughly city-loving girl, who didn't always seem at one with the rural aspects of the trip. Delhi must have made her feel really at home. Since then I have occasionally wondered if Ian found she was taking drugs: it would have explained his mood and her brusque departure. All we did know was that now we were without our designated nurse.

But it had been a tiring day and we had a packed sight-seeing programme tomorrow. I for one was ready for bed, and I slept well, despite the background odours, and occasional initial gasps and squeals from the washroom as my fellow travelling companions experienced the odd enlivening electric shock!

Next morning we were up at six to be off soon after seven. Our shopping stop was on the outskirts of Agra, where there was a very lively and crowded market arcade. Vegetables were displayed in huge wickerwork baskets, the salesmen to the fore wielding their scales, so that customers could put their chosen potatoes or onions in to be weighed. It was extremely photogenic, but I was equally attracted to the apparently underfed holy cow eyeing up the pomegranates in a handcart just outside. I wondered what percentage of takings market stall keepers allowed for the feeding of these street beasts.

There was a snake charmer out on the pavement here too. In fact there were two men working this time, one piping his wailing note, as Virginia and I had seen at the Sikh temple in Delhi, and the other providing hand drum accompaniment, the background rhythm adding a certain air of tension to the action. By now I had gathered that this was one of those jobs in India that someone did for life, and that it probably depended on caste too. As James Cameron writes,

> "In India the educated [or those of a higher caste such as Brahmins] may do many things, run many businesses, diversify and prosper, but the baser workers are specialists of the most precise and narrow kind; the more menial the task the more exclusive its nature."[94]

So these men were specialists in their work and I'm not sure they valued our presence that day. It was just as we were leaving town that we drew alongside them and Ian stopped the truck knowing we'd want to take photographs, whereupon the audience, which included a fair number of children, rather lost interest in the snakes and gazed at us instead. I wasn't sure we should find it complimentary to be considered more alluring than a snake, but that's how it appeared!

---

[94] *An Indian Summer* (1974), page 40.

We continued to Fatehpur Sikri, an elaborate red sandstone walled city that we were told had been Emperor Akbar's capital for only fourteen years (from 1571 to 1585) before it was abandoned for lack of water. (I have since found this to be slightly inaccurate. It continued as a city, though the water supply was never very good, until Akbar died there in 1605 after which it was abandoned, as a city of little importance now he was gone.) But why had Akbar moved the court from the established city of Agra to build a new capital at the village of Sikri 25 miles away, equivalent to a full day's march distant? One story went that Akbar had consulted a Sufi saint there who had correctly foretold the birth of an heir to the Mughal throne. Akbar decided to build a mosque at Sikri in thanksgiving for this, and he ended up creating much more.

However Richards explains the situation further in *The Mughal Empire*: Agra and Fatehpur Sikri were in reality joint capitals.

> "The newly constructed city bore a similarity to the moveable imperial encampment also designed by Akbar. Fatehpur Sikri was an urban form in transition between camp and imperial metropolis."

It was a useful refuge. In dire circumstances "the court, harem and treasury could be quickly removed to Agra for safety". It was also "a courtly city whose architecture and public spaces were very much an expression of the young ruler's passion for building and design."[95] Indeed the place, now eerily empty except for tourists and their guides, was obviously beautifully constructed and had a sense of harmony, Akbar's personal idea of harmony. Agra was already established and Akbar had a wish, I think, to make of Sikri something absolutely his. After his death it had become overgrown by the surrounding jungle but now, mostly restored from the invasion of nature, was amazingly intact and serene.

V.S.Naipaul relates how a travel agent in the foyer of his Delhi hotel querulously asked him, "Why do you want to go to Fatehpur Sikri? There is *nothing* there."[96] There is very much something there. An abandoned city reawakened is full of memories and I got a feeling of this as I

---

[95] *The Mughal Empire* (1995), page 29.
[96] *An Area of Darkness* (1995), page 217.

wandered round. The stone was warm under our feet; the marble pillars supporting arcades much cooler. It would be reasonably pleasant in the summer heat. Just as an ancient piece of music conjures up an atmosphere of the past so this fortified city on a hill, with its terraced slopes where homes and gardens had once been, created an atmosphere of past Mughal times.

I walked downhill, accompanied by Jane and Liz, to take a closer look at the so-called Elephant Tower by the city wall, built to commemorate the life of a favourite war elephant. The tower walls appeared prickled with thorns at a distance. Close to, the thorns turned out to be stone projections carved to resemble elephant tusks. We climbed the spiral staircase inside the tower and got an excellent view of the whole site from that vantage point. Around us were the green flashes and strange cries of parakeets and peacocks flitting above the jungle-overgrown buildings at the periphery of the site. Yes, the place had real atmosphere.

I returned up the hill to buy a couple of postcards and was groped in passing by one of the guides! Was it my sun hat again that was attracting him? I hurried after the others back to the truck, and we soon left for the Taj Mahal.

Several of us had not heard of Fatehpur Sikri before, but all of us had seen pictures and heard of the Taj, a beautiful mausoleum generally regarded as one of the wonders of the world today. When he heard such praise Naipaul became very cynical:

> "...it is only a despot's monument to a woman, not of India, who bore a child every year for fifteen years. It took twenty-two years to build; and the guide will tell you how many millions it cost."[97]

To his mind the time and money could have been spent to improve the lot of the Indian population. His complaint was that India had never been conquered for the real benefit of the Indians. It rankled with Naipaul too that Mumtaz Mahal, for whom the Taj was erected, was not even Indian, but from an aristocratic Persian family. In 1975 I and my friends never

[97] *An Area of Darkness* (1995), page 220.

considered this I'm afraid. We were simply excited to see what we understood to be Shah Jahan's romantic memorial to his beloved wife.

We approached the Taj, passing large schools and offices, long veranda-fronted buildings, to reach a tree-lined road near the River Yamuna, where we parked in the shade, along with rickshaws full of colourful Indian ladies. The Taj Mahal stood white and gleaming beyond a red sandstone outer courtyard and gates. I found it a truly wonderful place and we all gazed in admiration at this glorious mausoleum.

We walked the length of the long narrow pool in front of the building, its white central dome's reflection shimmering there. As we drew nearer I saw that what I had imagined was pure white marble was actually highly decorated in subtle coloured designs. At the last pool before we reached the doorway into the Taj's interior I was delighted to find an Indian family had decided to rest on a marble bench. They and their reflections in front of the building made an ideal photograph. The great domed crown of marble, flanked by its slender minarets was a superb backdrop for the subdued colours of the seated ladies' saris and the grey and cream of their menfolk's clothing alongside.

We mounted the steps to the doorway to take a closer look at the mosaic frescos in the marble of the walls. Beautifully entwined vines and flowers were traced around the arched entrance and delineated in the carved marble blocks of the mausoleum. We walked through the main archway and into the cenotaph chamber. It had struck us, as we entered, that today was actually November 11th, Armistice Day in Britain, a day of ceremony at our own national cenotaph, but of-course this chamber's cenotaphs were not military. A central slim-line one was for Mumtaz Mahal and a larger one that for Shah Jahan himself, with beautiful floral decoration on the glistening marble. The whole was enclosed by an intricately fretted marble screen. An ornamental lamp hung above, made of silver, gold, copper and brass: it had been presented by Lord Curzon, the Viceroy of India at the start of the twentieth century.

This upper chamber was for show only however. To see where the actual tombs were we went down to the crypt area. Incense sticks were set in the walls but the lower chamber was not open to the public. Walking the cool marble corridors was pleasant relief after the heat outside, but soon we exited the Taj once more to lunch in the park nearby, after which I returned to buy a few postcards. Once again this was a different experience to what I expected, but in a pleasanter way this time. A young boy was riding an Atlas bike as I approached the stall. I watched him with obvious interest and he surprised me by offering me a ride. I accepted with thanks and had a quick ride to ensure I hadn't forgotten the art: not at all bad! It helped me decide, once in Kathmandu, to hire a bike there to help with my sight-seeing. (I had enjoyed cycling at the weekend and on holiday at home, and on my return to England I was to cycle to work for a number of years, rather than learn to drive).

Back at the truck once more, it was time to make the short journey into Agra to explore the Red Fort. As its name suggested it was constructed of a dark red sandstone, and looked very much the fortress, four-square and strong. Nice and cool though it was in the arcades round the central courtyard, we soon climbed to higher levels to see the views. At first we looked round on our own, but several of us soon realised that a party just ahead had an excellent guide. Following him as discreetly as possible, we reached the point in one of the towers where we could see the Taj Mahal in the distance, down the Yamuna river.

We were surprised to learn from the guide that Shah Jahan had been put under house arrest up here by Aurangzeb, one of his younger sons, for the last eight years of his life. It seemed to be a very disloyal way to treat one's father, but it had to be remembered that Shah Jahan himself had begun his reign by killing his brothers and their male heirs.[98] Such were the customs of Mughal royalty! In fact Aurangzeb had shown himself kinder than most. In one respect indeed he was extremely thoughtful. He had a diamond fixed in place on one of the pillars of the tower to reflect the image of the Taj so that his father, whose sight was failing, could still see the memorial he had erected to the love of his life.

We were told there had once been a tunnel connecting the Fort to the Taj, but gathered that it was never used by Shah Jahan in his situation of house arrest. This tunnel was eventually blocked by the British for fear of the

---

[98] *Shah Jahan* (2009).

cobras living down there. The British also did work to replace the precious stones that had originally been part of the Fort's decoration, but which had been stolen. These they replaced with semi-precious stones that shine in moonlight when it lights up the walls. We went on to the small plain marble mosque and then to the audience chamber, where the acoustics were such that it was possible to hear the guide strike a match from quite a distance away. We chatted with him afterwards, a very interesting man, and then got side-tracked by ices for sale. I had a choc ice and a milk drink with nuts; I was getting used to these lovely treats. I hoped the ice cream was up to the standard of Kwality's!

We left Agra to drive towards the ferry over the Chambel. There was a slender bridge crossing the river here, but its central three arched section had collapsed and sunk two years before; hence the ferry trip. However we found a truck had got stuck on the far side - not a very good omen. It required heavy work to recover it, which meant our journey would have to be tomorrow. So we returned to the local Dak bungalow for the night. Built by the British, these were originally post houses, but now more commonly act as country guest houses. This one was in a lovely setting. We camped on the lawn under trees with startlingly white bark, which Scott informed us were gum trees, new to me then.

I ate a good tea, though still suffering from mild diarrhoea. Ian tickled me in the ribs and told me not to get a tan or I'd be taken for an Indian! Indeed I wish I'd been able to weigh myself for I think I was the lightest then that I've ever been. But a corner had been turned health-wise I felt. I yodelled with Heidi and Hannah, the Swiss girls, in the shower; then wrote some postcards before joining Virginia in our tent. We agreed that it had been an amazing day.

***   ***   ***

When we started to take our tent down early next morning we found a squashed, but still hopping, frog underneath! I'd had a similar find when camping near a river in France, but somehow hadn't expected to experience this in India. Again we would have expected something more exotic... but were delighted it wasn't!

After breakfast we moved off towards the ferry once more. I travelled in the cab, James driving: Lucas was in the hot seat, Jim and Sue, myself and Luigi sitting behind. At the ferry we waited for a load of water buffaloes to cross with their herdsmen. The bulls had wonderfully curved horns, but the cows appeared remarkably downcast, perhaps because their ears and heads hung down. Without due reason, for they were plump and appeared healthy enough, I felt sorry for them.

But as I watched their passage I began to feel sorry for our drivers too. We got out of the trucks and went over first, and even without the vehicles' weight we seemed pretty low in the water. Then the ferry returned for each truck and its driver in turn. Unsurprisingly the whole procedure drew quite a crowd. When the orange truck arrived it looked to have had a pretty hazardous crossing for the trailer was almost in the drink! The disembarkation planks the trucks were going to come down didn't appear too strong either, but I was amused to see Ian and Rob jumping up and down on them to test their strength. The planks were to take about 11 tons or so of weight with the truck and trailer as they rolled onto the river bank from the ferry, so Ian and Rob's perhaps combined 28 stone at most wasn't much of a test! However the operation went unexpectedly well, and we were soon on our way again.

We were now driving south, aiming for Gwalior, one of the oldest cities in India with a noted fortress. The region appeared prosperous, with well-kept cornfields and plenty palm trees. I also noticed some strange creatures though. There must have been a recent animal kill in the area for we saw a whole field covered with vultures, grim looking birds of prey that they are. I also noted in my diary that I saw 'Painted and peacock-plumed cows'. They sound weird enough to remember, but I cannot for the life of me say what these were ... decorations somewhere or real cattle? Very peculiar, and sadly my memory is no help with this entry!

Gwalior is a railway junction, so it's not so strange that we saw an old steam train going past at one point in our journey that day. Stranger to us westerners was the sight of women washing and slapping clothes on the stones by a slime-covered pool. As in Afghanistan we found it incredible that these women achieved the pristine whiteness of a lot of the clothing we had seen, for the waters where they did their laundry were anything but clean.

Then James took us down the wrong road and Ian, sitting in the back of the orange truck, signalled him to stop and took over to get us through Gwalior. However, this route seemed to bypass the shops, which didn't please the cooks! Then we went over an unsigned, vicious speed reducing hump. We were thrown every which way in the cab, but it was worse for Helen, the bluie, who was in the back of our truck that day with her husband, Stephen. He rang us to stop, for she had hit her head on a ceiling bar as she was thrown upwards. The bump had also resulted in the smashing of two bottles of beer! Poor Helen wasn't seeing double, but had quite a lump on her head following this debacle. As the blue truck was following us and Ben had seen what had happened, he was able to slow sufficiently.

We continued past a large military academy and the road then inexplicably narrowed to the width of the truck, so that it was a battle of wills between Ian and other drivers as to who left the road! We'd met this game of 'chicken' before, vehicles driving straight at each other and then nipping quickly to the side at the last moment, onto the red brick verge to avoid a collision. It made for an exciting ride up in the cab, but can't have helped Helen's head feel any better and certainly shook everyone up even more in the back. Zigzagging in and out of billowing clouds of red dust they had quite a fairground ride!

It was time to buy some food though, and we made a brief stop in a village near Jhansi to satisfy the cooks. Several of the rest of us, including James, bought bananas and we were amused to see James caught in the first few mouthfuls, having to negotiate with a holy cow who fancied his fruit! But it was time for him to do some work again. Ian had had a fairly rough morning of it since Gwalior, so he called on James to take over at the wheel once more.

By now we were into undulating country, almost every hill crowned with a shrine, a fort or some temples. We asked James to stop so that we could take photos of one or two of the most spectacular. It was amazing how many of these quite exceptional ancient buildings there were around, no longer strongholds from the Mughal era in this region. These shrines were likely to be Hindu or Jain in origin: the scene had changed. This was Uttar Pradesh, the realm of princely states, where Maharajas had ruled under the Raj.

We stopped for lunch, but had an unexpected problem. All our cooks had elected to swop with bluies that morning and the blue truck hadn't arrived yet. It says something for the cohesion of the group by now that everyone proceeded to work together to help get a meal under way, and we managed really well considering. It was just as we'd finished and were clearing away that the blue truck, plus our cooks, appeared at last! So we all had a bit of a wait while they sorted themselves out.

We then continued the long drive to Khajuraho, our next port of call. On the way we got stopped at a level crossing and I watched another steam train chuff past. I wondered if it might be a good idea to take a train trip across India at some time in the future. Luigi and James rather put me off though with their stories of crowded carriages and long waits in stations.

We were making slower progress than usual and had to drive on quite late. Not used to continuing after dark, we found things got really interesting in the cab as dusk fell, for several groups of striped-faced monkeys were to be seen in the light of our head lamps. We reached the Tourist Bungalow at last around 7pm. I helped with the evening meal, as I had helped at lunch, this time because Abby, on cook duty, had cystitis. James estimated she had been buzzing for a loo stop every ten kms. or so for the last two hours of the drive. This was why we had run late. It was certainly an embarrassing condition to suffer on a long road trip like ours.

Later in the evening she had an interesting story to tell us though, which led to considerable discussion. Her problem had continued of course after we arrived and set up camp. She went to the loo in the woodland near her tent, lit still by the lights of the Bungalow, and she began to notice a couple of times that a certain man was watching her. It was a sign of a more populous country that we were now aware of others visiting nature for a similar purpose to ours. Country people might well have been doing this in Iran and Afghanistan too but it was in India that we noticed that there were often other people around when we went to the toilet in natural settings; that was why most of us girls by now had invested in long skirts to hide proceedings. Locals usually moved away respectfully when they became aware of what was going on, but this man didn't and still seemed to watch. It quite unnerved Abby.

The third time she had to go she looked carefully to see if he was there again, but this time there was a woman watching her, and when she had finished the woman approached her. She told Abby that her husband had asked her to come and verify what he thought was amiss. "You see", she said, "we are both doctors and we think you may have cystitis. We have some medicine which could really help you." Abby was invited to accompany her to their house nearby and received the medicine and some useful advice from them, which helped her recover much more quickly. She felt she had learnt a lot from this encounter. It had made her question her attitude of suspicion, she said. It was often difficult for us to come alongside local people as we travelled, to see them as really similar to us despite different customs. There was an inclination to view them as too different, aliens almost. It was when we allowed them to approach us more that communication was thoroughly enabled at last and good came of it.

Dervla Murphy has commented on this "strange unconsciousness of the unity of mankind" that causes some travellers to hold themselves aloof from the people they are travelling among.

> "Is this something... our age does - on the one hand make communication easier than ever before, while on the other hand widening the gulf between those who are 'developed' and those who are not?"[99]

Musing on this and whether I could try harder to understand how the people around me lived, I returned to writing some more postcards; there would have to be a bumper posting before long. Then I chatted with Ian, Liz and Jane. We discussed what we had seen over the last few days and Ian told us more about the extension of the trip to Assam. Virginia was to go on this further jaunt and I must say I was feeling rather sorry to miss out on it, though my continuing journey to Australia and New Zealand was exciting enough!

***   ***   ***

---

[99] *Full Tilt* (1965), page 95.

We were up at 6am and cleared away quickly to indulge in banana pancakes for breakfast, a lovely treat, thanks to our bulk buying of bananas the morning before, near Jhansi.

Then we set off for a two hour visit to the Khajuraho 'love' temples. There had been eighty-five temples originally erected here by the Chandella kings in the tenth and eleventh centuries to various Hindu gods[100], but there now remained only twenty two. Each consisted of two or three towers of granite or sandstone gradually rising to the tallest spire, covered with decorative high relief sculpture. These walls surrounded the shrine to the particular god and were accessed by steep steps to the basic dais.

We went round a few of the best preserved with a guide who was quite a scream with his description of the various "erotics" on view! The amazingly explicit carvings of human love-making in every conceivable contortionist's positioning, and the exuberant portrayal of naked humanity was something new to those of us who had not dipped into the Kama Sutra. "Here you see exceptional ladies ... breasts like melons!" was one of our guide's favourite descriptions of the ultra-curvaceous females we saw on the walls of the temples.

And animals got in on the act too - elephants, serpents, horses and camels. Lukas couldn't get enough of this! He was tempted to climb up the temple sides to get close-up shots with his smart camera. "Mein Gott!" he'd exclaim from time to time, "Come and look at this fellow - at it with a horse!"

The Lakshman and Kandariya Mahadeva temples were probably the most interesting and looked wonderful from some distance away, for they were surrounded by a bank of red roses, which we thought very appropriate to the subject of love. To the Christian or Muslim this show of sexual adventures would seem thoroughly sinful, but the Hindu celebrates love as part of the best of life, the senses regarded as on a par with spiritual essence. Considering that the area had been invaded by Muslims in the thirteenth century, with their dislike of representations of the human form

---

[100] *Kathmandu by Truck* (1976), page 90.

(the damage done to saints' faces at Göreme came to mind), it was amazing that these temples remained in such good condition.

As we left the site we came upon an elephant taking tourists for rides at 5 rupees per person. This was expensive but, I thought, not to be missed. Bluies Gloria and Anne joined Virginia, Jane and myself to try this experience. She was a female elephant, named Sundry, with rather ragged ears, and of a certain age (about twenty-five). Markings on her head and back suggested that she had carried processional howdahs a fair bit in the past. She had a sedate but slightly syncopated rhythm in her walk which almost made you do a swaying dance up on her back and was good to sing to - yes, I had a go - once you got used to it!

We then started our long drive to Benares. Ian warned us there was to be no lunch stop, but we would make a short halt to shop for fruit and biscuits. I also sampled a small omelette at one food stall. We were going through pleasant country and it was not too hot. I enjoyed reading more of *The Pass beyond Kashmir*. Around mid-afternoon we descended from one plateau level to another with sparser vegetation.

Then the truck's engine failed! We waited an hour for the blue truck to catch up with us, for we were out of diesel and would need towing to the nearest fuel station. We camped on the stony, thorny ground alongside. It was too late to reach Benares that day.

Chapter 20. By Holy Ganga and the Sacred Fish's Tail

The next day was Friday 14th November, originally to have been our expected date of arrival in Kathmandu. I was flying out to Bangkok on the 22nd. I hoped I'd have sufficient time to see what I wanted of Kathmandu before I left!

Rising at seven, we once more made good time at the start of our cooking day. Our vehicle set off limpingly, towed by the blue truck. We went right through the crowded streets of Mirzapur, battling with rickshaws and bicycles. Every little boy we came across, and the majority of the male population of Mirzapur too it seemed, followed us applauding as we searched for the petrol station. We then watched astounded as the poor fuel attendant hand-pumped the diesel into the orange truck's tank! He managed to do it with hardly a break too, though it took much longer than usual of course.

Then we went on to reach Benares just before lunch, which we had quickly before taking a rickshaw to do the shopping – minus Sarah, who had sprained a knee. It was the easiest shop yet, for we bought all our fruit and vegetables at one stall, and the bread at the next. Then we were taken on to the rickshaw-boy's relatives' silk shop - a situation we'd been told to watch out for! But we all profited that day. I bought a really lovely blue/green shot silk sari, a very tasteful silk tie (excellent Christmas presents) and a wrap-around long skirt for myself! The latter was great. My trousers were too loose because I'd lost weight, and this skirt (with a neat edging of tiny elephants to remind me of Sundry) tied more securely round my waist. Virginia and Tim similarly bought presents for themselves and the members of their families.

Going through the town we had noticed that it was more than usually crowded and frankly pretty smelly, perhaps not surprisingly considering its reputation as a favoured cremation site on the river Ganges, a stretch of water sacred for Hindus. Benares is now more commonly known as Varanasi and this change of name was just beginning to be the custom when we visited. In geography lessons at school I had never registered such strange renaming situations, though working in Switzerland I found cities often had two names according to language, when they were on the border between the country's German-speaking and French-speaking populations – Biel/Bienne for example. How confusing for the inhabitants, I had thought. I was to meet with it in stricter form, according to regime change, fifteen years later, when Leningrad became St Petersburg. In the case of Varanasi it was more to do with getting back to an original name it seemed, Benares being seen as a corruption of Varanasi. When they learnt of the alteration Maddie and Ros rather wickedly tweaked Varanasi to become 'Very-Nasty'! And indeed there were some extraordinary and, to us at any rate, rather unpleasant activities going on around the Ganges here that we would be introduced to next morning.

In the meantime I needed to get the stack of postcards I'd been writing to the post at last; they went to my parents and cousins, work mates in two countries, and friends at home and abroad, seventeen cards in all. Most would hear from me next in a new continent I realised with a thrill.

I washed some underwear, and then my hair, lazing afterwards in the tent till it was time to start tea. But when Virginia and I gathered with Sarah and Tim at the truck we found it was jacked up as Ian and Ben were working on it. We couldn't get at the kitchen equipment and cooker for a quarter of an hour, and then had to get everything out including the gas. Also we had no decent light. It was anything but an easy job that night.

We finally got tea ready by 7.30 ... not helped by Sarah's blandly exiting the scene a little earlier! Virginia and I went for a coffee afterwards, and were looking round the cheap ivory for sale nearby when we were joined by Ben and Luigi. I summoned up my courage and asked the former if I could travel with him in the bluies' cab the next day. I had to do it once during the trip I felt. Then I would have tried travelling everywhere Encounter had to offer us.

***   ***   ***

We were up at 4.30am and I joined Ben in the blue cab to set off at 5.30 for the Ganges waterfront. We got lost twice, but made it in time for sunrise, when the sun's light cast a golden shimmering reflection over orangey red waters. I could understand devout Hindu believers thinking of the river as divine at this time of day.

The plan was to take a boat trip down the Ganges - ever popular with tourists - to watch the various events Benares was famous for. Hindus see the river as the holy Ganga, equivalent to a water goddess that nourishes the north of India. For two and a half thousand years pilgrims had come to bathe and worship in the mother river, at dawn in particular. As John Finnemore colourfully put it,

> "…all wish to enter the water at that instant when the sun… pours a flood of golden splendour over the wide stream, and lights up the long row of temples and palaces which face him as he rises."[101]

We gathered by the quays and piled in six to a boat to be rowed along the river. It gave an extraordinary glimpse of Hindu practise, taking in both the ritual bathing in the holy waters of the river and the cremations on the neighbouring ghats. I could hardly credit the number of people, of all ages, who thronged the steep stairs leading down to the water's edge from street level.[102] Men together with women (something we had grown unaccustomed to seeing in Asia thus far), they were in every state of undress, readying to take a dip or drying themselves after doing so. Towels, bathing sarongs and other clothing hung from balconies high up alongside the steps down to the river and well-used dingy and patched parasols had been erected to protect the more sensitive from the sun. Some were washing their clothes or scrubbing pots and pans. Others supped the holy waters while offering puja (Hindu prayers).

All this was happening just along the waterfront from where bodies were being burnt; you could see the smoke rising from the funeral pyres. I shouldn't have wanted to lower myself under the river surface where the odd strand of charred hair or toenail of a corpse might be floating, let alone drink here! Quite apart from this, statistics have since shown that pollution of the ghat areas in Varanasi appears to be increasing year on

---

[101] *India* (1915) page 47.
[102] See photograph on page 172.

year, with human excrement being one of the major problems ... yes, 'Very-Nasty' indeed![103]

We were rowed quite close to the cremation ghats, which made me feel uncomfortable. I had felt rather embarrassed to be staring at the praying bathers: now I felt worse. It seemed thoroughly inappropriate to peer at and photograph mourners at such a time. A Hindu cremation occurs within 24 hours of a death, so loss is still very raw, though Hindus believe that only the body burns, the soul continuing to reincarnation. Two men in working clothes were adjusting the pyre with long poles, as Kapuściński explains "to direct a better draft so the cremation can proceed faster"[104], there always being a queue of cremations to get through. Male relatives of the dead person being cremated stood or sat disconsolately around in their mostly white funeral garb. No women attended the actual cremation as far as we could see.

Meanwhile monkeys were leaping from roof to roof, ever on the lookout for the odd scrap of food, and as we came away from the ghats we couldn't miss seeing the beggars lining every road to the river. They each carried a bowl, I thought at first for money, but soon it became clear that they waited for the more well-off to put rice in their bowls. It struck me as an excellent idea. We had been told by Ian to avoid giving money to beggars on the Indian streets, some of whom had been specifically placed there to collect money for corrupt institutions; they were evidently even occasionally maimed in some way, so that they would arose the pity of passers-by and collect more cash. To give food then seemed a very useful course of action, to at least help sustain them in their enslavement.

There was a moment of excitement on the quay when Virginia suddenly realised she had left her bag on the boat, but very luckily managed to find it again before it was too late! Otherwise on our return from the waterfront, and after we'd had breakfast (our group's last cook of the trip), we had an enforced wait for Lynn to return from a visit to the local hospital to check out what seemed to be a bout of food poisoning. This, to her disgust was re-diagnosed as 'indigestion'.

---

[103] *City Development Plan for Varanasi 2041* (2015), 'Sanitation', page 104.
[104] *Travels with Herodotus* (2008), page 25.

During the time we waited, a snake charmer arrived. He worked with a baby king cobra and three other cobras, as well as showing off a boneless two-headed snake, in which, he told us, the head changed end of the snake's body every six months. I doubted this very much, but it was certainly an unusual specimen. Then he introduced Virginia and myself to a six month-old python, "still only four feet long". Virginia wasn't too keen to handle the reptile, but I rather fancied seeing what it felt like. The snake charmer placed the creature round my neck and gave me instructions on how to hold its head. After 'testing my neck for collar size' it twisted round my body another couple of turns till it was comfortable. It felt dry and cold, not slimy at all as I'd feared, and it had slightly loose skin. Virginia took a photo of me with it in situ and I'm obviously having difficulty getting the snake to face the camera. It kept trying to turn and look at me which was a little unnerving! The charmer also showed us an anti-snake charm and encouraged us to watch a fight between a mongoose and a snake. I wasn't so keen about this, for it seemed a foregone conclusion that the mongoose would win in unpleasant style, but the charmer was careful to abort the match in time!

Back in the blue truck's cab with Ben, I wrote a quick letter, before I forgot details, to a friend who'd asked me specifically about what went on in Benares, and then settled down to watch the route. I had brief chats with Ben, and even helped find the way at one point. We saw a working elephant crossing the new bridge at Ghaghara, and also glimpsed monkeys and saw warthogs nosing among rubbish left by the road. Parrots and a vulture flew close to the cab.

We were travelling due north towards Gorakhpur. The countryside was flat, but the farming seemed very reasonable. There were some good acres of cultivated land and also green pasture, while pleasant trees often lined the route. I lunched with the blue truck crowd on the edge of a rice paddy, young shoots just coming up, the water of the flooded arable field having evaporated since the monsoon.

We stopped so that Ben could do an oil check and I took a photo in the wing mirror of two Indians watching the truck. As usual these men were some miles from the nearest town and, after a brief chat, walked on leaning on their long staffs. There was a loud rap on the side of the truck a little later and Ben was immediately very worried that we had struck a pedestrian's staff and maybe hurt one of these nomadic characters. No-one in the back had noticed anything to suggest this however, so it must have been a stone thrown up from the road.

The orange truck got lost and finally caught up as we waited outside a diesel station. I amused myself chatting with some Indian children coming home from school during this interlude. They were delighted to show off their English and I was taken through their notebook lessons on the subject. Ben had to shoo them away to get me back in the cab.

Once on our way again, Ben got properly lost in the smoky rush-hour of Gorakhpur. It meant we had to retrace our steps and it was pure hell trying to turn round against the stream of bikes, tricycle rickshaws and pedestrians. Eventually we were on track once more and we joined the orange truck to camp between trees not far out of town. On serving tea we soon had the local neighbourhood round! Four very smiling ladies brought their children to see us and to enjoy a cup of something warm. There were at least eight children who gazed at us in wonder. "How can they be so pale and exist properly on such strange food?" they seemed to be thinking. We on the other hand commented afterwards on their beautiful eyes, so expressive in their dark faces.

The evening continued with the usual pre-border chat from Ian on Nepal. It was incredible to think that we were almost at our destination. I couldn't wait to see the mountains.

***   ***   ***

We only rose at 4.45 but managed to get going as expected by six. It was, as my Scottish mother would have said, 'mare bi luck than guid guidance' for Virginia and me. I noted in my diary: Virginia will have to buck up for the Assam trip!

We watched the red globe of the sun rise above the misty plain very soon after setting off. We were mostly quiet, some dozing, others like me reading as we traversed the last of the flat lands. The rumbling vibrations of the truck we were so used to by now had as background the plopping rhythm of water pumps irrigating the fields, high children's voices calling after us and weird bird cries.

We reached the Nepalese border at 8am. The first changes I noticed were what I regarded as the Tibetan-type looks of the salesman from whom I bought bananas and glucose biscuits with my last rupees, reminding me of the Mongolian features of some people in Northern Afghanistan. He had a caged parrot by his counter that squawked in a strange way when I spoke to it. Was I listening to a warped version of Nepali for the first time, I wondered.

We were over into Nepal two hours later and had quite a long wait here too. We girls watched with interest as a female official checked the truck while the customs guard played with his children: role reversal in operation it seemed. Then a book of particulars had to be filled in (despite our having completed entry forms). Finally rupee notes had to be changed at the bank. At noon we left in the direction of the hills which gradually appeared ahead out of a 'cloud bank'. We drove into a narrow cut in the rising ground and entered another world.

We were in a wooded valley at first, with the odd thatched shack house with red mud walls, from which came the scent of pine wood fires. As we started to climb higher, we passed fewer people walking by the roadside, but these often carried heavy loads on their backs. Yet what we took to be a strangely mobile haystack would turn, smile and wave at us as we passed. Generally we got the impression of a more cheerful, exuberant population up here in the hilly terrain. Beautifully arranged paddy fields and scallop-terraced cultivation showed far up the slopes on either side, with rice out drying in neat piles on ledges.

We lunched by the road. I walked further on briefly to get a view of the valley with a farm below and came across a large blue and black butterfly. This of course was strange to me, but many of the plants around here were not. I had seen them at home, but on a different scale. I was used to seeing pots of poinsettias at Christmas for instance, their top leaves or bracts Yuletide red. Here they were growing wild, the size of small trees, their scarlet foliage adding colour to the scene.

A pleasant local custom appeared to be to decorate the pinnacles of haystacks with these leaves or a red flower or two, so that they reminded me of the cherry-topped buns my mother sometimes baked when I was a child. There were also some weird 'single branch-like' trees – a thin trunk with clusters of leaves up it. There were plenty of friendly, fit, smiling children *and* adults: in India the children might smile, any accompanying adults remaining invariably solemn. Little boys here would race behind the truck as it moved uphill! We hadn't seen such energy on the plain.

It was not a wonderful road. There were rock slides in several places, making it narrow, twisting and bumpy. It was fairly dusty too. There were lovely views far down into the gorge though, to waterfalls, cliffs and distant mountain peaks.

We stopped by a drying rice paddy at dusk, some 65kms south of Pokhara. We chatted with the local children – or rather exchanged noises with them. They were very easily pleased! After tea I got the addresses of some of my companions and we had a sing-song with Rob and Michael. James arrived in just his underpants (all formality was vanishing as we realised the end of our co-habitation was near) to tape us singing *On the Road to Kathmandu*!

***   ***   ***

Next day, Monday the 17th November, was our last morning of camping. How weird it felt to be staying in one place for a few days once we reached Kathmandu! Of course we had experienced this in Kashmir, but now camping would soon be a thing of the past. I was rather surprised to find I should almost miss it!

But today we were up at 5am and got rolling an hour later, as we were now very accustomed to doing. I travelled in the cab, James at the wheel. Liz was in the hot seat, while Jane, Lukas, Virginia and I were behind. This was certainly a day to be in the cab getting the very best views, our first glimpses of the Himalayas.

It was very misty. We still had some climbing to do, travelling between small banana trees and cactus hedges. The south-facing slopes here must

231

get fairly warm to allow these plants to grow well, I thought. Sure enough, just before 8am we began to see the sun filtering through the mist, and then drove out of the clouds to see a fantastic panorama, the Himalayas. Our first sightings were of the Annapurna mountain range and then of Machapuchare.

This translates from Nepali as 'fish's tail', as the mountain has a double peak, but it's also sometimes dubbed the Himalayan Matterhorn being, from the south, similar in outline to the Swiss mountain. It's almost twice as high though at 22, 943 ft or 6,993 metres. An extremely difficult mountain to climb[105], Machapuchare is also considered by the locals to be the home of Lord Shiva, the Hindu god, and so is seen as a sacred mountain. Ascents are not encouraged. Being nearer than the Annapurna its sharp triangular peak seemed to dwarf them, though one or two of the surrounding range are in fact higher.

These wonderful snowy heights we glimpsed from the viewpoint of the road above the town of Pokhara, which turned out to be a rather straggling town, spreading over quite a wide area. We drew up near the airstrip, a very simple affair in 1975. This still exists but has been superseded by an International Airport. When we stopped there towards the end of our trip it was in order to shop at the Monday morning market in progress there.[106] The sales men and women lined the road, and behind them were shacks with steep-sided roofs made of what looked like animal skins. Piles of wood were stacked here, stored chopped into useful logs for everyday fires. I wondered if it was ready to be flown out to other places in the country, perhaps above the tree line.

Goods for the market had been brought along on wheeled trolleys that now served as tables, or carried in large baskets on the vendors' backs. (These baskets reminded me strongly of ones used in a similar fashion during the grape harvesting in Switzerland.) I was fascinated by the Tibetan-type looks of the people who had spread out matting on which to display their fruit by the roadside, sometimes under umbrellas to protect them from the sun. Women sported the odd bangle and large-stoned ring,

---

[105] Noyce, W. (1958).
[106] See photograph on page 173.

but also sometimes a nose stud. They had scarves wound round their heads, while the men wore turbans or neat oriental skull caps. They crouched barefoot or sat cross-legged at the edge of their mats and smiled at us winningly as we passed.

Or most of the time they did. I had noticed a couple, selling their fruit side by side, who were obviously the best of friends, sharing a joke their faces wreathed in smiles. It would make a great photo. I stepped forward and as usual asked if it would be OK to take a photograph of them. Though she made no sign that she didn't want her photo taken, the woman's smile wiped off her face immediately so that she looked as sour as the limes on her stall (but no, these were the green oranges again). By contrast her male neighbour's smile increased, with a sideways glance at her. What was the back-story here? Why did she so obviously dislike and he relish this situation? Had I interrupted something? I took the photograph anyway but not for the first time swore to myself that I would invest in a telephoto lens such as Hannah, Lukas and James had. The answer was surely to take pictures like this at a distance.

To make myself feel better I gave myself the real treat of two '5-star' chocolate bars and a pineapple juice! They tasted all the better for being enjoyed while I gazed at snowy Machapuchare, visible above the low clouds on the northern horizon. I vowed then and there to return to explore this region another day ... and indeed managed to six years later.

We had our lunch stop by a bridge not much further on, on the British road completed two years previously, which had a very good surface. I took the opportunity to explore our lunch site a little, climbing down to the river valley below the bridge and crossing to the 'jungle' on the far side. There were prickly trees and clinging bushes everywhere, but some really beautiful butterflies. With a shudder I imagined how in the wet season I might very well have picked up leeches galore, or so I had heard from the others: as it was, I collected only plenty burrs and grass seeds.

As it was our last lunch stop several of us were taking photos to mark the occasion. On my return to the group I too took two or three shots rather haphazardly and quite by accident got one of Stephen from the blue truck in the process of taking his trousers off! His wife, Helen, was ready with his shorts. Also watching him was Ian, sitting cross-legged with his back to me. But - did my eyes deceive me? Was he really in just his briefs (a rich shade of purple) and his cap? This naturally called for comment and I was in time to hear:

Geoff/Luigi: "Aah! What ghastly sight is this? The big white chief in his underpants and cap!"

Driver Ben: "It could have been worse ... just in his cap!"

We were soon on our way once more, Ian (back in his trousers) at the wheel. The road ran through lovely sunny valleys. About half way to our destination we came on a road leading left to Gorkha. Liz noticed the sign first and immediately recognised that it might be the hill village that gave the Gurkha soldiers their name. Ian confirmed this and told us a little of the history of this regiment.

The men hereabouts had caused such vigorous resistance to northern expansion of the East India Company towards the end of the eighteenth century that the Governor General had actually declared war on Nepal in 1814. A peace treaty was eventually signed two years later, but ...

"During the war a deep feeling of mutual respect and admiration had developed between the British and their adversaries, the British being much impressed by the fighting and other fine qualities of the Gurkha soldier."[107]

Under the terms of the peace treaty they were encouraged to volunteer in the East India Company's army and they have proved themselves time and again to be thoroughly worthy of the trust the British put in them. A magnificent fighting troop by all accounts, the Brigade of Gurkhas are known as Britain's 'oldest ally' in Asia.

From here we followed a river for a few miles, the Himalayan peaks peeping over the hills on the left, but later only the foothills were visible. We were constantly stopped by tolls, the aim evidently being to finance

---

[107] *Gurkha History* (2020).

and maintain the new road's excellent condition. These charges were quite expensive for large vehicles. I was to use this road again a few years later travelling in the opposite direction, from Kathmandu to Pokhara by bus. The friend I was travelling with then, living locally at that time, recommended that I sit behind the back wheels of the bus, as this ensured a smoother ride. I'm afraid the tolls had not been entirely effective in keeping up the condition of the road since our 1975 overland trip.

As dusk fell we had our last loo stop, a poignant and quite emotional occasion, in the grounds of an agricultural college. We rather sentimentally joined hands, for all the world like saying the Grace at the end of a prayer meeting ... and with something of the same reverence. It was a convivial moment in every sense of the word! Not for the first time there was chat imagining how it would be if we continued to act at home as we had on this trip. I kept quiet about the loo stops I had experienced on childhood journeys north of Inverness. I even remembered my father leaping over a wall in his hurry to return to the car when chased by a bull!

More outrageous were imaginings of what would happen at home if we tried bartering in Marks and Spencer's, say. An irate "*How* much?! It's not worth *half* that" while marching towards the door, would be regarded as the height of rudeness and would get us nowhere. Nor would we get away with taking a dip in our underwear in any old river or fairly clean pond we came across. No, things might have to become decorous and conventional again once we were back home - worse luck! Strange that I should feel like adding that last thought, but I had become almost emotionally attached to our nomadic existence.

Under way again, we began to notice that the nearer we were to Kathmandu the more diverting and varied the toll stops. Some children entertained us to a concert, singing to the accompaniment of Asian-type fiddles, perhaps sitars or sarods, during one of the final halts - for baksheesh naturally. They seemed to be more used to tourists the nearer we got to the capital. Of-course Kathmandu was a very popular venue for tourists, a city boasting temples of every conceivable form, or so it seemed from our guide books.

The Asian Greyhound brochure was even more graphic.

"Without a shadow of a doubt one of the world's most fascinating cities, Kathmandu is rich in both Buddhist and Hindu shrines and temples ... The city welcomes all tourists and offers very low priced hotels and restaurants, but be prepared for an almost total lack of hygiene. Kathmandu is not a clean well serviced city, but more than compensates in friendliness."

Ian had suggested that we might find it cleaner than usual, as the coronation of King Birendra of Nepal had taken place in February and things had been smartened up for the occasion.

By now though most of us were willing to put up with a degree of dirt! No, generally it was excited expectation that we felt. It was difficult to realise fully that we had almost reached our destination. How strange it was going to be to be able to get up later in the morning and not to have to worry about getting the tent up and down reasonably fast. It would feel really strange to be without our money-belt at times too – certainly when in our sleeping bags. Life was going to change ... but not back to normal just yet.

On we went, Lukas using our old fire engine spotlight to show up the road ahead, which was of a worse condition now. We had rarely travelled after dark for long, and in my memory never with the spotlight illuminating the surrounding countryside. At last we saw the twinkling lights of Kathmandu ahead: like Bunyan's 'Celestial City' it looked quite magical. And indeed it almost felt like the end of a kind of pilgrimage. Tomorrow we would have been on the road for twelve weeks and we had attained our aspiration, the final goal of our slow circuiting of the globe, experiencing life in some fascinating countries.

Chapter 21. To the Roof of the World

We threaded our way into Kathmandu's busy streets, Ian pointing out useful places en route. We were making for Encounter's headquarters in the city, Kathmandu Guest House, and here Ian had a lot of trouble turning the truck into the rather narrow entrance in near darkness. Virginia, who was sitting behind him in the cab, made herself thoroughly unpopular by sticking her head out of the window to see the problem in the rear, thereby completely blocking his view. Unsurprisingly this caused her to be shouted at! Ian was, I'm sure, ready for a good long rest by now, his temper easily frayed.

We descended and sought our luggage, but on entering the quite spacious building found the Guest House extremely crowded. We were arriving later than expected and others had been catered for, so there were no rooms free. However we were given space in their ballroom at 5 rupees a night. This was a palatial spot, a very large room with plaster ceiling decoration, suggesting that the Guest House had had a more stylish reputation in the days of Empire. We laid out our sleeping bags near chairs where we could put our clothes, neatened up a little, and joined several of the others for a Chinese meal at a neighbouring restaurant well known to overlanders. Sweet and sour chicken with rice, and lemon meringue pie to follow, was a delicious finale to our last travelling day together.

We didn't indulge in too long a lie next morning. The floor had been hard so I was glad to rise. We got our names on the waiting list for rooms at the Guest House desk and then went to have breakfast. Cornflakes, two boiled eggs, buttered toast and coffee – oh, the luxury of nearing home ideals! Butter in particular we relished: apart from on the houseboats in Kashmir it had been almost two months since we had last tasted it.

Virginia and I were given a room after breakfast and I soon got my laundry sent off. Then we helped the others get the tents out to dry, and did some mending and sorting of the camp beds before helping to stack away food on the orange truck. Everything needed to be shipshape for the Assam trip.

By now it was lunch time. Several of us went for the Chinese option again. Then we took a rickshaw to the post office, just in time to collect our mail before it closed at 2pm. Delightfully, there was not just one, but *two* letters from my parents – great! We window-shopped down to the Nepalese Bank, where I changed some travellers' cheques, which I now intended to spend to very good purpose. For lastly, and most importantly, I dropped in on Royal Nepal Airlines and booked an Everest flight for the exorbitant price of £15! I was going to view the 'roof of the world' closer up. It had been my dream ever since I heard about the trip. Only Abby and Dave of the others joined me in lashing out. Like me they just couldn't wait … but we would have to be patient a little longer. The flight was in two days' time, on the Thursday as I left for Bangkok and Australia on the Saturday.

Then we were nicely in time for the afternoon Folk Dancing Concert we'd heard would happen in the City Hall. There was an exhibition of Nepalese culture at the entrance, handicrafts, jewellery, prayer wheels and some rather lovely stamps. It was unfortunate that I decided to try the toilet facilities before the show, for they were absolutely horrible. I noted in my diary that they were so bad that "I stood on the toilet seat"! In the street Asian Greyhound's comments had seemed rather too harsh: not so now.

But the show itself was fun. There was very decorative dancing from girls holding candles. This was followed by the character dances – a grimacing witch doctor, strutting peacocks, Tibetan and heavy-footed yak dances as well as courtship displays. There was an amusing compère and altogether it was a pleasant production.

We returned to the Guest House to change for the last meal out on Encounter Overland – wonton soup, sweet and sour prawns with rice, apple pie, lemon tea and coffee. A superb spread! But sadly we were too many to all fit in the same room. Some of us had to sit out away from the main party. It only took a couple of visits to the main table to get most people's addresses though. I certainly meant to keep in touch with a few of these special travelling companions if possible. Fleming I found to be surprisingly right to comment that "A hard journey makes you curiously tender to even your most maddening companions"[108], and there were

---

[108] *News from Tartary* (1936), page 162.

those here who, on the contrary, had enhanced the trip considerably for me.

Back in our room I also managed to finish Berkely Mather's *The Pass beyond Kashmir*, before going to sleep. Neat timing. I'd give it to a second hand book shop here before I travelled on. I needed to lighten my rucksack as much as I could.

***   ***   ***

So now all we had to do was to relax and get to know Kathmandu a little. Virginia and I managed the first part of this just fine: we barely got to breakfast by ten o'clock next morning! As we chatted with a few others who were around we found that Meg, like us, was keen to hire a bike to explore the city sights. Ian had pointed out where to go for this, so as soon as we'd finished we made our way there. We were given men's bikes, but they went well when we briefly tested them and hire was only the equivalent of 20p a day. This would be excellent exercise after sitting in our orange truck for so long.

One thing we knew to test before we set off. Ian had said it was of prime importance that the bell should work, for we would find pedestrians took no notice of us otherwise. No problem there; the bells jangled beautifully and would soon alert any troublesome jaywalkers.

Our first thought though was to get off the main busy streets and ride to the edge of town. The obvious place to visit was Boudhanath Stupa, the Buddhist shrine on the ancient trade route from Tibet that skirted the more modern main city, some five or six miles out from the centre. A stupa, we had learned, was a hemispherical mound containing relics, and used mainly as a site for Buddhist meditation. According to the guide books this one was well worth a visit, being one of the largest stupas in the world. Tibetan merchants were said to have rested and offered prayers here for many centuries and when refugees came to Nepal from Tibet in the 1950s, many decided to live around Boudhanath.

Using the maps that the Guest House had provided we set off towards the Royal Palace. It had been misty when we rose that morning, but around eight thirty the sun had started to come through and by now it was quite warm. There were few motor vehicles around on the roads we followed, but bicycles and pedestrians were numerous: I used my bell almost continuously.

In Durbar Square the Palace, Gaddi Durbar, gleamed white in the sun. It had been constructed less than 70 years before by the politicians in charge of Nepal at the time, men strongly influenced by European design. At the time it reminded me of a grand version of one of the Southern Plantation houses I'd seen in Hollywood films like *Gone with the Wind*, rather than any Asian building I'd seen to date. It contrasted hugely with the surrounding darker three-tiered wooden pagodas of much earlier date.

The square was crowded with sightseers and it was difficult to decide on the way forward. Having lost our way a few times in the narrow streets off the shopping district, we finally managed to reach Gyaneshwor, notable for being the half-way point of our journey on our maps. The streets here had no pavements. The terraces of houses' dark and dingy entrances led straight out over plank bridges across the drainage ditches-cum-sewers lining the road and we prayed no child would suddenly run out in front of us. The upper stories of these terraces were more interesting, for it was here that there were windows, occasional terracotta or cream-painted walls, and shading provided by wooden-supported awning-type overhanging roofs. Women drew water into washing bowls from brick pumps alongside the gutter, elderly men sat in their doorways in the sun and children followed their mothers on their way towards a street market.

We peddled on into Chabahil, a more countrified district. There was sparser housing, and grass grew on many of the roofs. There were less cyclists by now and we passed the odd square with a small stone shrine set under trees. Briefly we foundd ourselves by a river and I found a prettily-marked stone on the bank that I took for my cousin: this would do nicely as her requested 'stone from Kathmandu'.

A little way on we came on a larger brick home beyond some greenery, including a fruit-bearing tree. Were these green fruit guava as Meg suggested? Virginia and I had never heard of them. Leaning my bike against a roadside pole, I took a photo to check later, but then heard a splash behind me. My bike had fallen into the roadside sewer! The others helped me with their wet wipes to get it clean once more.

Another twenty minutes jolting along the often rough-surfaced lanes north from here and we met the wider road leading to the stupa. The great sacred mound shone white in the sunshine, lines of prayer flags fluttering gently above. It was set on an octagonal terraced base and surrounded by a circular way. Here we found attractive-looking craft shops where women were at work producing goods for tourists. Grains and grasses had been laid out around the ring, against the outer wall of the stupa, to dry in the sun.

What immediately caught the attention however was the four-sided and befringed tower topping the stupa. It was from this that the prayer flags were strung. But on each wall of the tower's base, just above the swelling of the mound, were a pair of mesmerising hooded eyes, the 'all-seeing eyes of Buddha', gazing out over the surrounding landscape. It certainly gave anyone moving around in the vicinity the impression of being watched disapprovingly. Shades of George Orwell's *1984*!

We had a quick look into some of the shops, where I bought a wooden prayer wheel which is still a prized possession. We then set about climbing the Stupa for we could see people on the terraces above and tiny figures walking round the foot of the dome itself. The climb up there was well worth our trouble. The views were superb, particularly to the north. Beyond the three-storied terraced dwellings and shops of the circular way stretched fields, then another row or two of bigger houses. Behind them we saw the sturdy foothills and then the snow-capped Himalayas themselves. It was almost unbelievable that these great peaks of some 23,000 ft. were within forty miles or so of us, at our meagre 4,500 ft. level.

We slowly returned to ground level, peeping into alcoves within which were images of the Buddha and passing several prayer wheels. We lunched nearby on Tibetan vegetable chow-chow with crushed orange to drink. The latter was not a hit with me: my diary commented:

Too much pith and too many pips!

We now aimed to compare the Buddhist shrine with a well-known Hindu one not too far away – Pashupatinath temple. In meant cycling directly south towards another river, a larger one than that at Chabahil. This temple was perhaps Nepal's most sacred Hindu site, on the banks of the holy Bagmati river. Like the site on the Ganges at Varanasi, it was also an important cremation ground.

On our arrival a pleasant little man elected to guide us round, beginning rather grimly by leading us past the burning bodies of an adult and a child, to climb the nearest hill to get a view of the Boudhanath Stupa once more. The mound stood out white across the valley against the further Himalayan foothills. Coming back down the hill to view what we could of the temple (non-Hindus were not allowed in) we came across a heavily-white-bearded yogi in orange garb carrying a trident, also tipped with orange ribbon. He suggested I might like to take his photo – "for only one rupee", with which I complied, as he did look very exotic. However our guide muttered, "Holy men no good. Smoke hashish every day. Come from India."

We were hastily led on to try and see the statue of a golden bull, one of the forms reputedly taken by the Lord Shiva that stood before the temple doors here. Of this bulky structure, actually made of bronze, we caught but a glimpse across the river. There seemed a great many buildings, almost a village, jumbled up close around the white-walled two-tiered shrine.

Personally I found the local monkeys of more interest. There were one or two families of them nearby. One father monkey fell in the river and had to swim out to sit in wet chagrin beside his mate. I loved the baby monkeys they had with them. It was appropriate that they should be here, for the manifestation of Shiva, Pashupati that the temple was dedicated to is known as the Lord of Animals. I was not so happy though to learn that there was even a temple here for animal sacrifices.

It was a relatively short ride back to the Guest House from here and rather atmospheric at twilight. Once back, I did some washing and had a shower in the condensation-moist and dimly-lit hole that acted as our bathroom. Then Virginia was going to a meeting for the Assam extension trip at 8pm, so I went to the Chinese restaurant a little earlier. The service was not up to its usual brisk standard though and the soup arrived at the same time as the main course, the rice of which consequently got cold. On returning to the Guest House I had another nasty moment too. My hired bike was not in the place I'd left it. I wondered briefly if it had been stolen but soon realised that it had only been moved to another stand for some obscure reason.

***   ***   ***

This was to give me further trouble next morning, for when I tried to free it from the stand at six o'clock I found it thoroughly stuck in position! So how was I to get to the airport for my trip to see Everest? I decided to walk to Royal Nepal Airlines HQ for a 3 rupee bus to the airport. This was a peculiarly surreal experience. In the half-light, for it was misty once more, I found myself following a couple, weirdly singing their way along, for all the world as though we were in a musical!

Once at the airport I made for the domestic flight terminal and booked a seat reservation with the aid of a helpful older man there. Dave and Abby had arrived already, so we chatted in the sun till the mist was properly up at 9.30. At this point we were allowed onto the aircraft. Rather typically in my experience a large number of smarter tourists had managed to book the best seats and one of the port engines interfered with my view.

But I had the mountains on my side as we took off and flew towards the north east. Straight away I actually recognised something, Boudhanath stupa just north of the airstrip, its mound a tame rounded reflection of the more jagged peaks just appearing on the skyline. We moved over it towards the lines of foothills and the towering Himalayas themselves. The wonderful snow-clad range shone clear against a blue cloudless sky. No wonder November was a good time of year to climb Everest, I thought.

I photographed one of the prominent mountains you could see from Kathmandu, Dorje Lakpa (22,854 ft) and then the plane turned a few degrees east to fly parallel with the mountains and there was Everest, the only one in the range to have a swirl of snow rising up from its peak, like a flag to say 'Here is the highest!'[109] Wonderful! I had reached my longed-for view of the roof of the world.

From then on passengers were allowed to go into the cockpit one by one to take photos. My turn came as we banked round towards the mountains, in preparation for our return home. The result was a challenging view of Everest on its side! Some light misty clouds still remained in the valley below the great vertical cliffs crowned with the features I'd read about in Sir John Hunt's book[110] – Mounts Nuptse and Lhotse with Mount Everest itself sharp between them. I even fancied I could distinguish the Cwm glacier which had featured in their approach to climbing the mountain.

With, I'm sure, a hugely satisfied smile on my face I returned to my seat and sank back content. This had been a major goal of the last three months' travel. I had seen the magnificent highest point on our beautiful planet Earth. It was a moment to treasure and remind myself of when feeling at all low.

The mountains were now on the far side of the plane, so I only got the odd peep at them on the way back to Kathmandu. Instead I watched the valleys and red hills pass below. Then on the southern slopes of the foothills the strange contour patterns of paddy fields appeared, like those we'd seen when climbing to Nepal from the Indian plain.

On leaving the aircraft we were given a prayer-wheel charm and a certificate to say we had made the trip. But Abby, Dave and I were feeling hungry and decided to experience an early lunch at the airport - egg and ham, plus rolls, butter, jam and tea. OK it cost 17.50 rupees but the service was good and, on a high as we were, it tasted marvellous!

I bid the others goodbye and walked back into town. My way took me by a rather decrepit small farm and past one of the most undernourished bull calves I'd ever seen. It was eating well enough now, but looked to have been half starved for a while. From here I was soon in the outskirts of Kathmandu and came on a shop for tourists, including some second hand

---

[109] *See photograph on page 173.*
[110] *The Ascent of Everest* (1953).

books. I bought three of them. I was ready with the Mather book, but could not resist some Thomas Hardy short stories, Chris Bonington on Everest and *To Kill a Mocking Bird*. So much for my ideas of lessening my load for travelling onward! But they were useful reading during the two nights I spent in airport lounges during my journey ahead.

Back at the Guest House before 2pm, I joined other late diners from our group for chicken noodle soup as a second light lunch. I then looked again at my bike and managed to prise it from its stand. Hooray, it would take me shopping. I cycled towards the centre and confirmed my flight in two days' time at the airline offices. I then visited some of the craft shops in the old town round Durbar Square. I was looking for something in filigree work for my mother but ended up buying her an unusually decorative copper-banded teapot. Then I moved on to explore the area of the old Royal Palace.

It's worth mentioning some of the more recent history of the Nepalese monarchy since my stay in 1975 at this point. King Birendra had been crowned King of Nepal only nine months before, having reigned since 1972. It's interesting to note how the Nepali Times saw the era of the 1970s from the end of 2000, thirty years on.

> "In 1972, the country was still largely road-less, and travelling from one part of Nepal to another invariably required crossing over into India ... Nepal's infant mortality rate has been slashed from 172 per 1,000 live births to less than 90 today. The country's literacy rate has risen from 15 per cent thirty years ago to nearly half the population today. Annual per capita income has gone up from $80 when King Birendra came to the throne to $210, even though the population has also doubled from 12 million to 24 million."[111]

Of-course Kathmandu had changed for the worse in some ways too, becoming very vehicle-busy and polluted compared to the city I knew. But one could say that the population were fond of their king, which made what happened next all the more shocking. King Birendra and all his closest relatives died in a massacre during a reunion dinner of the royal

---

[111] *Thirty Years of King Birendra's Reign* (2001).

family in July 2001, only six months after the above article was written. The assassin appeared to be Crown Prince Dipendra, but had he really gunned down nine members of his own family? That he too died, presumably having finally shot himself, was made problematic by the fact that he had two bullets in his brain, not just one.

There are still several suggestions about what happened. It's quite a mystery. The absence from the royal reunion dinner of Dipendra's uncle who now came to the throne, Prince Gyanendra, gave rise to suspicions for instance, as did the fact that the latter's son and wife survived their lighter injuries. All this meant that the Kingdom of Nepal had become unstable enough to be dissolved seven years later in 2008. By that time it was the last Hindu monarchy in the world. Again our trip had been well timed: we saw it in its heyday.

Back in November 1975, as I explored the Palace region, I came upon Meg and Virginia, and they'd witnessed another strange phenomenon we'd heard existed in Kathmandu, the daily appearance of the Kumari, or Living Goddess. Chosen specially by priests as an infant, this girl was thought to be the incarnation of Durga, the more fierce form of the Hindu goddess Parvati. Durga was usually portrayed mounted on a tiger or lion, having several arms and brandishing spears and knives in her many hands ready to slay demons. In discussion on the truck we had thought it not very good for a youngster to be so unnaturally pampered as the Kumari must be, for who would dare to invoke the wrath of an incarnation of Durga? Worse still, as soon as she started menstruating she would be sent back home and a new Kumari selected, but her reputation as an ex-Living Goddess would have made her unlucky: there were few young men who would wish to marry a one-time Kumari. Her main task each day as Goddess seemed to be to appear to waiting crowds at a particular window, in traditional bright dress and make-up. This is where Virginia and Meg had seen her. They had thought she looked rather unhappy. I thought I could understand that.

Leaving Durbar Square we cycled through the chaotic narrow back streets. They were terrible to cycle through in the busy afternoon, but there was no possibility of turning round to go back the way we'd come. We had to keep with the tide of cycle and pedestrian traffic. I re-hired the bike for the following day before returning to the Guest House. The others had had enough of it, so I should be on my own, but there was still at least one place to visit on my last day here, if not in the city then at least in the surrounding countryside. I had written to my parents:

Kathmandu city is NOT full of hippies [*for they had wondered about this*] and is quite interesting, but the surrounding countryside is great!

Yes, I was thoroughly enjoying the exercise and the freedom of choosing where to go.

It had given me an appetite too. I tried Kothey for my evening meal that night. This was a dish of savoury meat balls - fried pork mince. I found it very filling. Luckily I could now work it off a little: Liz was suffering from back stiffness, so I gave her a final massage and some exercises. Then I settled for a while to read one of my new Hardy short stories. It had been a very full and thoroughly rewarding day.

*** *** ***

I got going slowly next morning, gradually organising myself for departure. I wrote final cards to my parents and friends, cycled to the Post Office to send them off, and to check for any incoming mail, and changed my last Swiss Franc travellers' cheque at the bank. With a picnic lunch ready in my bag, I was now free to explore the Kathmandu valley's amazing collection of temples and shrines for a last time.

There was little doubt in my mind that it was Swayambhu, the monkey temple that I should visit. I rode there in bright sunshine and was soon feeling very hot indeed, for it was a hilly run. Unlike Boudhanath, Swayambhu stood among trees atop a steep hill, a taller 13-tiered gold spire rising from its whitewashed dome, reminding the Buddhist of the thirteen stages they needed to follow to attain nirvana. Two great white towers stood, one on each side of the stupa too. It certainly looked impressive as I approached on the road below.

I left my bike at the foot of the hill, where a steep wide set of some three hundred steps went straight up to the stupa. But I made my way further round and up a narrower path towards one of the side towers, because of what I saw ahead there. Swayambhu was not called the monkey temple for nothing. There were monkeys everywhere on these steps out of the way of the main route, picking up any titbits of food left by humans. At the top, they were to be seen tearing apart and gorging, juice running down their chins, on any fruit left at the numerous small shrines to be found gathered round the stupa itself. I found this strangely grisly at a holy site, but it was clearly encouraged, for I saw a couple of ladies in beautiful saris throwing them food as people do the pigeons in Trafalgar Square.

There were one or two souvenir stalls up near the stupa. I bought a snuff pot and a tiger's claw as presents, before moving across to the balustrade where I joined a group of women with marked Tibetan features, in warm shawls and boots, admiring the magnificent view. Once again it showed the Kathmandu valley fringed by hills, the snowy Himalayan peaks just visible beyond.

Near them, outside the central worship area, were a group of monks, their heads shaven, wearing wine-red robes and brown mantles. As I watched them I was startled by a growling at my shoulder, only to find another monk gesticulating that I should enter the shrine to see the Buddha there. I moved to where he indicated and saw a central statue shining gold.

After the bright light outside it was difficult to see fully at first but when I began to adjust to the shrine's dim atmosphere the Buddha before me didn't seem typical to me. In the west we tend to think of Buddha as a smiling rotund character. This was a solemn rather feminine version, wearing a highly decorated gilded crown and having golden snakes uncoiling up from the shoulder alongside each of its over-large ears. It had been given colourful necklaces in addition, which looked a little out of place, homemade and makeshift against all the gold. If I were to visit it today I should look with more interest at the hand positions of the Buddha: for I have learnt that they all have a tale to tell – of meditation, teaching or enlightenment. But I wonder if this Buddha still exists, for the Swayambhu site suffered badly in the 2015 Nepalese earthquake, though the main stupa was not much damaged.

After a look at some of the other surrounding smaller shrines and their attendant monkeys I set off down towards the road again and ate my picnic lunch on a lawn alongside the steps, half way down. I soon realised I was being gazed at wistfully by four skinny children, so they shared my biscuits. I had a treat myself too, for as I cycled back into Kathmandu I came on a dairy and bought a good slice of Dutch cheese – the first cheese I'd seen for many weeks – which I nibbled on the way to the bike hire offices. (I remembered to check it wasn't solid marzipan as I'd experienced back in Turkey!) I then bade farewell to my bicycle and walked on to have a pre-journey shower and hair wash and do my final packing at the Guest House.

Virginia and I joined the two American girls, Gloria and Meg, sisters Chloe and Alice, and Anne later for a farewell meal. Liz, Jane and Sarah joined me too as we were all to leave the next morning. We had chicken mushroom and rice with pancakes to follow, and Gloria added a treat, a rum and coke each. Her final advice to me was "Remember, you've gotta go Afro, Daphne!" She had suggested this to me a week or two previously when I complained that I hadn't had a haircut in ages. I actually took her advice when I got home again and it worked pretty well for a while.

Tim and Geoff found us and said they were going to the local disco and they needed us girls to come too. I described the place in my diary as "a very dark, jazzy hole" but many of our travelling companions were there, including Ian, so we had a good bop once it warmed up a bit. It was a suitably relaxed last celebration of our time together.

We returned to the Guest House in the small hours of November 22nd and I was up reasonably early once more to complete the packing by 8.15. The final task was to get my sleeping-bag roll safely on top of my rucksack. It still looked a shade unwieldy. Then Virginia and I went to have breakfast and I made my last farewells, kissing and hugging everyone. It was then that I tried to get my rucksack on my back and almost fell over! But I succeeded in getting into the taxi with Michael, plus guitar, who was flying back to Canada, and Peg and Mark, returning home to Sydney. I was travelling with them that far, for I was to change in Sydney next day for my flight to Melbourne. It seemed strange to contemplate traversing half the globe in such a short time, after becoming habituated to journeying so comparatively slowly across Asia.

What a variety of amazing experiences we had had though! It had undoubtedly changed me. I knew I could cope better with life in its rougher aspects now and I had dealt with new situations that would be extremely useful in future, possibly solo, travel. This trip had whetted my appetite to see more of Asia and of further afield of-course, especially places off the beaten track. I had been fascinated by my glimpse of how others lived and had learnt to question some of my own assumptions of the best way to live too. I also knew a little more where help was needed on the planet and meant to do something about it if I could. Above all my journey had truly been the never-to-be-forgotten trip of a lifetime, and had successfully lifted me to view the roof of the world! What could be better than that?

Thumbnail Sketches of My Companions

(To preserve confidentiality I have given everyone false names, though nicknames are correct)

Orange Truck

STAFF

Ian   Group Leader and orange truck driver. Took an electrical engineering degree and tried an office job briefly but couldn't settle, so started trekking. Had four years' experience, mainly in Asia and Africa. Blond, red-bearded and of medium height, he tended to amble, head down. Gregarious, he was a great drinker and joke-teller. Generally a good leader though, tough when necessary.

James   Driver of the orange truck. Slightly effeminate 'upper class' Englishman, a barrister by training, though he'd never practised. On his first Encounter Overland trip as a driver, having experienced the Asia journey as a passenger the year before. Slim, darkish with a sparse beard and moustache, he tended to mince along, with rolled-up trousers ("ready for the big squat" as he put it!). He was poorly tolerated by Ian and quietly laughed at by Ben (the Blue Truck's driver). His redeeming feature – being pleasantly chatty and generally a laugh!

COUPLES

Sabrina   Darkly handsome and pleasant girl. At 20, the youngest on the trip. She and her boyfriend, Dieter, started the journey dressed identically.

Dieter   Dark, rather haggard, bearded, quiet Swiss. A good mechanic, he wanted to farm in NZ.

Peg   Attractive slim brunette, a secretary, who'd been travelling with her husband (known from childhood) round Europe for 3 years. A good cook, she was usually quietly pleasant and charming, but didn't suffer fools gladly – James and Lukas both came under fire!

Mark	Her husband, an architect from Sydney. The Scandinavian bearded type, the red in his beard a sign of a brisk temper, though he was generally quietly pleasant with a nice streak of boyish gaiety and humour.
Sue	Mid-thirties Cockney with a thin horse-face, buck teeth and dyed red hair. Could be miserable, but had plenty common sense. Travelling with her fiancé ...
Jim	From northern Australia. He and Sue were to get married out there. He'd been away from home for 8 years, recently working as a mining foreman in South Africa. He was nice, but many years younger than Sue, and also pretty tactless at times with an interestingly rich vocabulary! Would the partnership work?

FRIENDS

Maddie	Nickname – 'Scrumpy'. Very open, honest and amusing small, plump person from the West Country. Taught for about 3 years in a poor district of London and must have been a good teacher with her enthusiasm, gaiety, good sense and uninhibited character. She had an excellent sense of humour and got a real kick out of life.
Rosie (Ros)	Maddie's next door neighbour in Balham. Came from Newcastle and worked for the Inland Revenue. Better looking than Maddie, but also more subdued, with less character. Fairly small with long brown hair, she was practical, loyal to her friends and liked a good joke.
Jane	Slim, practical American nurse. The only girl with 4 brothers in her family, she was a little boyish. Had worked in London with…
Liz	Another nurse, but from Australia, who was going to visit her mother, but aimed to return to the UK to live. Rather quiet but helpful and kind. Tended to suffer from a bad back.
Dave	Nicknamed 'Sponge-cake'. Attractive New Zealander, from Christchurch, where he was a Post Office official. Of

medium height, bearded, with sexy eyes and mouth, he enjoyed wine, women – and song, for he played the guitar. Could be spontaneously very kind and was often first to lend a hand when needed. Loved a bawdy joke.

Rob	Otherwise known as 'Lamb-chop'. Dave's more straight-forward, but less physically attractive companion, Rob worked in a bank in Christchurch. Sang and played the guitar well, and liked company. Wore contact lenses, which sometimes gave him red eyes and hence the nickname, 'Spaghetti Junction'!
Myself	Yorkshire-born physiotherapist who had been working in Switzerland for two years and aimed to visit friends to Australia and New Zealand.
Virginia	Irish radiographer who had lived next to me in Lausanne. Could vanish in times of need! Not too bad company in the tent the majority of the time though.

SINGLES

Meg	Plump pleasant little American from California. Had worked in a bank, but then decided to take an English degree course.
Abby	Well-spoken English girl, though she could appear both bawdy and rude, she was so direct. She'd held a position as an editor in publishing in London, and I could imagine she would stand no nonsense! But she was very practical, and a kind and sensible friend-in-need on occasion.
Lynn	An Australian girl, she was practical with plenty determination and character. Also she had a Geography degree. She was, perhaps surprisingly for she was not a particularly good-looking girl, successful with men. She danced well, but drank heavily. This might have been the main cause for her occasional health issues.
Sarah	A nursing sister from Charing Cross Hospital. Came across as intelligent and pleasant at first meeting, but not

a very reliable member of a team and could be very condescending to the 'natives'.

Geoff   Otherwise known as 'Luigi'. Humorous, moustached bachelor, a 'three men in a boat'- type. He'd travelled as far as Kashmir already, and was often seen in his Jordanian headdress from a previous trip in the Middle East.

Tim   Tall, quiet lad from the Kent coast, Electronics his subject at Uni. Had helped cook in hotels during the summers, and so was an asset on our cooking team.

Scott   Quiet, darkly good-looking, Australian from Melbourne. Rare, in that he started the trip clean-shaven. Could fly a plane before he drove a car, and was keen on both forms of transport ... also more unusually on Eastern jewellery and china.

Lukas   An eccentric Austrian who, at 37, was the oldest on the trip. He joined the trip late, in Salzburg. Charmingly extrovert, but could sometimes be a little insensitive. However, he generally got on fine with the local people we met. He was also an excellent photographer.

Blue Truck ('Bluies')

STAFF

Ben   Blue truck driver. He was a car mechanic running his own business, but pretty well travelled. Dark, long-haired and bearded, with a snub nose and a twinkle in his eye, he was not a mixer. He was reliable and kept himself to himself, rarely drinking a lot, and driving superbly well for long stretches at a time. He was not at his best in the morning, but became quite relaxed of an evening.

COUPLES

Helen   Bright and pleasant. A good cook and household manager type. Well suited to her husband…

Stephen	Well-educated Englishman from London. A bit of a charmer with women.
Lindy	A slim, good-looking Australian girl but rather lacking in humour, travelling with...
Mike	Her husband, a handsome Australian architect. Very sure of himself. They joined the trip last, in Thessalonica.
Anne	Fair, pleasant Cockney lass. Chatty and good fun. Had come rather blindly with her very good friend, an office colleague.
Roger	'Lean & hungry' good-looker from London. Had packed in his office job and decided to take this trip with Anne.

FRIENDS

Heidi	Rosy-cheeked, pleasant Swiss girl from the Lake Zurich region. Pretty good at English. Travelling with her friend...
Hannah	Another Swiss girl, a more practical, hardy type than Heidi and even better at English. Perhaps it was her job as a social worker that made her extra good at getting to know local people and photographing them well. [I should like to thank Hannah for her two photographs of the trucks on pages 85 and 172 of this volume].
Michael	Bearded, quiet Canadian chiropractor from Toronto. Another one who sang and played the guitar. Travelling with...
Derek	His blond brother-in-law. Married with 3 children in Toronto. Quietly humorous. (Turned out to be a dentist, but wisely kept that quiet.)
Chloe	A French teacher from London. Smart and attractive. Travelling with her sister...
Alice	Sexy Lisa Minelli look-alike. Very pleasant and easy to talk to. Ex-nurse, barmaid, and now a student teacher. She and her sister were originally from Wales.

SINGLES

Gloria	A gorgeously different American from San Francisco! Kind and extrovert, she sang to her own accompaniment on the guitar. Was an individual dresser, with great earrings, and rings on her toes. The only authentic hippie of the group.
Cynthia	An ex-Bunny girl and magazine editor's secretary in London, who was very smart-dressing and acting. Soon swept James off his feet! More practical than she looked though.
Jan	From Melbourne, but had been working as a secretary in London for 2 years. Platinum blond and sometimes a bit loud, but mostly very pleasant company.
Sharon	London nurse and the designated one for the trip (ie. she was responsible for all the medications we were carrying). Dark and quite sexy; a city-loving girl, who didn't always seem at one with the rural aspects of the trip.
Graham	Bespectacled and dark-bearded, he was ever pleasant and gallant - the typical old-fashioned Englishman. Sometimes insufferably slow however.
Daniel	Nicknamed 'Treeman' (never got to know why – a conservationist??) Bearded Englishman - bit of an odd guy! Evidently his mother 'let him come on the trip'!
Howard	Very quiet, rather nice-looking bearded Englishman. It was said he could be fun, but he wasn't particularly out-going.

Bibliography

Ahmadi H., Nazari Samani A., Malekian A. (2010). *The Qanat: A Living History in Iran.* In: Schneier-Madanes G., Courel MF. (eds) Water and Sustainability in Arid Regions. Springer, Dordrecht. https://doi.org/10.1007/978-90-481-2776-4_8

A.L.J. for Encounter Overland (1975). *To the Roof of the World.* London: Westminster Printing.

Allen, Charles [ed.] (1985). *Plain Tales from the Raj.* London: Century Publishing Co.

Bragg, Melvyn (2018) *Persepolis.* 'In Our Time', 7th June on BBC Radio 4.

The British Army (2020). *Gurkha History.* Retrieved 24.10.20, from the website https://www.army.mod.uk/who-we-are/corps-regiments-and-units/brigade-of-gurkhas/gurkha-history/

BritishBattles,com (2020). Battle of Kabul 1842. Retrieved 15.4.20, from https://www.britishbattles.com/first-afghan-war/battle-of-kabul-1842/

Cameron, James (1974). *An Indian Summer.* London: Macmillan.

Carroll, Michael (1960). *From a Persian Tea House.* London: John Murray.

Çetingüleç, M. (2014). *Turkey's Tourism Renaissance.* Retrieved 4.1.17 from www.al-monitor.com/pulse/originals/2014/07/cetingulec-turkey-tourism-revenues-arab-japanese-antalya.html (posted 31.7.14)

Cooke, Peter (1987). *Bagpipes in India.* Retrieved 20.7.20 from https://www.drpetercooke.uk/wp-content/uploads/2015/11/Bagpipes-in-India.pdf (written for the spring 1987 edition of Inter Arts magazine)

dangerousroads (2020). *Kabul-Jalalabad Highway, a breathtaking chasm of mountains and cliffs.* Retrieved 12.4.20, from https://www.dangerousroads.org/asia/afghanistan/3217-kabul-jalalabad-highway.html

Dubin, M. & Richardson, T. (2010). *The Rough Guide to Turkey.* London: Rough Guides (Penguin Books).

Durrell, Lawrence (1980). *The Greek Islands.* London: Faber and Faber.

Editors of Encyclopaedia Britannica (2020). *Amritsar.* Retrieved 26.4.20, from www.britannica.com

Elliot, Jason (2006). *Mirrors of the Unseen: Journeys in Iran.* London: Picador.

Finnemore, John (1915). *India.* London: A. & C. Black.

Flecker, James Elroy (1913). *The Golden Journey to Samarkand.*

Fleming, Peter (1936). *News from Tartary: A Journey from Peking to Kashmir.* London: Jonathan Cape.

Flintoff, Corey (2011). *In India, Snake Charmers are Losing Their Sway*. Retrieved 27.7.20, from https://www.npr.org/2011/08/08/139086119/in-india-snake-charmers-are-losing-their-sway?t=1595849730520 (posted 8.8.11)

Gaunle, Shiva (2001). Thirty Years of King Birendra's Reign. *Nepali Times, #23*. Retrieved 31.1.21, from archive.nepalitimes.com/news.php?id=11394.

Güzelgöz, Muammer & Memduh (1975). *A Historical Guide to Cappadocia and Goreme*. Ankara: Ayyildiz Matbaasi.

Habashi, Fathi (2019). *Golden Temple in Amritsar, Punjab, India*. Retrieved 23.4.20, from https://works.bepress.com/fathi_habashi/474/ (posted 18.9.19)

Haenraets, J., Schwann, A. & Hollingsworth, M. (2010). *Paradise in Conflict: reexamining and safeguarding the genius of the Mughal Gardens of Kashmir*. Retrieved 10.5.20, from https://thecela.org/wp-content/uploads/PARADISE-IN-CONFLICT.pdf

Hatzopoulos, Dionysios (2013). *The Fall of Constantinople 1453*. Retrieved 29.2.16, from https://pneymatiko.wordpress.com/2013/05/28/the-fall-of-constantinople-1453 (posted 28.5.13)

Heid, Roger (2015). *The Rheingold Express*. Retrieved 22.2.16, from http://blog.reynaulds.com/index.php/the-rheingold-express

Higgins, Brian (2019). *Where are the Hanging Lakes in the World Located?* Retrieved 10.4.20, from https://www.quora.com/Where-are-the-hanging-lakes-in-the-world-located (posted 11.11.19)

Hoad, Phil (2018). Mashhad in the spotlight: Inequality plagues Iran's Holy City. *The Guardian*, Monday 22nd January.

Hunt, J. (1953). *The Ascent of Everest*. London: Hodder & Stoughton.

Hureau, Jean [ed.] (1974) *Iran Pocket Guide*. Holland: Jeune Afrique.

Kapuściński, Ryszard (2008). *Travels with Herodotus*. London: Penguin.

Karwiese, Stefan (1985). *Der Numismatiker – Archäologe*. Retrieved 6.3.16, from http://www.openbibart.fr/item/display/10068/1249961

Khayyám, Omar, translated into English by Edward FitzGerald, 1859 (1940). *The Rubáiyát of Omar Khayyám*. London: George G. Harrop.

Kipling, Rudyard & Balestier, Walcott, 1892 (2001). *The Naulahka: a Story of East and West*. Leeds: House of Stratus.

Lamplugh, Barbara (1976). *Kathmandu by Truck*. Guildford: Biddles.

Lendering, Jona (2004). *Pasargadae*. Retrieved 22.1.17, from http://www.livius.org/articles/place/pasargadae/ (last modified 12.12.16)

Marnham, Patrick (1971). *Road to Katmandu*. London: Macmillan

Mather, Berkely (1960). *The Pass beyond Kashmir*. London: Companion Book Club.

Ministry for Urban Development, Government of India (2015) *City Development Plan for Varanasi, 2041 (Final City Development Plan)*. Retrieved 12.9.20, from https://www. nnvns.org/data/Final%20CDP%20Varanasi.pdf.

Moghaddam, Dariush (2002). *Parse or Persepolis: Ancient Capital of Persian -Achaemenid-Empire*. Retrieved 9.3.17, from http://www.iranchamber.com/history/persepolis/persepolis1.php

Molavi, Afshin (2005). *The Soul of Iran*. New York: W. W. Norton & Co.

Murphy, Dervla (2010). *Full Tilt*. London: Eland.

Naipaul, V.S. (1995). *An Area of Darkness*. London: Picador.

Newby, Eric (1958). *A Short Walk in the Hindu Kush*. London: Secker & Warburg.

Newman, Bernard (1962). *Turkey and the Turks*. London: Methuen.

Nicoll, Fergus (2009). *Shah Jahan: The Rise and Fall of the Mughal Empire*. New Delhi: Penguin Books India Pvt. Ltd.

Noyce, Wilfred (1958). *Asia, Nepal, Machapuchare*. Retrieved 26.9.20, from http://publications.americanalpineclub.org/articles/12195811800/Asia-Nepal-Machapuchare

Omrani, B., Leeming, M. & Chatwin, E. (2011). *Afghanistan: a Companion and Guide* [2nd ed.]. Hong Kong: Odyssey.

Orwell, George (1949). *Nineteen Eighty-Four*. London: Secker & Warburg.

Paine, Sheila (1994). *The Afghan Amulet: Travels from the Hindu Kush*. New York: St Martin's Press.

Peake, Mervyn (1946). *Titus Groan*. London: Eyre & Spottiswoode.

Pletcher, Kenneth (2020). *Jallianwala Bagh Massacre*. Retrieved 23.4.20, from https://www.britannica.com/event/Jallianwala-Bagh-Massacre (last updated 8.4.20)

Podelco, Grant (2002). *Monuments of Herat, Afghanistan's Ancient Cultural Capital, in Danger of Destruction*. Retrieved 1.3.19, from https://www.rferl.org/a/1101519.html

Pope, Arthur U. (1965). *Persian Architecture*. London: Thames and Hudson.

Pullman, Michael (2017). *The Houseboats of Kashmir*. Retrieved 30.4.20, from https://www.wildfrontierstravel.com/en_GB/community/blog/post/the-houseboats-of-kashmir-1 (posted 7.4.17)

Remarque, Erich Maria, 1929 (2011). *All Quiet on the Western Front*. London: Vintage.

Richards, John F. (1995). *The Mughul Empire*. Cambridge: Cambridge University Press

Rod-ari, Melody (2015). *Bamiyan Buddhas*. Retrieved 4.4.20, from: https://www.khanacademy.org/humanities/ap-art-history/west-and-central-asia-apahh/central-asia/a/bamiyan-buddhas

Ron, James (1995). Weapons Transfers and Violations of the Laws of War in Turkey. *Human Rights Watch*, pp. 120–121.

Simpson, St John (2012). *Afghanistan: A Cultural History*. London: The British Museum Press.

Sodha, Allison (2020). *The Bold and Beautiful Laxmi Narayan Temple*. Retrieved 12.7.20, from https://www.afar.com/places/laxmi-narayan-mandir-new-delhi

Stevens, Roger (1962). *The Land of the Great Sophy*. New York: Methuen.

Stewart, Rory (2004). *The Places In Between*. London: Picador.

Stuart, Dorothy Margaret (1926). *The Book of Other Lands*. London: George G. Harrop.

Thubron, Colin (2006). *Shadow of the Silk Road*. London: Chatto & Windus.

Time Note (2021). *Nepalese Royal Massacre*. Retreived 11.1.21, from https://timenote.info/en/events/Nepalese-Royal-Massacre

Tyre News (January 1974). *London to Kathmandu with Asian Greyhound (Swagman Tours)*. Retrieved 24.7.15, from www.Indiaoverland.biz/overland/asiangreyhound.html

White, Jon (2016). *Anglican Churches in Iran?* Retrieved 15.1.17 from https://www.episcopalcafe.com/anglican-churches-in-iran/ (posted 3.3.16)

Worrall, Jill (2011). *Two Wings of a Nightingale*. Auckland: Exisle.